T0301647

Privatization and Labor

Privatization and Labor

Responses and Consequences in
Global Perspective

Edited by

Marsha Pripstein Posusney
Linda J. Cook

Edward Elgar
Cheltenham, UK • Northampton, MA, USA

Published by
Edward Elgar Publishing Limited
Glensanda House
Montpellier Parade
Cheltenham
Glos GL50 1UA
UK

Edward Elgar Publishing, Inc.
136 West Street
Suite 202
Northampton
Massachusetts 01060
USA

A catalogue record for this book is available from the British Library

Library of Congress Cataloguing in Publication Data

Privatization and labor: responses and consequences in global perspective / edited by Linda J. Cook, Marsha Pripstein Posusney.
    p.cm.
  Includes index.
   1. Labor market. 2. Privatization. I. Cook, Linda J., 1952 - II. Posusney, Marsha Pripstein.

HD5706 .P736 2002
331.12 – dc21

                               2001040965

ISBN   1 84064 435 4

Printed and bound in Great Britain by MPG Books Ltd, Bodmin, Cornwall

Contents

List of Figures

List of Tables

Acknowledgments

This volume grew out of a conference that was organized by the editors and held at the Watson Institute for International Studies at Brown University in March, 1999. The editors and authors would like to thank the following for their sponsorship and financial support of the conference: the Watson Institute for International Studies, the Department of Political Science, and the C.V. Starr Lectureship Fund, all of Brown University, the Center for International Business at Bryant College, and the International Studies Association through its workshop grant program. We are also grateful to the Watson Institute for providing additional financial support for the preparation and publication of this volume, and to Bryant College for providing clerical support.

The chapter by Martín Rama originally appeared in the *World Bank Economic Review*, **13**, 1, (January, 1999). It has been edited slightly to fit the format of this volume. We are grateful to the World Bank for granting us permission to republish this article.

List of Contributors

Chris Alexander is Associate Director of the International Studies Program at Texas A&M University. His most recent publication, 'Opportunities, organizations, and ideas: Islamists and workers in Algeria and Tunisia', appears in the November, 2000 issue of the *International Journal of Middle East Studies*. He is currently completing a manuscript comparing contemporary state–labor relations in Algeria, Tunisia, and Morocco.

Christopher Candland is Assistant Professor of Political Science at Wellesley College, where he teaches comparative and South Asian politics. He is co-editor, with Rudra Sil, of *Labor Politics in a Global Age: Continuity and Change in the Industrial Relations of Late-Industrializing and Post-Socialist Economies* (Oxford University Press, 2001), and co-author, with Junya Yimprasert, of 'Can corporate codes of conduct improve labor standards? Evidence from the Thai footwear industry', a report for the Asia Monitor Resource Center.

Linda J. Cook is Professor of the Political Science department at Brown University, and a faculty associate of Brown's Watson Institute for International Studies and the Davis Center for Russian Studies at Harvard University. She previously authored *The Soviet Social Contract and Why It Failed* (Harvard University Press, 1993) and *Labor and Liberalization: Trade Unions in the New Russia* (Twentieth Century Fund, 1997). She is currently at work on a project titled 'Restructuring the Welfare State: The Politics of Safety Net Reform in the Russian Federation'.

Corinna-Barbara Francis is Assistant Professor in the Political Science department of the University of Missouri-Columbia. She has published articles in *China Quarterly*, *Comparative Politics*, *Asian Survey*, and other journals.

Preston Keat earned his Ph.D. in Political Science at the University of California at Los Angeles in 2001. His doctoral dissertation is titled, 'Playing Favorites: Government Aid and Industrial Restructuring in Post-Socialist Poland'. His most recent publication is 'Penalizing the reformers: Polish steel and European integration', *Communist and Post-Communist Studies,* **33** (2000).

Brendan Martin is director of Public World, a London-based international consultancy specializing in the labor and social dimensions of privatization and public service reform. A member of the Advisory Group on Privatization of the OECD, Martin is author of *In the Public Interest? Privatization and Public Sector Reform* (Zed Books, 1994). He is currently completing a manuscript provisionally titled *Redesigning Public Services: A Partnership Approach* (Zed Books, forthcoming).

Craig Murphy is Professor and Chair of Political Science at Wellesley College and Research Professor at Brown University's Watson Institute of International Studies. His current work includes a two-year project, 'Gender in International Relations: From Seeing Women and Recognizing Gender to Transforming Policy Research', funded by the Ford Foundation. Recent publications include *International Organization and Industrial Change: Global Governance since 1850* (Polity Press, 1994), and 'Global governance: poorly done and poorly understood', *International Affairs* (2000). He is a founding editor of *Global Governance*, and is currently President of the International Studies Association.

José Pineda earned his Ph.D in Economics at the University of Maryland in 2001. He has presented papers at the annual conferences of the American Economic Association and the Latin American and Caribbean Economic Association.

Marsha Pripstein Posusney is Associate Professor of Political Science at Bryant College and Adjunct Associate Professor of International Relations (Research) at the Watson Institute for International Studies at Brown University. Her first book, *Labor and the State in Egypt: Workers, Unions, and Economic Restructuring* (Columbia University Press, 1997) was co-winner of the Middle East Studies Association's 1998 Albert Hourani award for outstanding original scholarly research on the Middle East. She is now working on a comparative study of the effects of privatization on employment and labor protection programs in Tunisia, Morocco, Jordan, and Egypt.

Martín Rama is a Lead Economist with the Development Research Group of the World Bank. He did his undergraduate studies at the Universidad de la Republica, Uruguay, and obtained his Ph.D. in Economics from the Universite de Paris I, France. His research deals mainly with labor issues in developing countries.

Martin Rein is Professor of Social Policy in the department of Urban Studies at Massachusetts Institute of Technology, where he works primarily in the field of comparative social policy. His most recent books are *Rethinking the Welfare State* (Edward Elgar Publishers, forthcoming, 2002), and *The Public–Private Mix in Pension Reform*, co-edited with Winfried Schmahl (Cambridge University Press, forthcoming).

Francisco Rodríguez is Assistant Professor of Economics at the University of Maryland. He is currently on leave while serving as Chief Economist of the

Venezuelan National Assembly. Recent publications include 'Does distributional skewness lead to redistribution? Evidence from the United States', *Economics and Politics* (1999) and (with Dani Rodrik) 'Trade policy and economic growth: a skeptic's guide to the cross-national evidence' in *NBER Macroeconomics Annual* (2000).

Elena Vinogradova holds a Ph.D. in Economics from Moscow State University and is a senior research fellow with the Institute for Socio-Economic Studies and Demography, Russian Academy of Science. She has participated in numerous research and policy advice projects dealing in the Russian Federation, under funding from agencies including the World Bank and the Carnegie Endowment. She has published numerous articles in various Russian journals.

1. Introduction

Linda J. Cook and Craig Murphy

1. Introduction

The 1997 *World Development Report* outlines a program for strengthening the capacity of national governments to catalyze economic growth through privatization and deregulation. At the center of the report is a political analysis of the most efficient means to transform third world societies and societies in transition to achieve these ends. The potential allies supporting the Bank's program of lean government, deregulation, and privatization are identified as 'consumers', Treasury ministries, financial interests, employers, younger workers, local administrators, small businesses, and 'taxpayers'. The natural opponents are identified as the rest of the central government, government employees, trade unions, pensioners, and all other workers whose jobs or sectors are protected by interventionist state policies.[1]

Over the past decade versions of this program have been implemented widely in formerly socialist and mixed economies, transforming relationships among the state, labor, and management, removing the state from its role as large-scale owner and employer, substituting private corporations and market institutions. The present volume brings together a multi-disciplinary group of scholars from political science, sociology, and economics, as well as policy practitioners to look, empirically and comparatively, at privatization processes across a broad range of countries and regions. It presents a set of case studies focused on the politics of economic restructuring programs and their social consequences.

Because privatization programs affect labor most directly, we concentrate on blue-collar industrial and service workers and their unions. The first group of chapters elucidates the responses of trade unions, and of labor more broadly, to the privatization programs initiated by governments. The second group focuses on social welfare, viewing the welfare consequences of both enterprise privatization and related programs to transfer social provision from the state and enterprises to the private sector.

As the 1997 *Report* highlights, the current wave of privatization and deregulation is a political program, the result of a strategy designed to serve one set of interests as opposed to another. Like any political program it had a history; it did not fall from the sky, nor was it an inevitability. International institutions played roles in designing, promoting, and implementing that political program. They were not the only forces involved, but they were significant forces. Furthering marketization – the shift of social activities toward the market – the IMF (International Monetary Fund), World Bank, and FAO (Food and Agricultural Organization of the United Nations) have promoted deregulation nationally (for example, the weakening of regulations on pesticides, pharmaceuticals, tobacco, and, to a lesser extent, on labor in Africa in the 1970s). They have also promoted deregulation internationally, i.e., the ending of commodity agreements; opening economies to international competition by lowering trade barriers, removing capital controls and domestic content and ownership rules; and privatizing state and parastatal industry, especially doing so in such a way that anyone in the world can purchase the industry.

International institutions became effective promoters of marketization and privatization through conditionality, policy coordination, and the hegemony of a particular form of liberal economics. These became part of African policy programs in the late 1970s as both debts and conditional funds from abroad increased. To a lesser extent the same broad-stroke story is true in richer places, though of course there are also places that have not been in debt traps and have also adopted these policies. From the late 1970s onward, in the wake of the downturn of the world economy, intergovernmental and bilateral aid donors attempted to get more bang for the buck. This was done via coordination, via setting lead agencies (i.e., determining that one agency, usually the UNDP or the World Bank, would take ultimate responsibility for coordinating all donors operating in a particular country), and via coordination in the field. The effect was to marshal aid resources behind the neoliberal, marketizing agenda in country after country. Donors promoted privatization and deregulation, the core of the neoliberal agenda, in virtually every nation that received international assistance.

Critics of privatization contend that this policy is inimical to the interests of labor unions and of most, if not all, workers. In their view privatization, especially in the developing world, shrinks the public sector in which workers have achieved the highest levels of organization and wages, job security, and decent working conditions. It generally brings lay-offs and downsizing, erosion of other protections or their removal from labor codes, increased repression of workers, and the consequent weakening of unions. Governments accede to privatization programs in large part because of the pressures from international financial institutions (IFIs) that are discussed above. These programs do not always bring growth and generally bring negative distributional effects for organized sectors; they do bring a host of specific problems, including the spread of diseases and growing abuses related to weakening and non-monitoring of labor standards. Industrial centers and older sectors are especially damaged. Critics assume that workers will oppose these programs and, where unions are sufficiently powerful and responsive to their rank-and-file, they will try to block their implementation.

Proponents of privatization argue that it is a necessary antidote to bloated, inefficient, and debt-ridden public sectors. In their view, organized public sector workers seek rents from the state in the forms of overstaffing, generous pay and benefits, and restrictive and inflexible labor contracts. They block efficient allocation of economic resources, and crowd out spending on the social needs of the unorganized poor. Governments adopt privatization programs in order to end wasteful subsidies that are bankrupting their economies, and to stimulate economic recovery and growth. Many proponents, including those from the IFIs (see, for example, Kikera, 1997), are nevertheless sensitive to the politics and social costs of privatization. They propose that labor unions be brought into the privatization process, invited to help design compensation and transition policies for affected workers. They argue that even for public sector workers the results of privatization are at worst mixed, with some earning higher wages in the more efficient post-privatization enterprises, though others may lose permanently.

While the majority of chapters in this volume tend more to the 'critic' than to the 'proponent' view of privatization, their empirically-grounded case studies in the end suggest a more nuanced perspective. All see privatization as having real costs for organized labor in both post-socialist and developing nations, but costs and benefits may be quite different for various sectors of the labor force. The impacts of privatization on employment and social welfare, while seen by most of the authors as broadly negative, also show variation. Moreover, some of the authors argue that the costs and inefficiencies of internationally-promoted programs are greater than they need be, and propose alternatives that pay more attention to national contexts. We will turn now to look at the case studies, first a set of chapters on trade unions, social movements, and privatization struggles, then a set on privatization's employment and social welfare consequences.

2. Trade Unions, Social Movements, and Privatization Struggles

The chapters in this section look closely at labor's responses to privatization in Eastern Europe, Africa, and South Asia. All show unions or workers protesting aspects of privatization policies, but the types and extent of protests, as well as their effects, are shaped in complex ways by the structure of the national labor movements, and by their relationships with both the state and other social and political movements. The political context in which privatization programs are initiated influences the propensity of workers to resist sell-off schemes, as well as the forms such resistance might take. The relationships among labor unions, and between the leaders of peak organizations and their rank-and-file, also matter greatly.

The presence or absence of genuine partisan political competition is a crucial variable. In the two democratic cases, Poland and India, unions exercised the greatest influence on the privatization programs because they provided key support to governing political parties or coalitions. Yet this influence produced dramatically different outcomes: in India politically powerful unions virtually blocked government-initiated privatization programs. In Poland unions accepted privatization because they were confident in their strength to limit the costs workers would pay.

Where privatization is initiated by authoritarian governments, labor's response depends partly on whether union leaders have been coopted and on whether the rank-and-file have been repressed. Coopted leaders tend to focus their energies on bargaining over benefits and transitional aid for displaced workers, and are at risk of losing credibility with their membership. If repression is not extreme, workers who are affected most directly by privatization may respond more assertively than their unions. Privatization also has effects on the organization and solidarity of labor movements, and implications for the forms of organization that best protect workers. Singular, national confederations are better positioned to resist, or negotiate the terms of, privatization schemes. Decentralized unions are able to respond more quickly to situations in individual plants or industries, and may better serve the interests of workers after privatization has been implemented.

In 'Unions in Transition: Why Organized Labor Embraced Economic Reform in Poland (1989–99)', Preston Keat argues that, against analysts' expectations, Polish labor consented to a reform program that brought high unemployment, falling wages and rapid restructuring of the economy. Keat contends that Poland's unions, first and foremost Solidarity, accepted reform precisely because they were strong, confident that they could block the most adverse effects of reform and extract compensation for losers. His study shows that the unions in fact did so: from the outset Employee Councils limited large-scale privatization; after two years of painful reforms unions mounted a strike movement that extracted concessions; and elections produced a government that was more accommodating to labor. Keat also shows that the responses of different industrial sectors varied: in the coal industry, where reform meant extinction, workers and managers combined to block reform. In steel and ship building, where success was 'feasible but uncertain', unions cooperated and the government 'consistently built compromise into its restructuring plans'

(p. 29). Two striking conclusions come from this study: First, a successful negotiated privatization strategy was possible, indeed facilitated, in the presence of strong unions in a democratic polity. Secondly, as Keat's evidence makes clear, in sectors with uncertain prospects those workers who cooperated with restructuring plans won, and those who resisted, most famously the Gdansk shipyard workers, lost.

Egypt presents a striking contrast with Poland. As Marsha Pripstein Posusney shows in 'Egyptian Labor Struggles in the Era of Privatization', Egyptian governments and unions had historically opposed privatization of the country's large public sector. When the IMF successfully pressured Mubarak to adopt a privatization program in the 1990s union leaders initially resisted, and called for expanded workers' rights. The government responded by removing recalcitrant leaders, insulating cooperative ones, and making it clear that labor would have little veto over the process; it could only negotiate some transitional aid for displaced workers. Union leaders, either believing the battle lost or unwilling to fight, focused their energies on modest aid programs such as early retirement, and on labor code revisions.

The rank-and-file did hold localized protests at every stage of the privatization process, mobilizing 'from below' without official union support. Though these efforts have proved unable to preserve the public sector, they have succeeded in slowing the privatization process. In Egypt privatization imposed big costs on workers and unions: workers found themselves more vulnerable to unemployment, wage reductions, and higher prices as the economy shifted toward market orthodoxy. Union leaders, already divorced from the rank-and-file, became further discredited; and workers, lacking organizational support and coordination, could only resort to isolated informal, ultimately symbolic protests.

In 'The Political Element in Economic Reform: Institutions and Privatization Patterns in South Asia', Christopher Candland argues that similar economic policies had widely-differing effects in the different institutional environments of India and Pakistan. In these once-unified polities, he points out, virtually identical IMF-sponsored privatization programs had opposite results: Pakistan privatized rapidly, India hardly at all. Candland finds the central explanation in differing labor institutions. In democratic India unions had for decades served as electoral vehicles for political parties, creating strong party-affiliated trade union confederations that used their influence to block and reverse the government's privatization decisions. In authoritarian Pakistan, by contrast, civic associations had been repressed and destroyed, trade unions depoliticized. Rapid privatization was carried out through labor's exclusion. These two cases would seem to illustrate the once-conventional wisdom that authoritarian governments are more effective at neoliberal reform because they can ignore social and political costs, while democracies are hamstrung, but we have seen that Poland contradicts this logic.

Drawing on the cases of Bangladesh and Sri Lanka as well, Candland also reminds us that state sector workers constitute a very small and privileged part of South Asia's labor force, and their unions, however effective, benefit only this small sector: 'In all of South Asia, public sector workers and the unionists who negotiate privatization bargain from a position of legally-protected, formal employment. The concessions fall only to them, *not* to the general labor force' (p. 79). He stresses that 'labor' in this region is not a single interest but a segmented one, divided by class, caste, ethnicity, and gender. The politics of privatization hurts and benefits only the top strata of workers. Structural adjustment programs and privatization have been accompanied by striking increases in the numbers of women working in the rapidly-growing, unregulated informal sectors of South Asia's economies.

Finally, in a chapter titled, 'Enterprise Reform and Labor in North Africa', Christopher Alexander looks at the effects of enterprise restructuring and privatization on organized labor in Tunisia, Algeria, and Morocco. The three cases share a broad cultural affinity, earlier development strategies that created large public sectors, and unions based in these sectors that had played important political roles despite their authoritarian environments. Alexander asks whether reform presented similar challenges in the three cases, whether workers' organizations responded similarly, and whether reform had a homogenizing effect on unions. Like Candland, he concludes that differences in the organization of labor and in the history of state–labor relations across the cases shaped labor's differing responses and outcomes.

Algeria, with the largest public sector in the region, has had the sharpest conflicts over privatization. The government's refusal to involve unions seriously in its privatization plans led to growing unrest. When the major union (UGTA) nevertheless supported the government against the Islamists it lost credibility with the rank-and-file, even as threats to workers' security drew blue-collar and professional workers together. The result has been grass-roots activism, formation of new unions, and serious worker opposition to restructuring.

Tunisia, with a much smaller state sector, slower privatization, and greater repression, has experienced the least conflict. Here the major union confederation (UGTT) saw itself in part as a social counterwight to the Islamists. Conflict between government and Islamists in the early 1990s led the government to moderate its reform program and the UGTT to mute its criticism. A new wave of privatization has brought some increase in grass-roots unrest and dissension in the UGTT, but the author doubts that Tunisia's labor movement will become much more assertive soon. Morocco presents some 21 unions, comparatively low standards of social welfare, and the highest levels of worker unrest in the region. Until recently three major confederations competed for membership and influence in often-politicized struggles. Privatization in Morocco sparked both grass-roots militancy and a new spirit of cooperation among the unions, though labor leaders rarely challenge privatization directly.

Alexander concludes that, despite their differences, in all three cases major unions were excluded from privatization policy-making. This exclusion tended to hurt their credibility with members and led to more intense worker militancy as well as tendencies toward fragmentation and the formation of new unions. Unions in North Africa now face two new challenges: a need for more decentralized bargaining structures in their more privatized economies, and the need to adapt to partial democratization, in particular the growing influence of legislative politics.

3. Employment and Social Welfare Effects of Privatization

The second set of chapters in the volume focuses on employment and other social welfare effects of privatization efforts. Three focus on the post-socialist world: Poland, Hungary, Russia, and China, one on West Africa, and two make general arguments about privatization's effects on employment, welfare, and growth. Most show privatization to have more costs than benefits for workers. Their more trenchant shared observation, though, has to do with the intrinsic difficulties, poor designs, and over-expectancy of results that seem endemic to privatization policies, especially those designed by international organizations with limited local consultation and too little regard for the economic and political contexts in which they are implemented. The final chapter takes issue with a fundamental assumption of the neoliberal model: that privatization is good for economic growth.

In the first chapter 'Public Sector Downsizing: An Introduction', Martín Rama presents the view of a World Bank employee who is committed to designing cost-efficient and fair procedures for downsizing of labor forces. Rama takes it as a given that state-led development strategies, in both the socialist and third worlds, 'left a legacy of bloated bureaucracies and overstaffed public enterprises' (p. 111) and that these must be cut order to increase productivity and lower budget deficits and tax burdens. But Rama also recognizes that this is a difficult task, politically but even more so in terms of policy design, and that past downsizing programs have had a decidedly mixed record when subject to cost–benefit analyses. The voluntary approach to reductions – essentially paying workers to leave – is the most popular with governments, and is now broadly supported by IFIs (International Financial Institutions). But the costs of the needed severance pay and other safety-net enhancements – early retirement, counseling, retraining – may be greater than the financial and economic benefits. Retrenchment programs are also subject to adverse selection: all the most productive workers may leave, or mainly those with few prospects for re-employment.

Drawing on a large number of World Bank commissioned as well as other studies on comparative experiences with retrenchment and downsizing, Rama proposes a five-step procedure to determine fair compensation for displaced workers, taking into account their lost earnings and benefits. His procedure is designed to provide incentives for downsizing without overpaying redundant workers at the expense of the broader society, and to limit spending on often-useless job training programs run by other state bureaucracies. Rama's proposals are sensitive to the social context of different countries: he recognizes that, while state workers are seldom poor, in some countries they support extended families including members who are poor. He takes into account the broader ramifications of downsizing in one-company towns, arguing for additional compensation to the community. He is sensitive to the possibility that downsized workers may simply move to other state bureaucracies, and ends with the trenchant observation that downsizing cannot be limited to 'isolated endeavors', but must become part of a transformation toward professionalism and efficiency in state institutions broadly.

Brendan Martin presents an empirical study of restructuring and privatization in the railways of two West African countries, Ghana and the Ivory Coast. His data show large-scale labor force reductions in both cases, though these are much larger in the Ivory Coast's full-fledged privatization program than in the more limited restructuring that was implemented in Ghana. But Martin points out that the significance of these cuts for workers is not straightforward, in part because the railways contracted out much of the work that had been performed by dismissed workers, giving preference to companies formed by former workers. It is equally difficult to assess the effects on wages and benefits; Martin cites the case of medical benefits in the Ivory Coast, in which the new privatized insurance program appears to disadvantage workers, but may in fact be better than the comparatively generous old state program that often had empty coffers. The author also shows that the railways were in decline before restructuring/privatization, and proposes that privatization is less a cause of dismissals than a way to make them politically feasible. Martin concludes that, given that the extent to which privatization per se imposes costs on workers varies depending upon the goals of the political, economic, and social policies it is designed to serve and on particular circumstances, it is more significant to critically examine those policies than to attempt to arrive at a general rule about the impact of privatization, as a policy instrument, on labor.

Martin also provides an insightful commentary on the role of labor unions in these two cases. While the unions were committed to bargaining for policies that would cushion the effects on their members – severance pay, early retirement programs, and help in labor force re-entry – they were not necessarily opposed to restructuring. However the World Bank, which supported and funded restructuring as part of its Structural Adjustment Programs, treated the unions as purely self-interested opponents and refused to consult with them on the design of reforms. Martin views this as a lost opportunity, arguing that dismissals were sometimes poorly planned and left the railways bereft of necessary personnel, and more broadly that input from the workers could have resulted in better-designed and more successful programs.

In 'China's Post-Socialist Housing Privatization', Corinna-Barbara Francis takes a critical view of privatization's effects on workers. In the socialist period, the vast majority of China's urban housing was built, owned, and allocated by work units (danwei), rendering workers dependent on their employers for housing. Housing privatization was supposed to benefit workers by reducing this dependence, facilitating labor mobility and helping workers to become independent property owners. Francis argues persuasively that instead it handed employers new levers of control, for two main reasons. First, because the danwei owned most of the existing urban housing, the government had to rely on them to privatize it. This allowed managers to distort privatization policies in ways that sustained their control over most housing, even as increased access to extra-budgetary funding allowed enterprises to increase their housing stock. Secondly, wages for the vast majority of workers were simply too low to allow them to purchase housing on their own, even through the very limited government-sponsored mortgage programs. Instead they had to rely on subsidies from employers, who in turn gained the right to withhold part of wages in personal 'housing accounts' which workers could not access or transfer and to claim buy-back rights even to apartments workers managed to purchase. Paradoxically, then, the program, for all its promises of independence and ownership, left workers more dependent and vulnerable.

In a related chapter Elena Vinogradova examines divestiture of enterprises' social assets to municipalities in post-socialist Russia. Vinogradova shows clearly that enterprises' provision of social goods and services, i.e., housing, medical care, kindergartens, etc., has declined rather drastically as the result of explicit government policies and legislation requiring that they divest these assets. Like housing privatization in China, divestiture was supposed to free workers from dependence on their enterprises for social provision.

Relying on a 1998 TACIS survey of managers' experiences and attitudes that the author conducted, she shows that, here also, the expected benefits of privatization have mainly failed to materialize. Reformers anticipated that divestiture would raise the profitability and competitiveness of enterprises, allow them to pay higher wages so that their workers could afford to provide for themselves, and allow municipalities to run social services more equitably and effectively.

In fact the positive effects for enterprises were few, only a small percentage increased wages, and municipalities were overwhelmed by the costs of running divested property and services. Enterprises were in fact often pressed into financing divested social assets, undermining both the intent of the program and the transparency of financing. Many facilities were left abandoned and deteriorating, with municipalities lacking the means to maintain them and enterprises unwilling to invest in facilities they can no longer own.

These two chapters present fascinating parallel perspectives on the failures of privatization programs in the post-socialist context, and on their ultimately high costs for workers. Both point to structural factors inherited from the socialist period – enterprises, deeply involved in the social sector as owners, funders, and allocators, could not be easily pushed out, and their societies proved too poor to take over their property. Chinese workers ended up more dependent and vulnerable, Russians with much-reduced access to social services. Francis sees this outcome as an inevitable result of the reform, while Vinogradova seeks ways to improve on it. The managers that she surveys are willing to provide, or help fund, many types of social services, especially if the legal prohibitions on enterprise ownership are removed, and this she proposes. In other words, the costs for workers could be lowered if Western models were adapted more to post-socialist realities.

In his chapter on 'The Political Economy of Pension Reform: Poland and Hungary', Martin Rein examines changes in this key benefit program in two relatively successfully post-socialist, largely privatized economies. Rein argues that Esping-Anderson's classic 'worlds of welfare capitalism' do not fit Eastern Europe, because those worlds assume too great a degree of social and political stability. Rather, we should conceptualize social policy in terms of a shifting mix of regimes and pillars that may vary across policy domains, with state, market, and community as the three pillars on which social security can be built. Examining the causes of change and policy outcomes in Poland and Hungary, Rein is mainly concerned with the interaction of two factors: the historical legacies of the state socialist systems, and the influence of international actors, both national states and international organizations, which 'used and abused those legacies to create frames to legitimate their claims' (p. 210).

Rein concentrates on the diffusion of reform ideas, from neighboring European states, the World Bank, the ILO (International Labor Organization), the IMF, and the ways in which these actors have framed internal debates and shaped policy choices in Eastern Europe. He specifies, well and with attention to disagreements among and within these entities, their proposals for pension reform. The dominant interpretation at present is that the World Bank has been the major external influence in Eastern Europe, but Rein comes to a different conclusion. While conceding to this interpretation for Hungary, he sees the Swedish model as the most important for the Polish reform. Rein's study highlights three aspects of post-privatization social policy-making: first, the central importance of international actors and influences. While Rein argues that outcomes are negotiated domestically, that legacies matter and that both cases show numerous departures from the international models, in his words, 'borrowing versus innovation is the dominant story' (p. 229). Secondly, in the domestic politics as played out here, workers and labor unions are at best one participant, seemingly much less important than either international or state actors, in negotiating a policy that will have its central impact on the welfare of workers. Not only are society and politics less stable, labor as a social and political force is clearly much less important here than in the making of the classic European welfare states.

In the final chapter, 'Labor and the Politics of Human Capital Accumulation', two economists argue that privatization, by contributing to the decline of labor's political influence, ultimately hurts economic growth. The authors, José Pineda and Francisco Rodríguez, begin with the assumption that economic and political power are correlated, and that labor will use its political power to increase governments' social and redistributive spending while capital will press for reductions in both. Privatization, they argue, is accompanied by a loss of unions' membership and bargaining power, and consequent declines in government spending that would contribute to human capital accumulation. The authors show that, over the past two decades, some OECD (Organization for Economic Cooperation and Development) and developing countries have significantly decreased the amounts of resources they devote to social spending or investment in human capital accumulation (i.e., education, health, etc.) They then demonstrate a negative relationship between the share of resources in the hands of capital owners and the level of taxation directed at such spending. But most economists agree that human capital accumulation is an important source of contemporary economic growth, and cuts in such spending undermine growth. So, conclude Pineda and Rodríguez, more economic and thus political power in the hands of capital ultimately undermines growth. Conversely, 'Policies that protect or enhance the bargaining power of labor ... are also likely to have positive effects on the efficiency of the economic system at large ... because ... contrary to the commonly-held belief that unions put a damper on economic efficiency, ... Stronger unions will be able to pressure at the national level for policies towards human capital accumulation that are consistent with equity and economic efficiency' (p. 255).

4. Conclusion

The liberal economic policy agenda that has privatization at its core is not new. International institutions have effectively promoted this sort of liberal fundamentalism before, during specific historic moments. Lou Pauly has shown this via the financial orthodoxy imposed by the BIS and the League in the 1920s. This was tied to the 1916 decision to make post-war interallied economic policy the purview of business (source, date). If we look back to inter-American and inter-imperial responses to financial crises in the 1870s and 1880s we find again that an orthodoxy is imposed via financial constraint (source, date). Then a host of specific problems resulted: environmental degradation, abuses of labor due to non-monitoring of standards, etc. Social forces harmed by these practices responded: industrial centers, peripheries, older sectors such as farmers in Europe, labor, organizing, running anti-sweatshop campaigns. In the past re-regulatory agreements in all of these areas were established: European Coal and Steel Community, decolonization and development, GATT (General Agreement on Tarriffs and Trade) exceptions for agriculture and other industries, ILO core standards in the North, welfare support by GAS, etc.

The present chapters perhaps indicate the beginnings of a similar process, leading to the moderation of neoliberal models. Those who bear the costs of privatization, particularly workers, have in some cases defeated and delayed privatization programs, and more often gained concessions (such as severance pay, etc.) that cushion the costs. These concessions, as well as much greater attention to poverty, have now become part of World Bank sponsored adjustment policies, for example. Scholars that analyze and critique the effectiveness of these policies also have influence, and the critiques articulated, here and elsewhere in the scholarly and policy literature, should also lead to policy adaptation. International institutions can play a role in the support of labor in part via the reregulation of previously deregulated or privatized parts of the economy, This happened in the past. We are seeing movement toward that end in a variety of places in the present.

Note

1. Not mentioned are 'non-consumers' – the vast majority in most third world societies in transition who have no discretionary income – the unemployed and members of traditionally disad-

vantaged and excluded ethnic or religious groups, people who are most often not significant taxpayers or consumers.

2. Unions in Transition: Why Organized Labor Embraced Economic Reform in Poland (1989–99)

Preston Keat

1. Introduction

Poland is regarded as one of the biggest economic reform success stories in post-socialist Europe. It also has the most powerful trade-union movement in the region, led by Solidarity. The effects of rapid economic reform in post-socialist countries (e.g. unemployment, lowered living standards and industrial wages, declining social services) typically are disproportionately felt by workers in traditional, inefficient, state-owned enterprises (SOEs). To the extent that workers in these enterprises are unionized, well organized, and politically powerful (i.e. have direct links to effective political parties), as is the case in Poland, they might be expected to succeed in blocking market-based reforms. How was Poland, with the strongest, best organized, and most militant industrial labor force in the region, able to reform its economy so successfully?

In the first years of transition (1990–93), 'shock therapy' was implemented, industrial production fell dramatically, and unemployment reached almost 17%. In a context of great uncertainty about the prospects for successful reforms, and even greater uncertainty about the fate of industrial workers, labor supported change. While the market-based economic agenda was initially the product of reformist politicians, and not union leaders, Polish trade unions were generally supportive of a wide range of market-based macro- and microeconomic policies. They even accepted for the most part a wage taxation law (the *popiwek*) that essentially guaranteed real wage reductions for almost all industrial workers. One observer called the acceptability of this rule to the Solidarity rank and file, one of the 'great paradoxes' of the Polish reform program (Rodrik, 1994, p. 213).

How did this come to pass? In a context of extreme uncertainty about the future, it may make sense for politicians to eschew gradualism;[1] it may also make sense from a purely economic point of view. I argue that it can also make sense for workers, if they are well organized. In Poland, the relative strength of organized labor enabled it to take the risk of reform. At three key levels – in individual enterprises, in sectoral and national bargaining arrangements, and in close association with major national political parties – labor had signifi-cant institutional strength. Unions were secure in their ability to condition change and extract compensation for potential losers from the reforms, and were therefore willing to face the initial shocks inherent in a rapid shift to a market economy.

In this chapter I examine the varied and evolving nature of workers' institu-tional capacities and explore how these affected economic reform policy. In Section 2, I present my argument concerning the institutional strength of labor and its willingness to risk reform. Section 3 is an overview of economic re-form and privatization policies in Poland. Section 4 examines the complicated and evolving nature of labor's support for economic reform. In this section I present evidence concerning privatization and the role of Employee Councils, national and sectoral-level collective bargaining, strike activity, and the role of unions in national political parties. I also examine the negotiations over re-form in three key industrial sectors – steel, coal and shipbuilding – and suggest that while there was a generalized support of economic reforms, certain par-ticularly vulnerable sectors blocked reform from the outset, while in others resistance grew over time. Section 5 concludes.

2. Labor Strength and Organization

Prior to reform efforts, the conventional assumption was that because of the relative strength of Polish trade unions, and in particular Solidarity,[2] there would be strong, and perhaps insurmountable, resistance to rapid economic reform after 1990. In other words, strong trade unions could and probably would block (or at the very least dramatically slow) reform. In fact, the opposite has oc-curred, with Solidarity playing a leading and proactive role in the reform pro-cess.

In the context of an examination of the possibilities for class compromise in capitalist societies, Przeworski and Wallerstein (1985) suggest that workers will feel more secure, and therefore be more willing to reach agreement with 'capitalists', if several institutional conditions are met. These conditions in-clude the existence of: (a) monopoly (union) representation of workers; (b) institutionalized labor–capital relations (formal, national collective bargain-ing institutions, etc.); and (c) workers' political parties with national political influence.

While theirs is not an argument about the transition from socialism to capitalism, it does point to what are, at least in the case of Poland, important factors that facilitated the transition to a market system.[3] Powerful, organized trade unions had the benefit of each of the three conditions mentioned above – they held a monopoly of representation of workers in collective bargaining;[4] collective bargaining was institutionalized at the national and sectoral levels, with the main trade unions in each sector negotiating wage and employment agreements with representatives of government and management; and both of the main trade unions were closely linked with prominent national political parties.

Furthermore, at the firm level, Employee Councils had explicit legal authority to negotiate the terms of individual company reform plans. The pre-privatization structure of control rights within firms was a direct outgrowth of the evolution of the legal framework governing enterprises in the decades preceding the fall of communism. In 1956, Employee Councils were given legal (if not actual) powers to influence a wide array of internal firm practices. During the mid-1970s the central government severely curtailed the authority of Councils, and by 1980, most had been eliminated. However, one by-product of the Solidarity movement's success was the introduction, in 1981, of legislation that reintroduced the Councils, and gave them new powers and control rights. With the subsequent imposition of martial law, many of the gains of the Solidarity movement were rolled back, including some elements of the Councils and workplace democracy (e.g. firm self-management laws were suspended). However, after 1982, key aspects of the rules were reinstated, and new interpretations of enterprise ownership and autonomy were permitted.[5]

These conditions made the relative strength of unionized labor visible, credible, and stable. Labor had sufficient national and sectoral coverage to feel reasonably comfortable about its conditions in the short and medium term. They had the 'cover' of a partial wage and employment security umbrella, and the ability to hold up or even partially reverse reforms if they were not successful enough. In short, organized labor had enough institutionalized power to be willing to take the risk of reforming, because they believed they would be able to reconsider in the intermediate term. They could also block or slow down reforms when and where the effects were most adverse.

Fernandez and Rodrik (1991) explain why there may be a bias toward the status quo (a bias against economic reforms) whenever (some of) the individual gainers and losers from reform cannot be identified beforehand. Even if reforms will be beneficial to most, and receive broad support once adopted, they are often blocked before they are initiated. If, for example, 30% of industrial workers will be worse off after reform, but exactly which 30% is unclear, it will be difficult to get any of those who might potentially be among that 30% to risk reforming.

In Poland, the institutional strength of labor served as a mechanism to avoid this status quo trap. Before reforms were instituted, workers did not know which ones among them would be better off after reform. They did know, however, that those who did suffer could be compensated (i.e. that they could force the government to compensate them with side payments, slowed or modified reform, etc.). Except in rare instances (e.g. the coal sector) where it was obvious to all that reform would mean certain extinction, organized labor was therefore willing to take the risk of reform. Put somewhat differently, key groups of potential losers knew they could slow reforms or extract compensation in time period two, so they were more willing to risk reform in time period one.[6]

3. Economic Reform in Poland

The era of Communist rule in Poland came to an end in 1989.[7] One of the most daunting tasks facing the newly elected democratic leadership was an ongoing economic crisis. After years of intermittent troubles, the socialist, centrally planned economy had almost ground to a halt, as a partially implemented market reform led to rapidly increasing inflation and massive shortages.[8] The new government faced the twin tasks of implementing a near-term relief program, as well as the more daunting project of devising and managing a comprehensive overhaul of the national economic system.

In late 1989 and early 1990, a team of economic advisors offered advice on curing the macroeconomic crisis (inflation and shortages), as well as a broader reform strategy to deal with the core issues of declining efficiency and decreasing standards of living.[9]

The plan of action that was placed before the political leadership combined very rapid liberalization and deregulation, including price, trade and financial liberalization, unification of exchange rates and currency convertibility, and removal of centralized allocation of inputs. The plan also called for comprehensive institutional change – privatization of the state sector, open foreign investment, the elimination of domestic monopolies, the creation of an independent central bank, reform of the financial sector (banking, stock exchange, insurance, etc.), tax reform (improving tax collection, and introducing income and value-added taxes), a rationalizing of budgetary procedures, the creation of effective local government, and the establishment of a non-firm-based social safety net (Balcerowicz, 1994).

As initially conceived, the reforms were to have the following sequence: (a) stabilization, (b) privatization, (c) industrial restructuring. The reformers felt that stabilization could only be sustained if most firms were privatized. Until privatization had progressed sufficiently, the government would have to limit wage growth and investment outlays, because firms could not be trusted to manage this on their own (Dabrowski et al. 1991, p. 404). The economic reform law was passed in the last days of 1989, and the program went into effect in early 1990.[10]

These reforms, which have been called the boldest stabilization program implemented in any socialist country (Milanovic, 1992, p. 1), proved success-ful in several key areas. In 1990, convertibility at the fixed exchange rate was maintained; real interest rates became positive; the budget deficit went from 7% of GDP in 1989, to a small surplus in 1990; the (real) level of subsidies was cut by more than half; inflation decelerated from 19% per month in 1989, to around 5% at the end of 1990 (Milanovic, 1992, p. 1). The numbers in these areas have remained consistently good (BCE, 1990–99).

At the same time, there were clear tradeoffs associated with the early tran-sition period. In 1991, real industrial wages fell by more than 30%; unemploy-ment grew from around zero to 6.1%; industrial production in the state sector decreased by 25% (compared with 1989); and GDP per capita dropped by 12% (Milanovic, 1992, pp. 1–2, 7; BCE, 1999). In the first three years of transition, industrial employment declined from approximately 6.2 million to 5.4 million (GUS, 1998).

Industrial production recovered by 1993, and GDP growth became posi-tive in 1992. Unemployment peaked at 16.4% in 1993, and is currently at approximately 10% (BCE, 1999). The private sector share of industrial em-ployment has changed from 16.2% in 1989, to 60% in 1996. The pattern of private sector employment growth is even more pronounced for the economy as a whole. The private sector share of GDP has grown steadily, from 28.6% in 1989 to 70% in 1996 (see Table 2.1). These impressive figures have led many observers to regard Poland as one of the few genuine economic success stories in the region.

Privatization

Privatization in Poland has been a multifaceted endeavor, as a wide range of techniques has been employed to dispose of state assets (see Table 2.1). In the original privatization law, passed in July 1990 (six months after the other ini-tial reforms were begun), the government chose a combination of three basic approaches: (a) capital privatization – commercial sale of shares in state-owned enterprises, (b) direct privatization – employee ownership, and (c) mass privatization (voucher distribution). Larger enterprises typically were priva-tized on a case-by-case basis, and progress was very slow. Small and medium-sized enterprises were privatized via direct auction as well as employee buy-outs (via liquidation), and from 1995, a range of large and medium-sized com-

Table 2.1   Ownership Transfer in Poland (1990–95)

	1990	1991	1992	1993	1994	1995
Total number of state-owned enterprises	8453	8228	7245	5924	4955	4563
Liquidation						
Started	49	989	1576	1999	2287	2507
Completed	0	201	561	893	1248	1450
Converted to joint-stock companies	38	260	480	527	723	958
Capital privatization	6	27	51	99	134	160

panies became part of the National Investment Fund (NIF) program (Ministry of Privatization, 1995; Blaszczyk, 1996, p. 179).

One very successful component of the reform program has been 'small privatization', wherein some 97% of small shops, retail outlets, and restaurants were privatized (Blaszczyk, 1996, p. 181). Perhaps the most interesting form of privatization has been enterprise-led liquidations. This entails the lease or sale of enterprise assets to a newly created corporation made up primarily of the existing workforce. Over 1000 SOEs had been privatized via this method by 1996 (Blaszczyk, 1996, p. 201). Not only has this been a popular form of ownership transformation, it has also led to unanticipated levels of proactive enterprise restructuring.

Two factors have been central to the success of this approach. First, the legal and institutional arrangements at the firm level – the strength and development of Employee Councils – made this a logical path to privatization. This alone, however, may not have been enough to clear the way for such a large number of successful privatizations. An additional factor – that these newly private enterprises would be *exempted* from the wage tax – was a clear incentive that made taking the leap more attractive. In effect, opposition to one reform (the wage tax) was channeled into support for another (privatization). Whether this was a clever policy twist by the government, or merely a fortuitous accident, is unclear.

In November 1995, the government distributed coupons for a nominal fee to citizens that entitled them to shares in National Investment Funds (NIFs). The funds are run by a mixture of local and foreign-owned management companies. Eventually all will be listed on the Warsaw stock exchange.[11] The NIF program has generally been judged a success; however, most of the largest and politically sensitive companies were not included in the program as originally envisioned.

As of 1997, the government still controlled some 3700 companies (BCE, Oct. 1997, p. 31). Among these state assets, a group of 400 large enterprises accounted for most of the net worth (97% of the net worth of state-held enterprise assets, according to Blaszczyk, 1996).[12]

To summarize, most of the larger companies were excluded from the initial phases of privatization. Many of them were later 'commercialized' – brought under control of the state Treasury in order to restructure and prepare for privatization – but progress among these companies has been decidedly mixed. The state still controls a great many of the largest enterprises, including, for example, 13 of 24 steel mills and virtually all coal mines. Politicians have been hesitant to challenge many of the largest companies. However, direct privatization/liquidation has been very successful in small and medium-sized SOEs, and almost all smaller companies are now privately owned.

4. Organized Labor and Economic Reform

The early post-communist governments in Poland were comprised of and represented a complicated mixture of Poles who struggled to remove the communists from power. Organized labor was prominent amongst them. Indeed, throughout the transition period governing parties have been reliant on the political and institutional support of the largest trade unions. At the enterprise level, the legacy and special legal status of Employee Councils gave them a clear mechanism for influencing reform policy. Even as this power gradually eroded between 1990 and 1992 as most SMEs were privatized (thus abolishing councils), and clear divisions developed between political party leadership and factory-level workers, other institutional arrangements and tactics emerged. Beginning in 1992, industrial action became much more commonplace, as the strike rate rapidly increased in the face of worsening conditions for many workers. One response of the government was to institutionalize national and sectoral collective bargaining arrangements, thus guaranteeing more 'fairness' in the distribution of costs and benefits of reform. In 1993–94, a so-called 'social pact' gave industrial workers in the sectors most directly affected by reform new guarantees regarding wages, employment, and inclusion in corporate governance structures.

Solidarity and OPZZ

The historic round table agreements of 1989, conducted between Solidarity and the new post-communist government in February and March, and finalized in April, were an outgrowth of Solidarity-led strikes and demonstrations. At the beginning of the new era, the Solidarity trade union thus enjoyed a special place in the public mind; it had been instrumental in bringing down communism and had 'changed the world'. The most visible trade union leader, Lech Walesa, would become President of Poland in 1991.

However, in the aftermath of the imposition of martial law in 1981, the government moved to fill the shop-floor organizational vacuum by sponsoring its own 'official', legal union, OPZZ. This new union emerged in 1983, and, in spite of its explicit links with the communist government, added new members at a rapid pace. OPZZ survives to this day as the communist 'successor trade union,' and is linked politically with the Communist successor party, SLD. While it claims a larger membership (3 million members in 1998) than Solidarity (1.2 million members in 1998) and its spin-off unions (e.g. Solidarity '80, with 157,000 members) (*Polityka*, 7 June 1998), OPZZ is generally considered a more 'passive' union than Solidarity (and many of the other unions as well). It is less willing to call or initiate strike activities, less involved in national-level politics, and so forth. The reasons for this are perhaps complex, but in a most basic sense, it is a product of the history and tradition in the various unions.

At the national level there are clear differences (both cultural and political) and limited cooperation between Solidarity and OPZZ. In most cases, Solidarity has been seen as the more proactive union in terms of restructuring and reform – either blocking it or actively participating in it – both in terms of national politics and company-level issues.[13] However, at the branch, and especially the firm level, there has been much more cooperation. Although the dynamics of power and bargaining vary from firm to firm, with Solidarity being clearly dominant in many cases, there has, in general, been a high degree of cooperation among competing unions. This is borne out in numerous surveys of union leaders,[14] as well as in the author's company-level interviews.[15]

Labor, Political Parties, and National Government

In the initial phases of reform, workers were institutionally strong at the national level in terms of political party organization and their direct ties with Solidarity-related governments between 1989 and 1993. Governments in the first four years after communism were all controlled by parties from the 'Solidarity bloc'. The largest of these was the Democratic Union (UD), which later merged with several smaller parties, and took the name Union for Freedom (UW).

In 1990, the first post-communist government was able to implement almost all of the shock therapy plan – including exchange rate adjustment, incomes policy, interest rate hikes, deficit reduction, price liberalization, trade liberalization, as well as plans for privatizing most state-owned companies. In 1990 and 1991, as we have seen, the Mazowiecki and Bielecki governments made steady progress on macroeconomic reforms and privatization of SMEs.

Trade union leaders were not directly involved in the development of these early economic reform plans. Organized labor did, however, give its full support to the program, including the state sector wage tax. Hale (1999, pp. 91–4) argues that Solidarity union leaders supported initial reforms because they accepted the need to make a radical break with the centrally planned economy (this sentiment was linked closely to their fervent anti-communism), and because the economic situation was so dire. The nature of worker support for the reforms evolved, however, as the costs and dislocations grew. One area where the government clearly acceded to workers' demands was in the area of Employee Council rights.[16]

Poland held its first fully open parliamentary elections in September 1991.[17] The resulting parliament was very fragmented, and included some 29 different political groups. The first government of the new parliament lacked any real cabinet-level consensus, and proved to be very unstable. During the 10-month life of this government, the macroeconomic environment remained stable, but power over structural reform in industry devolved to the firm level, where the results were decidedly mixed.

In June 1992, a viable government coalition finally emerged, with Hanna Suchocka (UD) as Prime Minister. The Suchocka government brought economic reform back to the top of the agenda, as it tried to strengthen macroeconomic policies and to speed up the privatization process. At the same time it made what it thought were strategic concessions as it faced growing confrontation from organized interests. A strike wave began in the summer of 1992 and culminated with strikes by coal miners in December. Unemployment had risen to almost 14% by the end of 1992. In the new year the strikes continued and things only worsened for the government. It granted certain trade preferences to selected areas in agriculture and industry, and initiated the 'social pact' with unions and employers.

This proved to be too little, too late. In June, several Solidarity-affiliated members of parliament abstained from a critical vote of confidence over the annual budget, thereby causing the government to fall; the incumbent, reform wing of Solidarity lost by two votes. Solidarity members at the time said explicitly that this action was in response to a budget that cut aid and support for key industries. The unintended consequence was that the former communists won the general election that followed.

Two relatively large parties that were carry-overs from the communist period – the Peasants' Party (PSL) and the reformed communists, renamed the Social Democrats (SLD), ruled together in coalition from late 1993 until the fall of 1997.

The SLD-dominated coalition government moved quickly in the fall of 1994 to address key grievances of organized labor. It agreed to use a tripartite forum to resolve issues of 'social justice' associated with reform. One clear by-product of this government's approach to labor relations and to the demands of key unions was a dramatic reduction in strike activity (discussed below). The SLD approach embodied a combination of pragmatic accommodation with key sectoral union organizations as well as continued stability in the areas of fiscal, monetary, and trade policy. The private sector continued its rapid growth and the economy remained stable. Progress in reforming heavy industry, however, was limited. SLD did manage finally to implement the NIF program, which had been in the planning stages since 1992, but in spite of the program's overall success, most larger firms were not included in the Funds as initially envisioned.

SLD governments did enough to keep the reforms firmly on track, particularly in terms of macroeconomic policies, and initiated new programs dubbed the *Strategy for Poland* and *Package 2000*. The Finance Minister, and one of the principal architects of the SLD plans, stated that his government 'attached greater weight both to economic growth and to the social costs of stabilization and transformation' than did previous governments (Kolodko, 1998, p. 22). He argued that the early transition had 'grossly neglected the state sector' by imposing capital and wage taxes on SOEs, and that it was necessary to increase the role of the central government in promoting enterprise reform, via commercialization. Under SLD leadership, the central government was to play a much more prominent role in reorganizing firms (Kolodko, 1998, p. 25). With respect to bargaining with unions, the government established a national tripartite Commission for Socioeconomic Affairs, which allowed the government to abolish the wage tax (wages were negotiated quarterly in the Commission).

Depending on how one looks at it, the SLD attitude toward unions can be seen as creative accommodation with an emphasis on continued reforms, or strategic acquiescence for political reasons. One hears both interpretations from key SLD leaders who were involved in economic policy-making at the time. Needless to say, they take full credit for the recovery of industrial production and generally high GDP growth rates experienced between 1994 and 1997.

In the run-up to the 1997 parliamentary elections, the party system evolved and solidified somewhat. A fourth main party emerged from a group of smaller Solidarity-affiliated parties, named Solidarity Electoral Action (AWS).[18] In the fall of 1997, AWS scored a surprising victory in the general election. They joined UW to form a coalition that continues to the present day.

A number of scholars have examined the inherent tensions in the Solidarity movement, and the form they took in the early days of democratic rule.[19] These are tensions which were never fully resolved, and which persist in the governing AWS–UW coalition. In a very basic sense, the two parties represent the two main, contradictory tendencies in the Solidarity movement: AWS (or at least several of the core parties that are grouped under the AWS umbrella) are concerned with directly meeting the needs of rank-and-file workers, while UW is openly pro-free market – the head of AWS, Marian Krzaklewski, is also the head of the National Committee of Solidarity (the trade union), while the head of UW, Leszek Balcerowicz, is the architect of Poland's shock therapy. Their ongoing, internal struggles, and the mechanisms of their potential resolution, mirror the early struggles and bargains over economic reform. While both parties are committed to continuing the reform process, points of tension remain, particularly in the area of industrial restructuring.[20]

Labor Challenges the Reformist Agenda: Strikes Waves in 1992–93

In the first years of transition, the number of strikes in Poland was relatively small. In 1990 there were 250, and in 1991, 305 strikes occurred throughout the country. In 1992 and 1993 the number of strikes jumped dramatically, to 6351 and 7443 respectively. By 1994, strike activity had subsided, with just 429 incidents of official industrial action. The trend continued in a downward direction through 1996. The two years that obviously stand out in this picture are 1992 and 1993 (GUS, 1997, p. 115). Strike activity was increasingly adopted as a tactic by groups that were faring less well as a result of reforms. Many of these groups, which had *initially* supported reforms, were now taking to the streets in order to push the government to modify its policies.

Beginning in May 1992, the strike rate rose dramatically, as the cooperation that initially existed between the Mazowiecki and Bielecki governments and major trade unions evaporated.[21] These strikes were, in many cases, due to unhappiness with the effects of the reforms – in particular, falling real wages (in part due to the state sector wage freeze), and the restructuring/privatization process. To cite a few notable examples, the Ursus tractor factory struck to protest a government sponsored restructuring plan; coal miners struck in order to protest the sectoral reform package and the supposed low level of government credits (December 1992), steel workers went on strike for higher wages, and increased government capital investment.

In 1993, the budget process moved to the center of the national debate, and strike activity spread to include teachers, doctors, and railway workers. In February and March 1993, striking workers from a variety of sectors (including coal, steel, rail, and the building trades) marched to the parliament and Council of Ministers buildings to protest the government's activities regarding payroll taxes, unemployment, 'anti-inflation' policy, the workers' pension system, and healthcare and cultural funding. Needless to say, all of these were by-products of the economic reform program (*Rzeczpospolita*, 19 March 1993; *Gazeta Wyborcza*, 18 February 1993).

The national leadership of both Solidarity and OPZZ met with cabinet ministers of the Suchocka government in an attempt to gain better social guarantees for members hurt by the reforms. They asked specifically for a 'code of social guarantees', and took exception to the government's proposed budget (*Rzezcpospolita*, 15 April 1993; 8 April 1993). In May, key members of the Solidarity leadership threatened to call a general strike, and suggested that a new government be formed, which would better meet the needs of workers[22] (*Gazeta Bankowa*, 14 May 1993). In a national press interview during the run-up to the general election of October 1993, the national director of the Solidarity trade union talked openly of the union's willingness to call a general strike if the next government was not accommodating enough (*Rzeczpospolita*, 6 September 1993).

The rapid rise in strike activity in 1992 can in part be attributed to the fact that UD 'broke its agreement' with the trade unions.[23] Members of union leadership from that period expressed growing frustration with the tone, terms, and distribution of costs associated with the economic reform agenda. The honeymoon apparently was over, and certain components of the reform agenda appeared to be in serious jeopardy. In the midst of a parliamentary struggle over the 1993 budget, Solidarity MPs abstained from a critical vote of confidence and precipitated the fall of the UD government. Strike activity in the ensuing period (late 1993–97), when the governing coalition was led by the former communists (SLD), declined dramatically.

Towalski (1996) offers an insightful interpretation of these strike data. He argues that the drastic reduction in strike activity from 1993 to 1994 can be attributed primarily to two factors; one technical and one political. First, the system used for counting strikes was modified, thus somewhat reducing their number. However, this change, while important, does not account for most of the reduction. The dramatic fall-off in strike activity after 1993 is largely attributable to the policies of the new, SLD/PSL government. The new government was more accommodating to the main trade unions, particularly in heavy industry, because the SLD feared confrontation with the Solidarity and OPZZ trade unions, and agreed to many of their demands.

Interviews that I conducted with various high-ranking SLD political leaders confirmed this interpretation. These politicians were acutely aware that Solidarity's parliamentary representatives had been instrumental in toppling the previous government, and that escalating strike levels were in large measure due to dissatisfaction with various side-effects of economic reform. Furthermore, they realized that, as former communists, they needed to move quickly to reach accommodation with Solidarity unionists who, they feared, might shut down the economy as a protest against a 'communist return' (even if it was through a democratic electoral victory). In short, they felt that accommodation and, as one party leader put it, 'calm, open-minded, non-confrontational bargaining', was critical to their government's survival.

Labor Strength at the Firm Level: The Institutional Legacy of Employee Councils

In 1989, reformers were faced with a legacy of enterprise self-management and Employee Council laws that gave Councils uncommon control rights (e.g. they could fire managers, determine investment strategies, overrule ministries). After an initial honeymoon period, workers' resistance to the ownership transformation program forced decision-makers to modify it, changing its tempo and increasing the participation of state enterprise employees in the privatization of enterprises in which they worked (Jarosz, 1996, p. 6). One aspect of the privatization agenda that the Councils effectively blocked was commercialization. Employee Councils opposed state plans to commercialize firms (re-nationalization to be followed by sale), because once a firm was commercialized, employees no longer had any control.

In the 1990 privatization law, Councils were effectively ceded the right to veto privatization plans for their firms. The law also gave employees the right to legally dissolve their firms and rent, lease, or sell the assets to a new corporation created for that purpose. This new corporation could be solely owned by the employees (Levitas, 1993, p. 105).[24] The process of privatization thus was not merely a government, top-down endeavor, but was mediated through workers and managers in individual enterprises. In the early phases of transition, Employee Councils had control over firm-level decision making, and also had *de facto* veto authority regarding government decisions about the transfer of enterprise assets (privatization, etc.).

The liquidation process which led to employee-owned companies was the one privatization method that gave rank-and-file workers the most direct say in and control over the restructuring process. One key incentive that further speeded-up the privatization process in SMEs, was the wage tax exemption for employee-leased companies (liquidations). Not surprisingly, this became the most popular form of ownership transformation during the first years of transition[25] (see Table 2.1). However, the largest firms generally did not opt for this type of reform – probably because the scope of reform was so great that it was not at all clear to employees and managers that going it alone could work, and because larger firms had more political and organizational power, and could thus force the government to either continue subsidies or push reforms only gradually.

In the spring of 1993, the Suchocka government, along with trade unions and a newly formed employers' confederation, agreed to the Pact on State Enterprises. In solvent firms with more than 1000 employees (i.e. most large SOEs), the Pact required workers' representatives to choose among four variants of further restructuring: (1) sale to a large investor, (2) sale of stock in a public offering, (3) management/employee buy-out, (4) entrusting control of their portfolios to a bank or management fund. The first three options amounted to privatization, while the fourth was somewhat unclear, and eventually took the form of National Investment Funds[26] (Mujzel, 1993, pp. 140–42).

Capital privatization, the outright selling of large state companies, had been a failure in the capital-scarce environment of the early 1990s. In this context, the pact was designed both to speed enterprise reform and to strengthen the position of employees; it was a compromise designed to move reforms forward. Although these may seem to be contradictory aims, the government felt that further reform would not be possible without the explicit consent of employees – unions had made this abundantly clear via both their public statements to the government and the rapid rise in industrial action during 1992.

In order to get the social support necessary to radically accelerate the privatization process, the government agreed to give more economic privileges to workers (20% of company shares allocated free of charge), draw them into the process as a whole, and grant them a permanent place on the corporate boards of the privatized enterprises (Mujzel, 1993, pp. 140–42; Dabrowski, 1995, p. 78). The labor minister at the time (Jacek Kuron) called the pact 'a proposal for the workforce and the management of enterprises to join actively in deciding their future and so ensure the most rational transformation of enterprises and of the national economy' (Mujzel, 1993, p. 140).

To many in the government, this seemed like the only politically feasible way forward. Although the government fell in June 1993, before the pact could truly take effect, it was resurrected in February 1994 by the SLD-led coalition. This government was well served by the arrangement, as privatization went forward with the support of organized labor, which had been given a clearer institutionalized role in the process.

With the new 'Kodeks Pracy' (labor code) in 1996, the SLD government introduced new rules governing SOEs. The institutional power of organized labor had come full circle. Most SMEs were by now privatized, many of them as employee-owned companies, where Employee Councils had been abolished. The 1996 Labor Code has meant a *de facto* end to the Employee Councils. In the first years of transition they played a critical role, but at this stage, it was sectoral bargaining that had gained ascendancy, and the new law reflects the place of sectoral confederations, which are dominated by the larger firms (Kodeks Pracy, 1996).

The Emergence of National and Sectoral Collective Bargaining

The 1993 Pact on State Enterprises also called for the establishment of a tripartite national negotiating commission, wherein the government, leaders from seven national union confederations (including of course, Solidarity and OPZZ), and representatives from the employers' confederation would meet to determine, among other things, new guidelines for wage taxation (they would agree on wages each quarter). The prevailing system of government-enforced wage restraint in SOEs had become a volatile political issue among industrial workers, who saw their real wages plummeting in the face of moderate levels of inflation.[27]

When the SLD-led coalition revived the Pact, they also established an additional tripartite forum, the National Tripartite Commission on Socio-Economic Issues, which, according to SLD politicians who were involved in the commission, gave them another mechanism to 'ensure that social peace could be maintained' – it gave the communist-successor party a less political forum in which to hear and respond to Solidarity (union) concerns.

In the National Tripartite Commission negotiations, seven union confederations sit at the table. The two dominant players have been Solidarity and OPZZ, if for no other reason than their relative size. At the sectoral level, the same main unions participate, in addition to various industry-specific specialist unions (e.g. the Railway Locomotive Drivers' Union).

Key unions initially considered the Tripartite Commission to be an important institution that would guarantee them access to the industrial policy-making process. One particular issue that was to some extent depoliticized in the commission was the government's wage tax, which had been imposed in 1990. Under the terms of the tripartite body, wage tax rates were to be negotiated among all the players on a quarterly basis. At the time, this particular tax was a major issue to rank-and-file industrial workers. However, other firm and sectoral-level issues would become much more salient.

A number of authors have suggested that a form of national corporatist bargaining – bargaining among national-level peak associations for labor and management, and the government – was emergent and growing in importance (Iankova, 1998; Freeman, 1994; Lajtos, 1994; Bialecki and Heyns, 1993). In fact, these institutions have had a limited impact. To put it simply, so-called tripartism enabled the government to get past the tricky issue of the wage tax, and also eliminate some of the inertia that had emerged in the privatization process.

At the end of the day, however, more important negotiations were taking place at the sectoral (confederation) and firm level. Answers to key questions concerning the future of Polish industry were beginning to emerge, but not in the context of the tripartite forum. The real action lay in a combination of company-based responses to restructuring challenges and sectoral-level negotiations with the government. The experience in the steel, coal, and shipbuilding sectors (examined below) demonstrates that the tripartite institutions have been of limited importance.[28]

Unions and Reform in the Coal, Steel, and Shipbuilding Sectors

Evidence from three key sectors that I have examined – steel, coal, and shipbuilding – lends support to the argument outlined in Section 2. Where reform meant certain extinction, both unions and management blocked the government's attempts to restructure the industry. Where reform was feasible, but success was by no means guaranteed, unions agreed to the government's agenda. In these sectors, firm and sectoral-level bargaining became the norm, as governments consistently built compromise into their restructuring plans. In cases where the government was not credible in its commitment to reform, management and labor often resisted it successfully.

In the coal industry, unions blocked reforms from the outset. In steel and shipbuilding, where reforms had a chance to succeed (although there were certainly no guarantees of success), unions generally supported reform, but they conditioned the restructuring process at the firm level, and later extracted substantial side payments to compensate losers in their industries.

Coal. Among the major industrial sectors in Poland, coal mining has the most obvious problems with long-term viability. Economic ministers in the first postcommunist government in 1990 proposed far-reaching restructuring and rationalization of the industry, which was considered the single largest drain on the national budget (i.e. it was the most heavily subsidized industry). Policy-makers in the Ministry of Industry who devised the initial plan were anything but pleased with the outcome. In the face of explicit threats of sector-wide strikes, the government modified the reform plan in such a way as to defer the most difficult decisions, and allowed continued subsidies.

This initial confrontation and government retreat established a pattern that has continued to this day. Subsidies to the coal industry still account for almost 30% of all government pay-outs to industry (Ministry of the Economy, 1998). Successive governments have failed to push through serious restructuring programs. This is no great surprise, given the strength and determination of the coal sector confederations, which have presented a unified front and repeatedly demonstrated the ability and willingness to strike – in an economy whose power, steel, chemical, and shipbuilding industries are directly or indirectly dependent on Polish coal.

At joint negotiating sessions with government officials, the difference between coal and steel union confederations has been clear. Steel confederations had certain basic benchmarks in terms of the speed of employment reduction and pension plans, but generally had a flexible stance toward the government, and acknowledged that many of the toughest decisions would need to be taken at the firm level. Coal confederation negotiators, on the other hand, adopted a confrontational, and even accusatory, bargaining position, that betrayed the desperation felt in their industry. They demanded a continuation of subsidies, and investment and employment guarantees, and accused the government of attempting to ruin their 'sacred' industry (and so forth). Although coal sector employment has declined by some 40%, these reductions have been achieved through attrition, and have not been associated with proactive restructuring.[29]

Steel. The Polish steel sector is comprised of 25 separate enterprises (mills). Employment in the industry currently is about 90,000, down from almost 150,000 in 1989. Output declined dramatically between 1989 and 1991, from 10 to 4.5, and has now recovered to 6.8 (units are converted from tons of output, with 1989 as the benchmark year – 10). In 1989, all of the steel mills were state-owned enterprises (SOEs). Today, there are a variety of ownership forms, including joint stock/state treasury, state enterprise, National Investment Fund, and private; the government is still the sole owner of almost half of the enterprises, and most of the others have some form of joint private/bank/ government ownership structure.

Over the past eight years, as the reform process has progressed, there has been an array of outcomes in terms of restructuring and economic success. Several steel mills are performing quite well, and have achieved impressive productivity improvements. Others have taken a 'negative' path to restructuring, and have seen productivity and sales stagnate, even as employment has decreased. Roughly speaking, five or six firms are doing well, five or six are doing very badly, and the rest are somewhere in between.

Since late 1992, steel sector union confederations have played a central role in negotiating with the government over the terms of restructuring the industry. Sectoral agreements, covering employees across the industry, have been used to establish baselines for wages, and to set the terms for pensions, early retirements, and workforce reductions. At the same time, there has been a great deal of variation among the 24 steel mills in terms of their approach to, and success at, restructuring. Company reform agendas are initiated and negotiated at the firm level, among management and labor.

The deal being negotiated between Poland and the EU regarding steel highlights the political nature of industrial policy in both the East and the West. In effect, there will be a cartelization of steel production: overall country quotas will be set in Brussels, and the Polish Ministry of Economics will play a leading role in allocating production quotas to different steel producers. Efficient producers will get their piece of the pie, but so will the worst performers. Successful firms will not have their output determined by simple demand/market forces. The current deal enables Poland to 'keep' its steel industry, prop up key large and inefficient producers (without killing the efficient firms), and maintain labor peace via generous side payments to sectoral trade union confederations (the EU will pay much of the cost of pensions for some 30,000 early retirements, which probably will be controlled by the confederations). It is a good deal for both politicians and steel union confederations on both sides. The main losers are managers and employees of successful Polish firms (Keat, 2000).

Shipbuilding. The Polish shipbuilding sector is comprised of three main shipyards – Gdansk, Gdynia, and Szczecin. The Gdansk shipyard, birthplace of the Solidarity trade union movement, is a notable failure. Szczeczin is one of the country's most celebrated success stories, and Gdynia, while slower to reform, has restructured successfully. Both shipyards have dramatically improved productivity, have become quite profitable, and have full order books for the next several years. Gdansk recently completed bankruptcy proceedings, and the small portion of the company that remains active was purchased by the Gdynia shipyard.

The most notable difference in government policy toward these companies was that Gdansk, from 1990–95, continued to receive substantial state aid that was not linked to restructuring. In the other two shipyards, continuing government support was explicitly and credibly linked to proactive restructuring policies and was limited to a short, one to two year time frame. In each case, company-level unions were active in the reform process – in Szczeczin and Gdynia they actively participated in and supported reform; in Gdansk, they blocked it.

Not surprisingly, Solidarity trade unionists in the Gdansk shipyard had a clear sense of entitlement. As the other two shipyards restructured, they resisted reforms, and rebuffed several overtures from foreign investors. In the dying days of the shipyard (July 1998), active and former leaders expressed feelings of exasperation and betrayal. In their minds, they had been the focal point of years of struggle against the communist regime, and were being forgotten by an ungrateful public and government. One commented that, 'our political umbrella has finally been taken from us ... now we must salvage what we can from the wreckage of this once great shipyard'.

5. Conclusions

The newly elected democratic government (1989) inherited a vast, diverse, and crisis-ridden industrial sector. In the first years of transition the government was able to achieve most microeconomic reforms and many macroeconomic reforms (excellent stabilization plus decent adjustment), thus generating enough economic growth and stability to escape having to directly challenge the most vulnerable among organized industry. The government maintained union support and at the same time overcame potential reform-blocking coalitions via selective use of soft budget constraints, severance packages, and sectoral employment guarantees.

Stabilization (macroeconomic policies, including currency, budgetary and trade reform) turns out to have been much easier than certain aspects of adjustment (microstructural issues, such as restructuring heavy industry). Policies leading to a stable macroeconomic environment, general progress in privatization and institutional reforms, and booming growth in the private sector have given successive governments some flexibility in dealing with the most problematic sectors and firms. By reducing employment primarily through attrition in certain firms, government policy has amounted to 'putting the dinosaurs to sleep slowly'. The government used what discretionary funds were available – in the context of generally sound fiscal policy – to aid these sectors.[30] In other sectors, which were deemed less critical to the national economy and where unions were less well organized, workers felt the brunt of economic reforms.

Since 1990, organized labor has exercised its veto authority when it felt it was too directly threatened. The use of this authority has varied over time, and by sector. Throughout the transition, fiscal, monetary and trade policies have been consistently sound, and the growth of the private sector has been impressive (both in manufacturing and services). The other half of the story, however, is that governing politicians were held directly accountable for the costs of reform, particularly by organized labor. The steel and shipbuilding stories suggest that labor was willing to face the risks inherent in rapid reform, but also that they were willing to 'push back' in order to compensate losers from the initial shake-out years.

The multi-track privatization program clearly has been conditioned and constrained by organized labor. In fact, at various stages during the past nine years, the process of institutional reform of SOEs has in many ways reflected the preferences of workers. A combination of institutions emerged – ESOPs, NIFs, sectoral reform packages – that reflected the locus of relative labor strength at different points in time. In the earliest stages, when labor was institutionally strong at the firm level, employee leasing (ESOP) was the most common, and successful, component of the privatization program. In later years, as labor bargaining power grew at the sectoral level, reform guidelines were determined more often at this level.

The state sector wage tax stands out as a key policy issue in both the enterprise reform and tripartite bargaining stories. In the first years of transition, ESOP–liquidation became a popular avenue to privatization not only because Employee Councils had the legal authority and organizational capacity to embrace this approach, but also because this allowed these newly private firms to avoid the wage tax. Larger firms, for which liquidation seemed undesirable for structural reasons, eventually clashed with the government over the tax, and backed off only after tripartite wage-setting was instituted in 1994.

Labor was willing to 'take the risk' of agreeing to reform, because it was not nearly as great a risk as has been commonly assumed. It had the institutional power to slow or partially reverse reforms that hurt too much. In firms and sectors where reforms turned out well, (almost) everybody has ended up better off. In the situations where there has been a great deal of pain associated with transition, organized labor has pushed the government to provide at least basic security for the losers. Happily for Poland, the successes have far outweighed the failures, enabling successive governments to stay on a path to reform and economic growth.

Notes

1. Przeworski makes this argument in *Democracy and the Market* (1991).

2. Beginning in the the early 1970s, the nascent independent free trade union movement, which would later become known as Solidarity, challenged the communist regime as it demanded better wages and working conditions as well as political rights and freedoms. In 1980, Solidarity included some 10 million members, fully one-half of the working age population in Poland. Approximately 2 million of these were rank-and-file industrial workers, while the rest represented a braod cross-section of society that opposed the regime. During the historic events of 1980, Solidarity was the central organizing point around which a larger social movement was based. After being formally legalized in August 1980, the union was forced underground with the imposition of martial law in December 1981, and its leadership was imprisoned.

3. Przeworski (1991, p. 181) makes a comment in passing to the effect that the institutional strength of workers can be helpful in the reform process, but the point is peripheral to his argument.

4. In this context, the term monopoly refers to a closed shop situation than representation by a single union. In most firms several trade unions worked together during bargaining over the terms of reform.

5. Dabrowski et al. (1991) summarize these developments, and argue that in the process the government sought both to divide the labor movement and to decentralize economic decision-making.

6. One can envision three stylized scenarios (under conditions of uncertainty about the distribution of gainers and losers from reform, and with reformist politicians in power): (a) strong labor can veto reform now and ex post; (b) medium strength labor can veto now, but not ex post; (c) weak labor cannot veto reform at any point. In situations (a) and (c), reforms are more likely than in situation (b), where labor would veto 'now'. Along similar lines, Calmfors and Driffill (1988), and Rowthorn (1992) have suggested that *both* very centralized and very decentralized wage-setting systems (i.e. both very strong and very weak labor) seemconsistent with good economic performance in OECD countries.

7. The first democratic elections were held in June 1989, with the Communists resoundingly defeated. In September the first effective government was formed, with Tadeusz Mazowiecki serving as Prime Minister.

8. From October 1988, the Rakowski government had implemented partial, market-based reforms.

9. Three of the most prominent were then Finance Minister and Deputy Prime Minister, Leszek Balcerowicz, and American economists, Jeffrey Sachs and David Lipton.

10. For a description of the 'fast-track' nature of this legislation in the Polish Parliament, see Balcerowicz (1994, pp. 162–4).

11. NIFs have the following shareholding structure: 33% by NIF, 27% by all other NIFs, 25% state Treasury, 15% to employees (*Financial Times*, 23 November 1995; Text of MMP law – Ministry of Privatization, 1995).

12. According to Blascczyk (1996, p. 195), 'there is a group of giant state-owned enterprises, which remain unrestructured, highly in debt, avoiding the payment of taxes to the state budget and even to the (employee) insurance funds, and because of political reasons, remain untouchable ... the politicians have not been sufficiently resistant against the political pressure of these groups'.

13. This was very clear in case study research on individual firms in the steel, coal, and shipbuilding sectors.

14. The research team of the Faculty of Labor Sociology at the Warsaw School of Economics (SGH) has conducted several very informative surveys of union leadership, which speak directly to the issues of attitudes toward restructuring, strikes, and political participation. See the works by Gardawski (1997), Gilejko (1998), and Towalski (1997).

15. In the course of my research in Poland between 1995 and 1998, I conducted numerous interviews with politicians, policy-makers, factory managers, trade union leaders (at the national, sectoral, and enterprise levels), industry experts and academic researchers. Most of the interviews were conducted in 1997 and 1998, when I was in Poland for 12 months on a Fulbright research grant. These interviews form the basis for much of my analysis – in particular in the sections of the chapter dealing with bargaining, the steel, coal, and shipbuilding sectors, and political parties and reform.

16. Dabrowshi argues that this approach won out over a more straightforward commercialization–privatization program, because the political leadership feared that it would open up another

field of social conflict within firms at the same time that the Balcerowicz plan would radically reduced inflation, output, and real wages. It becase practically impossible to privatize state enterprises against the will of employee councils and managers (Dabrowski, 1995, 76–7).

17. The first elections, in 1990, were carried out according to the terms of the 1989 Round Table Agreement which guaranteed the communist party most of the seats in the lower house of parliament. The communists were defeated so resoundingly, however, in the races for the remaining Sejm seats and the full Senate, that they had little effective power, and dared not block reforms.

18. The long-term viability and cohesion of this party is still in question. AWS is in some sense a 'coalition' party – it is made up of a number of small parties affiliated variously, with the Solidarity trade union movement, splinter groups of politicians previously linked to UW, and Catholic and nationalist causes. The clear leader of the party, Marian Kzaklewski, has been the national director of the Solidarity trade union since 1993.

19. See, for example, Kowalik (1993) and Kemp-Welch (1991).

20. One of the liveliest public battles has been between the AWS Economics Minister (Steinhoff), who has advocated sectoral 'cartels', and the UW Finance Minister (Balcerowicz), who has pushed for stricter enforcement of bankruptcy laws for SOEs.

21. The number of strikes in a given year is a potentially flawed measure of labor activity and militancy. In this case, however, it is a useful summary measure of the labor relations climate of the time – by any measure, be it strikes, threatened strikes, demonstrations, marches, or protests in parliament by pro-labor MPs, organized labor was directly challenging the government's economic policies during 1992 and 1993.

22. They wanted a new government (coalition, ministers, etc.), not new elections.

23. *Polityka* (5 June 1993) gives a detailed outline of strike activity during the Suchocka government. Interviews with national Solidarity leaders echo the points above regarding the dissatisfaction with the Suchocka government's economic reform policies.

24. Dabrowski et al. (1991, pp. 404–5), argue that there was something of a standoff between Employee Councils and the government regarding ownership rights, and that the posr-communist state 'did not inherit either de facto or de jure title to its enterprises ... the problem of privatization is thus not about the simple transfer of state assets into private hands'.

25. Employee-owned companies have performed better than initially expected. And, somewhat suprisingly, they have been at least as willing as typical privately owned firms to shed labor and increase efficiency. Data from ongoing research projects on these companies suggests that they have adjusted and performed remarkably well (Jarosz, 1995, 1996; Dabrowski et al., 1992).

26. Although the NIF program did finally get off the ground in 1994, many of the largest companies were not included, and therefore were not actually facing one of these four options (BCE, 1999; Mujzel, 1993, pp. 140–42).

27. Inflation was 70%, 43%, and 35% in 199, 1992, and 1993 respectively.

28. Hale (1999, chapter 5) argues that in key industries that were 'vital to the economy', enterprise-level union organizations found ways to protect their workers. In other sectors, however, this was less often the case (e.g. textiles). the three sectors that I examine here tend to fall into the first category of sector, and in this sense are not illustrative of the entire industrial economy.

29. Coal sector employment has declined, through attrition, since 1989: 1989 – 415,000; 1992 – 334,000; 1995 – 275,000; 1998 – 230,000. Even under the current restructuring plan, just 11 of 65 mines are slated for closure (Ministry of the Economy, 1999).

30. Nobody has been 'fired' in coal, or railway transport (PKP), the two largest employers in the country. Sixty percent of industrial subsidies go to coal and PKP alone; steel by contrast gets 3% (Ministry of the Economy, 1998).

References

Adamski, Wladislaw (ed.) (1993), *Societal Conflict and Systemic Change: The Case of Poland (1980–1992)*, Warsaw: IFIS Publishers.

Balcerowicz, Leszek (1994), 'Poland' in John Williamson (ed.), *The Political Economy of Policy Reform*, Washington, DC: Institute for International Economics, 153–77.

Balcerowicz, Leszek (1994b), 'Understanding Postcommunist Transitions', *Journal of Democracy*, **5** (October).

Balcerowizc, Leszek and Alan Gelb (1994), 'Macro-policies in Transition to a Market Economy: a Three Year Perspective', *Proceedings of the World Bank Annual Conference on Development Economics*, 21–44.

Berg, Andrew and Jeffrey Sachs (1992), 'Structural Adjustment and International Trade in Eastern Europe: The Case of Poland', *Economic Policy*, **14** (April), 118–55.

Blais, Andre (1986), 'The Political Economy of Public Subsidies', *Comparative Political Studies*, **19**, 201–16.

Blacyca, George and Janusz Dabrowski (eds) (1995), *Monitoring Economic Transition: The Polish Case*, Brookfield: Avebury.

Blaszczyk, Barbara (1997), *Prywatyzacja w Polsce po Szedciu Latach*, Warsaw: CASE.

Blaszczyk, Barbara and Richard Woodward (eds) (1996), *Privatization in Post-Communist Countries; Volumes I and II*, Warsaw: CASE.

Boycko, Maxim, Andrei Shleifer and Robert Vishney (1995), *Privatizing Russia*. Cambridge, MA: MIT Press.

Business Central Europe (BCE)
    'Round Two', October 1997, pp. 31–2.
    'Slow Death' , April 1997, 11–2.
    'Key Data 1990–99' (data on various economic indicators, www.bcemag.com)

Centrum Badania Opinii Spolecznej (CBOS) (1994), *Pracownicy Przedsiębiorstw Panstwowych, Sprywatyzowanych I Prywatnych*, Warsaw: CBOS.

Centrum Badania Opinii Spolecznej (CBOS) (1995) (Czerwiec), 'Spoloczenstwo a Strajki', Warsaw: CBOS.

Dabrowski, Janusz, Michal Federowicz and Anthony Levitas (1991), 'Polish Enterprises and the Properties of Performance: Stabilization, Marketization, Privatization', *Politics and Society*, **19** (4), (December), 403–38.

Easterly, William (1997), 'When is Stabilization Expansionary', *Economic Policy*.

Fernandez, Raquel and Dani Rodrick (1991), 'Resistance to Reform: Status Quo Bias in the Presence of Individual-Specific Uncertainty', *American Economic Review*, **81** (December), 1146–55.

Fischer (1993), 'The Role of Macroeconomic Factors in Growth', *Journal of Monetary Economics*, **32** (December), 485–512.

Fischer and Gelb (1991), 'The Process of Socialist Economic Transformation', *Journal of Economic Perspectives*, **5** (4), (Fall), 91–105.

Fischer et al. (1996), 'Stabilization and Growth in Transition Economies: The Early Experience', *Journal of Economic Perspectives*, **10** (2), (Spring), 45–66.

Freeman, Richard (1994), 'What Direction for Labor Market Institutions in Eastern and Central Europe?' in Oliver Blanchard, Kenneth Froot and Jeffrey Sachs (eds), *The Transition in Eastern Europe, Volume 2, Restructuring*, Chicago: University of Chicago Press, 1–36.

Friedrich-Ebert-Stiftung (1993), Conference Proceedings, November 1993, Warsaw, Poland. *Privatization and Transformation in Eastern Europe: A Trade Union Perspective*, Warsaw: FES.

Gardawski, Juliusz (1997), *Zwiqzkowcy w Badaniach z Lat 1986-1996*, Warsaw: Szkola Glowna Handlowa (SGH).

Gardawski, Juliusz and Tomasz Ukowski (1994), *Robotnicy 1993*, Warsaw: Friedrich-Ebert-Stiftung.

Gardawski, Juliusz, Leszek Gilejko and Tomasz Ukowski (1994*), Zwiqzki Zawodowe w Przedsiêbiorstwach Przemyslowych*, Warsaw: Friedrich-Ebert-Stiftung.

Gazeta Bankowa
5/14/93, 'Jankowski Wyrusza na Rzad'

Gazeta Wyborcza
18 February 1998, 'Strajk Podatkowy', p. 1.
3 March 1998, 'Poszukam Nowych...', p. 26.

23 March 1998, 'Chcê...Nastêpn¹', p. 18.
26 April 1994, 'Praca Bez Mocy'
16 May 1994, 'Tyle Strajku I Co...', p. 14 (strike calendar).

Geddes, Barbara (1994b), 'How Politicians Decide Who Bears the Costs of Liberalization', in Ivan T. Berend (ed.), *Transition to a Market Economy at the End of the Twentieth Century*, Munich: Sudosteuropa-Gessellschaft, 203–28.

Golden, Miriam (1997), *Heroic Defeats*, Cambridge: Cambridge University Press.

Gieorge, Pawel (ed) (1998), *Zwiqzki Zawodowe w Okresie Przeobrazen Politycznych I Gospodarczych*, Warsaw: DIALOG.

Gilejko, Leszek (ed.) (1998), *Wlasność Pracownicza w Polsce*. Warsaw: SGH.

GUS (Glówny Urzad Statystyczny) (1997 and 1998), *Maly Rocznik Statystyczny*, Warsaw: GUS.

Hale, Lisa (1999), *Poland's Right Turn: Solidarity as Opposition, Government and Union in the Capitalist Transition*, Dissertation, Northwestern University.

Hethy, Lajos (1994), 'Tripartism in Eastern Europe', in Richard Hyman and Anthony Ferner (eds), *New Frontiers in European Industrial Relations*, Oxford: Blackwell, 312–36.

Iankova, Elena (1998), 'The Transformative Corporatism of Eastern Europe', *East European Politics and Societies*, **12** (2), (Spring), 222–64.

Jarosz, Maria (ed.) (1995), *Management Employee Buy-Outs in Poland*, Warsaw: Polish Academy of Sciences.

Jarosz, Maria (ed.) (1996), *Polish Employee-Owned Companies in 1995*, Warsaw: Polish Academy of Sciences.

Johnson, Simon and Marzena Kowalska (1994), 'Poland: The Political Economy of Shock Therapy', in Stephan Haggard and Steven B. Webb, *Voting for Reform*, Oxford: Oxford University Press, 185–241.

Keat, Preston (2000), 'Penalizing the Reformers: Polish Steel and European Integration', *Communist and Post-Communist Studies*, June.

Kemp-Welch, A. (1991), *The Birth of Solidarity*, 2nd edn, London: Macmillan.

Klaus, Vaclav (1994), *Rebirth of a Country: Five Years After*, Prague: Ringier.

Kodeks Pracy (1996), Polish Parliamentary Documents (Sejm), Warsaw.

Kolodko, Grzegorsz (1998), 'The Polish Transition', Manuscript, International Monetary Fund, Washington, DC.

Kowalik, Tadeusz (1993), 'Trade Unions' Attitude to Privatization', in Friedrich Ebert Stiftung, Conference Proceedings, November 1993, Warsaw, Poland, *Privatization and Transformation in Eastern Europe: A Trade Unions Perspective*, Warsaw: FES, 123–33.

Kozek, Wieslawa, Michal Federowicz and Witold Morawski (1995), 'Poland', in John Thirkell, Richard Scace and Sarah Vickerstaff, *Labour Relations and Political Change in Eastern Europe*, London: UCL Press, 109–36.

Kozminski, Andrzej (1993), *Catching Up? Organizational and Management Change in the Ex-Socialist Block*, Albany: SUNY Press.

Levitas, Anthony (1994), 'Rethinking Reform: Lessons from Polish Privatization', in Vedat Milor (ed.), *Changing Political Economies: Privatization in Post-Communist and Reforming States*, London: Lynne Rienner, 99–114.

Lipowski, Adam and Jan Macieja (1998), *Studia nad Restrukturyzacja Sektorów Przemyslowych w Polsce*, Warsaw: Instytut Nauk Ekonomicznych – Polska Akademia Nauk (INE-PAN).

Lipton, David and Jeffrey Sachs (1990), 'Creating a Market Economy in Eastern Europe: the Case of Poland', *Brookings Papers on Economic Activity*, 1, 75–133.

MacShane, Denis (1995), 'The Changing Countours of Trade Unionism in Eastern Europe and the CIS', in Richard Hyman and Anthony Ferner (eds), *New Frontiers in European Industrial Relations*, Cambridge, MA: Blackwell, 337–67.

Mason, Bob (1995), 'Industrial Relations in an Unstable Environment: The Case of Central and Eastern Europe', *European Journal of Industrial Relations*, 1 (3), 341–67.

Milanovic, Branko (1992), *Social Costs of Transition to Capitalism: Poland 1990–91*, Washington: World Bank.

Ministerstwo Skarbu Panstwa (Biuro Analiz Ekonomicznych) (1997), *Dynamika Przeksztalcen Wlasnosciowych* (No. 33), Warsaw: Czerwiec.

Ministerstwo Skarbu Panstwa (Biuro Analiz Ekonomicznych) (1997b), *Dynamika Przeksztalcen Wlasnosciowych* (No. 35), Warsaw: Grudzien.

Ministerstwo Skarbu Panstwa (1997c) (listopad), Kierunki Prywatyzacji w 1998 r, Warsaw.

Ministry of the Economy (1998), Draft Report on State Aid in Poland Granted in 1996, Warsaw.

Ministry of the Economy (1999), Draft Coal Restructuring Program, Warsaw.

Ministry of Privatization (1995), Text of Mass Privatization Programme, Warsaw.

Mujzel, Jan (1992), 'Privatization and Labour Autonomy: The Polish Case', in Friedrich-Ebert-Siftung, Conference Proceedings, November 1993, Warsaw, Poland, *Privatization and Transformation in Eastern Europe: A Trade Unions Perspective*, Warsaw: FES, 136–52.

Murell, Peter (1996), 'How Far Has the Transition Progressed', *Journal of Economic Perspectives*, **10** (2), (Spring), 25–44.

NSZZ Solidarnosc (1989), Porozumienia Okraglego Stolu, Gdansk: NSZZ Solidarnosc.

OECD (1992), *Industry in Poland: Structural Adjustment Issues and Policy Options*, Paris: OECD.

Polityka
   'Cudzym Kosztem', 6 June1998, 67–8.
   'Niebezpieczne Zwiazki', 7 July 1998, 26–8.
   'Zwiazkokracja', 12 December 1998, 3–8.
   'Odprawa Gornikow', 23 January 1999, 24–6.

Poznanski, Kazimierz (1996), *Poland's Protracted Transition: Institutional Change and Economic Growth in 1970–1994*, Cambridge: Cambridge University Press.

Poznanski, Kazimierz (1998), 'Rethinking Comparative Economics: From Organizational Simplicity to Institutional Complexity', *East European Politics and Societies*, **12** (1), (Winter), 171–99.

Przeworski, Adam (1985), *Capitalism and Social Democracy*, New York: Cambridge Uiversity Press (relevant chapter co-authored with Michael Wallerstein).

Przeworski, Adam (1991), *Democracy and the Market: Political and Economic Reforms in Eastern Europe and Latin America*, New York: Cambridge University Press.

Rodrik, Dani (1994), 'Comments on the European Periphery', in John Williamson (ed.), *The Political Economy of Economic Policy Reform*, Washington, DC: IIE, 212–16.

Rzeczpospolita
4 March 1993. 'Mielizny Korporatyzmy', 3.
11 March 1993, 'Solidarnœœæ przed protestem'.
19 March 1993, 'Dzwigami fo Sejmu I URM; Nowa Europa', 1.
8 April 1993, 'Karta Gwarancji Socialnych', 1.
15 April 1993, '"S" Odmawia Opiniowania', 'OPZZ- Rząd, Pokaza Sobie
    Karty', 'Ma Miare Mozliwodci', 7.
6 September 1993, 'Byc Przy Tworzeniu prawa: Rozmowa z Maieanem
    Krzaklewskim, Przewodniczacym NSZZ S', 3.
17 June 1996, 'Rzeczpospolita Zwiazkowa' (38 territorial orgs; 16 branch orgs –
    'S')
30 December 1996, 'Strajkow Coraz Mniej', 2.

Sachs, Jeffrey (1993), *Poland's Jump to the Market Economy*, Cambridge, MA: MIT
Press.

Shleifer, Andrei and Robert Vishny (1994), 'Politicians and Firms', *Quarterly
Journal of Economics*, 995–1025.

Slay, Ben (1993), 'Evolution of Industrial Policy in Poland Since 1989', *RFE/RL
Research Report*, **2** (2), (8 January), 21–8.

Stachowicz, Jan and Bogdan Wawrzyniak (1995), *Restrukturyzacja Sektor
Hutniczego w Polsce*, Warsaw: Polska Fundacja Promocji Kadr.

Szell, Gyorgy (ed.) (1992), *Labour Relations in Transition in Eastern Europe*, New
York: Walter de Gruyter.

Szomburg, Jan, (1995), 'The Political Constraints on Polish Privatization', in
George Blazyca and Janusz Dabrowski (eds), *Monitoring Economic Transition*,
Brookfield: Avebury, 75-85.

Thirkell, John, Richard Scace and Sarah Vickerstaff (eds) (1995), *Labour Relations
and Political Change in Eastern Europe*, London: University College Press.

Towalski, Rafal (1997), 'Strajki w Polsce (1989–1996)', Warsaw: SGH (manuscript).

Towrzecki, Hubert (1994), 'The Polish Parliamentary Elections of 1993', *Electoral
Studies*, **13** (2), (June), 180–5.

Vickers, John and Vincent Wright (eds) (1989), *The Politics of Privatization in
Western Europe*, London: Frank Cass.

Webb, W.L. (1992), 'The Polish General Election of 1991', *Electoral Studies*, **11**
(2), (June), 168–72.

Williamson, John (ed.) (1994), *The Political Economy of Policy Reform*, Washington, DC: Institute for International Economics.

World Bank (1995), *Poland: Policies for Growth with Equity*, Washington, DC: The World Bank.

3. Egyptian Labor Struggles in the Era of Privatization: The Moral Economy Thesis Revisited

Marsha Pripstein Posusney

1. Introduction

Although Egypt was one of the first developing countries to contemplate privatization – the first calls for it were heard as early as 1974 – only in the past several years has a sustained push to sell the country's state-owned enterprises (SOEs) been underway. The major legislation to facilitate privatization was not passed until 1991, and a variety of political and technical dilemmas delayed serious implementation until the spring of 1996. Since that time, about one-third of the 300 or so SOEs have been fully or partially sold.

The Egyptian labor movement played an integral part in forestalling privatization. For most of the 1970s and 1980s, opposition to diminishing the public sector was unified from the rank and file through the three levels of leadership of the singular labor confederation, the Egyptian Trade Union Federation (ETUF). The 1990s sell-off was enabled in part by the cooption of most of the senior ETUF leadership; those who proved recalcitrant were removed from office by the government. This has meant that further resistance to privatization is coming from below, and lacks the support and coordination that effective trade union organization can provide.

This chapter examines the effects of the recent privatization push on the Egyptian labor movement, and explores the changing nature of labor opposition to privatization. It is set against a condensed analysis of the nature of Egyptian labor protest in the previous decades, which demonstrates the operation of a moral economy. While there are some indications that this is gradually eroding, a considerable amount of worker resistance, informed by moral economy beliefs, still obtains. At the same time, the progress of privatization is putting pressure on the existing trade union structure, which is linked to the old economic relationships.

The next section elaborates on the operation of the Egyptian moral economy prior to the 1990s. Section 3 then traces the major developments with regard to Egyptian privatization and labor in the 1990s. Contemporary labor resis-

43

tance to privatization and its implications are evaluated, against these back-drops, in Section 4.

2. Pre-Privatization Egypt: Labor in a Moral Economy

In the moral economy perspective, collective actions are generated by viola-tions of norms and standards that a subaltern class has become accustomed to and expects the dominant elites to maintain.[1] Rather than reflecting some emerg-ing new consciousness, protests aim at resurrecting the status quo ante. They are precipitated by a passionate response – anger – over the perceived disrup-tion to previously established economic relationships.

In the Egyptian moral economy, workers viewed themselves in a patron–client relationship with the state. The latter was expected to guarantee workers a living wage through regulation of their paychecks as well as by controlling prices on basic necessities and ensuring equal treatment of workers perform-ing similar jobs. Workers, for their part, provided the state with political sup-port and contributed to the post-colonial national development project through their labor. This relationship was cemented during the years of Gamal Abd-al Nasir's rule, especially from the mid-1950s to the mid-1960s, when the government's role in the economy greatly expanded, and the regime explicitly appealed to workers' nationalist sentiments when encouraging them to increase their productive effort. Nasir's idea of reciprocal rights and responsibilities may have resonated with workers because of pre-existing moral economy be-liefs shaped during the country's long years as an agrarian society. Arguably it also tapped into Islamic notions of fairness and justice in employment rela-tionships (Pfeifer and Posusney, 1997).

In a social contract argument frequently applied to Egypt, some scholars argue that *all* Egyptian citizens surrendered their political freedoms to the re-gime in exchange for economic entitlements. The reciprocal rights and obliga-tions I am suggesting here were specifically between productive sector work-ers and the government, and the workers' side of the bargain was their labor power itself. While a lack of political freedoms per se was not part of this deal, restrictions on strikes and union activity were concomitant with this under-standing. Work stoppages were banned in the 1950s, and during the 1960s, Egyptian unions were corporatized into a single, hierarchically ordered con-federation whose leaders were carefully screened by the state. Because it im-plied that the government valued uninterrupted production, this repression also served to reinforce workers' belief that their toil represented a significant con-tribution to the state and entitled them to the provision of a living wage and standard social protections.

The moral economy was manifest in the timing as well as the nature of labor protest from the 1960s through the 1980s. First, the frequency of labor protest, in relation to overall economic conditions, appears to be the opposite of what standard neoclassical theory would predict. During periods of economic expansion and rising wages, labor protest was quite muted. Conversely, the greatest frequency of job actions occurred during times when real wages were falling.[2] Thus, these protests clash with the rational choice model of workers taking advantage of new opportunities to realize gains; rather, it seems that Egyptian workers were more apt to mobilize when their accustomed livelihood was threatened.

The specific motivations behind individual job actions also confirms the existence of a moral economy. Most of the protests were restorative in nature, precipitated by cutbacks in wages or other benefits. Such actions revealed that workers held a sense of entitlement, based on their perceived contributions to production. A second type of entitlement protest revolved around notions of fairness in the wages earned by different types of laborers. Egyptian workers demonstrated a belief in parity, i.e., that similar work should yield similar rewards. They also exhibited opposition to widening disparities between the wages of manual workers and those afforded to civil servants and company managers. Finally, workers were sometimes moved to action seeking gains to which they felt entitled because of promises made repeatedly, over time, by company management, the government, or the courts. Anger over unmet expectations was the impetus to these protests.

Workers' sense of entitlement was based on the belief that their labor was an essential contribution to the post-colonial national development project. They revealed their commitment to this project by trying to fulfill their side of the bargain even when they felt that the government was not meeting its obligations to them. This was manifested when workers eschewed actual work stoppages in favor of symbolic protests that demonstrated their sense of betrayal while not harming production. The closest alternative to striking was the plant occupation, during which management was ejected or ignored but workers continued running the factory on their own. A second popular technique was a boycott on cashing paychecks. It was particularly used in the public sector, where workers say it was effective because it interfered with government accounting procedures.

A third, still more mild form of symbolic protest involved sending telegrams to government officials seeking redress of grievances. Such messages sometimes provide further evidence about workers' expectations of themselves and the state. For example, railway workers in the 1980s, in a last ditch effort to avert an actual strike, sent this message to the president: 'We are all waiting here at the league headquarters. ... Some of the trains have already stopped running *in abandonment of our responsibilities*' (emphasis added).[3]

The view that workers who actually, or even seem poised to, cease production are harming the interests of the state was actively encouraged by successive regimes in Egypt. It was adopted by the new military rulers in 1952 well before the creation of the parastatals. Presidents Anwar Sadat (1970–81) and Husni Mubarak (1981–), even while trying to retract the expanded state role in the economy instituted under Nasir, perpetuated this philosophy. Sadat condemned a 1971 sit-in at the Helwan ironworks as 'an undemocratic act' and blamed both a 1976 bus drivers' strike and severe bread riots shortly thereafter on communist agitation, implying that loyal workers would never otherwise leave their jobs. A decade later, Mubarak vilified two large factory occupations as acts revealing 'a lack of nationalist responsibility' (El-Shafei, 1993, 56).

Moreover, despite their differences in overall economic strategy, the Nasir, Sadat, and Mubarak governments pursued very similar policies with regard to labor protest. The actions were quickly put down by both repression and concession. Only the largest incidents were ever mentioned in the official press, and these were customarily blamed on outside agitators. Preventing any escalation of the protest, and maintaining an image of national harmony and worker satisfaction thus seemed to be far more important to Egypt's rulers than minimizing financial concessions. The consequence of this carrot and stick combination was to reinforce the moral economy, and thereby pave the way for future protests.

The nature of punishment itself appeared to derive more from regime perceptions of the severity of the incident than from any precise legal framework. When only a small single plant was involved, the immediate handling of the problem was usually left to the discretion of local police, with national security agencies and government figures called in only if the protests could not be quickly broken up. However, protests which involved issues of national policy, large numbers of workers, and/or more than one plant, brought rapid intervention from the highest levels of government. The local police sometimes treated detained workers with particular brutality, but the volume of arrests appeared to be greater in the more prominent incidents. Also, in the latter cases, the state security forces often resorted to beatings and/or bullets to break up the protest. In addition, in both large and small incidents those accused of being the protests' ringleaders were typically either fired from their jobs or subjected to forced transfer to remote locations.

Unions in the Moral Economy

In addition to being largely symbolic, most of the labor protests of these pre-privatization decades reflected a lack of formal organization. Local union leadership was either not involved or actively hostile to these protests. Workers, in turn, increasingly accompanied their protests with attempts to invalidate the locals. And from above, federation and confederation leaders often ignored the protests, unless called upon by the government to represent the workers, in which case the senior unionists ritually began by condemning the workers' tactics first.

Workers occupy their positions because they have no choice; they lack the educational background and/or family connections necessary to obtain more desirable employment. It is the feelings of near-helplessness which this situation engenders that facilitates the development of a shared sense of oppression and a spirit of solidarity among workers. By contrast, union officials at all levels are there because they consciously decided to solicit a leadership position; they then act in accordance with the same set of preferences that led them to seek union office. For many, and especially those in senior leadership positions, these motivations are opportunistic, stemming from the power and material privileges associated with their posts. Loyal membership in the ruling National Democratic Party (NDP) is a prerequisite for such opportunists to obtain and maintain power. At the lower levels, some unionists are motivated by altruistic ideologies, but the government's screening of union leadership candidates makes it difficult for them to obtain their positions, much less move up to the upper ranks of the confederation.

But loyal union leaders are only useful to the ruling elite if they are able to control the rank and file, and some modicum of legitimacy is necessary for senior unionists to accomplish this. In the 1970s and 1980s, senior unionists dealt with this dilemma by appearing to champion causes that had widespread resonance among the base – national issues that affected large numbers of workers. Opposition to privatization was chief among these, and accounts in part for the setbacks that sell-off advocates within the government suffered during these years. It was issues at individual plants, affecting only a circumscribed number of workers, that the senior unionists effectively disowned.

Lacking the coordination of the national confederation, local struggles were isolated and, absent the moral, financial, and logistical support that unions could have provided, disgruntled workers had to rely on their own efforts. Sometimes other groups provided assistance; train drivers who struck in 1986 turned to their workers' league, a formal rival to the unions, for organization. Elsewhere, a leadership role by leftists, sometimes through informal rank and file organizations, was evident. But such organizations lacked the advantage of union dues to support their activities, which was especially felt following government crackdowns. In numerous cases, workers donated part of their salaries to support the families or pay the legal expenses of those detained or otherwise punished as a result of these incidents. Townspeople in the industrial mill areas often mobilized to support kinfolk and neighbors by sending food to workers occupying plants and joining in demonstrations.

It was against this backdrop that the Egyptian government turned toward privatization in the 1990s. Since the government's intended withdrawal from the economy represented a retraction of its obligations under the moral economy, an upsurge of labor militancy could be expected as the program was implemented. The next section traces the privatization process, emphasizing the regime's efforts to pre-empt labor protest, and the trade union response.

3. Privatization and Unions in the 1990s

In response to popular pressures against privatization, the Mubarak government in the early and mid-1980s vowed repeatedly that it would 'neither sell nor diminish the public sector'. However, the regime began to profess an openness to privatization beginning in 1989. This shift was clearly associated with pressure from the country's multilateral lenders, following the effective collapse of a standby agreement that Egypt had signed with the IMF in May 1987.[4] In the spring of 1988 the Fund refused to release the second tranche of the loan and, without that seal of approval, Egypt was precluded from negotiating a new debt rescheduling agreement with the Paris Club. By the fall of 1988 the country had already fallen into arrears on some payments, and the balance of payments situation continued to deteriorate. By the time negotiations for a new agreement with the Fund formally opened in 1989, the IMF was no longer exclusively concerned with its standard stabilization package, but had now joined the World Bank in pushing privatization.

Consequently, the Mubarak regime gradually softened its stance against privatization, submitting a new letter of intent to the IMF which pledged to reduce the government's stake in joint ventures with the private sector, and to sell off some small public sector concerns. The IMF rejected this letter as insufficient, however. Moreover, the Fund now insisted that many reforms be implemented *prior* to the signing of a new agreement.

As the talks continued, Mubarak's spokesmen frequently warned that rapid reform would increase the suffering of Egypt's lower classes, and could thereby lead to political unrest. In response to these concerns, the Bank proposed the creation of a 'social fund' to which Egypt's creditors would contribute, to ease the burdens of reform on the poor. Bank officials suggested that part of the money be earmarked for retraining public sector workers displaced by privatization. In addition, the regime formally embraced the idea of employee share in ownership (ESOP) plans as a way to make privatization more popular.

By early 1991, at least several hundred small establishments, mostly those previously owned by the governorates, had been sold. It is noteworthy that these were predominantly agriculturally based concerns, located in rural areas where the union movement has traditionally been weak. The government then submitted to parliament the legislation necessary to proceed with privatization of larger industrial establishments. The IMF signaled its approval of these measures by signing a new standby agreement, and a generous debt rescheduling accord with the Paris Club followed shortly thereafter. These deals included $600 million for establishing the Social Fund.

The 'public enterprise legislation', also known as Law 203, was passed in June 1991. In addition to paving the way for full or partial privatization of parastatals, the law also sought to make public sector firms operate more efficiently by grouping the SOEs into several dozen holding companies whose members would be appointed by the government, and who were expected to manage their portfolios according to market principles. While the holding companies themselves would be wholly state owned, their minimum share of equity in the subsidiary firms was set at 51%; the remaining 49% of the assets could be purchased by the private sector through subscriptions. The resulting joint ventures would still be considered part of the public enterprise sector. However, the holding companies could also decide to maintain only a minority share in a subsidiary, and in this case the firm would be considered a private sector joint venture subject to the terms of the private companies law. Finally, the holding companies were empowered to divest themselves of a subsidiary completely, or close it down.

In a significant departure from its past practice, the ETUF endorsed Law 203. However, union leaders did insist on several modifications to the original draft. One was that the prevailing requirement that 10% of company profits be distributed to workers remain intact; unionists also claim to have won removal of a previously existing cap on the nominal value of profit shares workers could receive annually. Secondly, the final version specified that existing national labor legislation, with its protections against arbitrary firing and mass lay-offs, and for health and accident insurance and pensions, would continue to apply unless and until overwritten by a new labor law. These modifications enabled both government and union spokesmen to proclaim that workers' interests would not be harmed by privatization.

Nevertheless, the multilaterals complained that the investment climate in Egypt, including these job security regulations, still posed a hindrance to privatization. Accordingly, in October 1991, the regime quietly established a committee to begin drafting new legislation that would replace Law 137 of 1981, the extant labor law, as well as the additional regulations binding only on the public enterprises. The committee consisted of representatives from the

ETUF, businessmen's organizations, the Ministry of Labor, the local legal community, and the International Labour Organization (ILO), which provided funding for the endeavor. Its role was to ensure that the new law did not contradict Egypt's participation in international agreements. Since the longstanding ban on strikes had already been proven to contradict Egypt's signature on the International Human Rights Agreement, the regime's consent to ILO participation signaled its willingness to consider legalizing strikes in some fashion as a *quid pro quo* to labor for liberalizing hiring, firing, and promotion regulations. Discussion of this explicit exchange increasingly appeared in the discourse of regime officials and union leaders, especially as the opposition press leaked news of the committee's supposedly secret deliberations.

There was, however, little progress in these efforts. Union leaders, under the spotlight of the opposition press, continued to resist the retraction of job security or other traditional benefits enjoyed by public sector workers. The government for its part sought to strictly contain the right to strike; cracking down during this period on the Islamic associations and their growing influence in the professional associations, the regime obviously feared that legalizing *any* form of collective protest could have a snowball effect.

In the meanwhile, the government continued to declare that its privatization program was geared toward protecting workers' jobs and livelihoods. No layoff clauses were specified in the agreements to sell SOEs, and the establishment of shareholders' collectives among SOE workers was vigorously promoted. Nevertheless, public sector managers were under pressure to make their firms more profitable, and their first line of attack was workers. Numerous firms which had earlier resorted to hiring temporary workers now began to lay them off. Other establishments simply declared that large numbers of their full-time, permanent employees were redundant, and therefore no longer entitled to supplementary wages. These supplements – incentive pay, productive bonuses, profit shares, and various 'compensations' for meals, uniforms, and/ or dangerous work – often amounted to two-thirds of a worker's take-home pay. This situation forms the backdrop for the rank and file protests over privatization in the first part of the decade.

At the same time, the pace of the sell-offs was rather slow. There were delays in developing the capital market and in the identification and valuation of the candidates for privatization. The multilaterals continued to complain publicly of government foot-dragging. Privately, Bank and IMF officials acknowledged that one reason for urging haste in the reform program was to deprive its opponents of sufficient time to mobilize resistance. The IMF allowed an extended finance facility (EFF) signed in 1993 to lapse in 1995, after repeatedly refusing to approve its first review. Although the primary bone of contention had been the Fund's demands for further currency devaluation, more rapid privatization was a second major issue, and it rose to the forefront in the spring of 1996 when the Fund dropped its demand for devaluation. Accordingly, the government announced new plans for more extensive and rapid privatization, and this marked the turning point in the sell-off program.

By May 1998 the IMF finally pronounced itself satisfied with the program's progress. Measured in terms of annual privatization receipts as a percentage of GDP, their report noted, Egypt ranked fourth internationally, trailing only Hungary, Malaysia, and the Czech Republic. Government figures indicate that, through the late 1990s, some 119 of the country's 314 SOEs had been fully or partially sold. These were mainly manufacturing ventures, but the government has pledged to offer many ventures previously considered of strategic or historic/cultural value, including utilities, public sector banks and insurance companies, maritime and telecommunications firms, and prominent tourist hotels.

The Union Movement and Privatization

The ETUF's endorsement of Law 203 represented a significant turnaround from its earlier opposition to privatization. Union acquiescence was achieved in part through heightened levels of coercion, combined with a continuation of the regime's customary cooptation techniques. Significant pressure was exerted on some union MPs to win their votes, and some nevertheless refused to support the bill. However, the confederation's ongoing cooperation was also purchased through concessions to labor's concerns which enabled some unionists to claim that privatization would not harm the interests of their membership.

For senior unionists, the contradiction between yielding to pressures from the regime, and maintaining some semblance of credibility with the rank and file, did not go away, and after the 1991 trade union elections the ETUF's leaders adopted a more oppositional posture again. Leftists opposed to privatization captured about 25% of the leadership positions in the public sector industrial locals, doubling their previous presence. The corporatist system protected senior union personnel from losing their posts in the elections – changes at the top occurred only due to retirements – but they appear to have been chastened by some significant NDP losses at the base.

Thereafter, the senior unionists did begin to draw more public and private battle lines around the maintenance of workers' customary rights and benefits. By the end of 1992 it was clear that the confederation, despite having endorsed Law 203, was at odds with the regime over its application. At its general assembly held in December the confederation passed a resolution condemning privatization and called for legalizing strikes if any workers did lose their jobs as a result of public sector diminution. The meeting also condemned the price increases resulting from lowered subsidies, and renewed the call for a high council on wages and prices to ensure that the former keep pace with the latter. Significantly, and for the first time in its history, the delegates refused to send the customary telegram of support to the government, and the decision rejecting this gesture was unanimous.

Nevertheless, while ETUF leaders warned publicly that massive lay-offs could produce a 'social explosion', they made no effort to mobilize the membership behind these implicit threats. Their actions, as in the past, were confined to public statements and behind-the-scenes lobbying of other regime elites. Moreover, much of 1993 saw the ETUF divided by, and preoccupied with, opportunistic power plays among the senior leadership.

In an effort to mollify the ETUF, the government began adding federation officials to the boards of holding companies for firms whose workers the unionists represented. This enabled unionists so inclined to carry on the struggle against privatization in another venue. However, it also put them into the same social circles as the business elites comprising much of these boards' membership, providing new avenues for corruption. It also appears that, whatever their private motivations and public demeanor, the senior unionists recognized that they had already lost the battle for preserving the public sector and its workforce, and now came to redefine their *raison d'être* as winning the best terms for workers who would be displaced or reclassified. Thus, while labor leaders' pronouncements continued to decry layoffs, a discussion of tradeoffs increasingly found its way into their public statements as they negotiated these with the regime in closed-door committees.

By 1994 ETUF opposition to privatization per se had receded, and confederation president Sayyid Rashid declared in 1995 that Egyptian workers supported privatization, in light of Mubarak's promises that it would not hurt them. In 1996 former ETUF president Ahmed al-'Amawi, then at the helm of the Labor Ministry, criticized the opposition press for questioning the veracity of Mubarak's slogans. A few senior unionists did prove more recalcitrant, trying to block sales from their positions on the holding company boards, and/or fighting for better terms for workers in the early retirement program. These leaders were removed by the regime in the fall, 1996 trade union elections.[5]

While these events were unfolding, the regime took steps to consolidate the position of the loyal unionists, further insulating them from rank and file pressures. Law 12 of 1995 revised the union laws to entrench the current crop of senior union personnel, by allowing them to remain in office past retirement age as well as by extending the term of union office from four to five years. Moreover, the latter provision was allowed to take immediate effect, thereby postponing for a full year the union elections that had been scheduled for the fall of 1995. The law further makes it likely that federation and confederation leaders will be divorced from the base by allowing them – but not lower level officials – to continue to hold union office even after promotion to senior management positions in their workplace establishments.

In numerous ways, the new union law tightens the control of the federations over the locals and makes it more difficult for new blood to enter the ranks of union leadership. Workers are now ineligible to run for union office until they have completed a full year of local membership, and a full term – now five years – of service on a local executive board is required before a worker can run for federation office. Federation leaders are given enhanced power to expel individuals from union membership, while the limited provisions for their accountability to the membership are further eroded. The proposed changes to the labor law would consolidate this trend.

Revising the Labor Laws?

While privatization went forward in the late1990s, the project to reform the labor laws stalled. At the end of 1994 the various parties involved in the negotiations over the new labor law finally agreed on their 16th draft. It would facilitate lay-offs in the public sector and newly privatized firms, and generally reduce the benefits and protections available in the public sector to those which actually prevail in the private sector. As signaled for several years, it would also legalize strikes for the first time in Egypt's post-coup history, although this *quid pro quo* for the sacrifice of job security is sharply constrained.[6] The bill was then expected to be passed in the spring of 1995.[7] Instead, it underwent four more revisions, and at the time of this writing in summer, 2001, it had not yet been discussed by Parliament.

The proposed new legislation requires that firms must obtain government approval for any mass workforce reductions. This provision also existed in the previous law, but in the past, such approval was almost never given. The new law signals a sea change in economic philosophy by stating explicitly that it is an employer's right to adjust the workforce according to economic conditions. The draft law would also considerably increases an employer's freedom to dismiss workers individually (Posusney, 1995).

The draft maintains the prevailing requirement that all workers must still be employed under written contract, which can be of indefinite ('permanent') or specified duration. However, it widens the range of serious worker infractions for which employers are entitled to break a contract. Moreover, the law enables employers to effectively force workers to resign by empowering them, 'for economic reasons', to lower the contractual wage and/or require employees to perform different jobs. This article, included at the insistence of the businessmen's organizations, nullifies the very essence of the work contract concept.

Finally, while Law 137 specifies that a temporary contract, if renewed, acquires indefinite status, the new law would permit multiple renewals. Many private sector employers had been evading the old protections against firing through techniques such as using only temporary contracts and terminating workers briefly before renewing them, or forcing workers to sign blank contracts or undated resignation letters upon hiring. The resulting disparity in job security between the two sectors has been the major reason why qualified workers have preferred public sector employment.[8] Under privatization pressure, public sector managers had increasingly resorted to temporary hiring to enhance profitability, but such employees could still aspire to permanent positions. The new law would make it unlikely that any temporary worker would ever achieve the security of permanent status, or that any new worker would be hired indefinitely.

The law's provisions for legalizing strikes would nevertheless render legal work stoppages rare. They require that two-thirds of a *federation's* leadership endorse a walkout at individual plants. Thus the law denies decision-making power to the locals, where militants have been most successful at gaining influence. In addition, strikes would still be prohibited while contracts are in effect, during mediation and arbitration, and in vital services. Moreover, union leaders would be required to give employers and the government 15 days written notice, as well as a justification, before declaring a strike.

These restrictions were endorsed, if not recommended, by the businessmen's representatives, but some employers remained unenthusiastic about the proposed law. Indeed, because smaller domestic entrepreneurs had historically evaded the labor laws, they stand to gain little from the right to strike/right to fire exchange. It would increase their management prerogatives legally, but not actually, while they would lose some claim to government assistance in suppressing labor protest.[9] At the same time, the repeated delays in issuing the law suggest that the regime itself is not anxious to legalize labor protest in even this sharply limited manner. With rank and file workers, labor activists, and leftist opposition parties having obvious (but contrasting) reasons for opposing the law, its only constituency appears to be the senior unionists whose control over the base would be tightened by its provisions.

Early Retirement

The regime itself apparently recognized that confederation complicity alone would not be a sufficient mechanism for pre-empting, or dousing outbreaks of, rank and file protest related to privatization. As the prospect of a massive diminution of the public sector workforce loomed, the government moved to ameliorate the deleterious consequences of job loss through an ambitious early retirement program.

In October 1993, just as the first industrial sales under Law 203 were being finalized, it was disclosed that ETUF delegates had participated in a committee to devise ways of eliminating redundant public sector workers. The committee included representatives from the Ministry of Labor, several insurance companies, and the Social Fund, which would finance the endeavor. They agreed to implement a pilot early retirement program, including a full-pension option for some workers and a lucrative severance package for others; this compensation would be earmarked for the establishment of a small business. There would also be a job retraining for younger redundant employees. The government began offering these alternatives in a limited way to workers in targeted establishments at the end of 1994.

Subsequently, as the privatization push gained steam but with the job security protections of the existing labor law not yet withdrawn, the government sought to expand the early retirement plan.[10] There were new negotiations, prolonged and often heated, with the ETUF leadership over the design of the program. These resulted in agreement that all workers accepting early retirement would receive a lump-sum payment, based on their years of service, and a monthly stipend. The agreed-upon package was to represent the minimum that workers could get, with individual plant managers and local leaders in some cases free to negotiate more lucrative packages for workers.[11]

The regime has been promoting the program as fulfillment of its promise that privatization can be achieved without harm to labor. For workers, however, a major problem is that the monthly stipend may be less than half the pension the worker would have received under the old system. Labor activists say it is insufficient for workers to meet regular expenses, and that their prospects for finding new employment to supplement the stipend are bleak. In addition, retiring workers risk eviction from cheap company housing complexes.

The official rationale for the lump sum approach is that recipients should invest in a small business, or in stocks, thus fostering economic growth. But many workers are tempted to spend the money on large-scale expenses, like those associated with marrying their children. Because the prospects of finding new employment are dim, those who do so spend their money rapidly, and those whose investment schemes fail, face a dismal future. Some workers also questioned whether their jobs could be saved if the government instead invested the early retirement funds in modernizing their factories.[12]

Reports in 1997 indicated that program enrollment was falling short of government targets, and labor activists charged that some workers were being pressured into enrolling under threat of wage cuts or transfer. By the end of

1998, however, the rate of acceptance had gone up dramatically; the Land Center for Human Rights (1999) claims that 130,000 public sector workers had been discharged under the program. While many workers may have welcomed the opportunity for early retirement, labor activists attributed the increase to workers' growing fear that once the new labor law was enacted they would risk being fired with no compensation whatsoever, in a country which lacks unemployment insurance.

Whether workers accepted early retirement with gratitude or reluctance, it is clear that they have been rendered more vulnerable as the Egyptian economy has shifted toward market orthodoxy. Given the authoritarian nature of government in Egypt, there is no reliable survey data that can provide an accurate breakdown of workers' responses to the progress of privatization. The prior existence of a moral economy suggests that many workers would feel betrayed by the government, and would be inclined to resist the sell-off. The defection of the ETUF leadership means, however, that protests against privatization would be rank and file efforts, resembling the isolated struggles over wages and working conditions in individual plants which characterized the pre-privatization era.

4. Rank and File Protests over Privatization

In spite of the regime's efforts to win workers over to privatization, and notwithstanding the ETUF's policy shift, the idea of selling off the public sector remained controversial among at least a sizeable proportion of workers.[13] The characteristics of labor protest in the 1990s suggest that a moral economy was indeed still operative in the minds of many workers. As the decade closed, however, there were indications that market logic was playing more of a role in shaping the nature of workers' collective action.

Entitlement Protests
Like the earlier, plant-based struggles over wages and working conditions, collective actions related to privatization are intrinsically restorative. Workers are objecting primarily to the prospective or actual loss of their jobs and the income security associated with them. The early retirement program, as explained above, does not fully substitute for public sector workers' accustomed income stream. Even for those workers who anticipate remaining employed after their firms are sold, there is an anticipated, if not actual, loss of the benefits customarily associated with public sector employment.

An incident in the summer of 1992 indicates that opposition to privatization was not limited to public sector workers, but that many of those employed privately viewed public sector employment as a future entitlement. It occurred in 10th of Ramadan city, one of several new industrial areas set up by the government in remote locales to both ease the population pressure on Cairo and encourage private enterprise. When the Minister of Labor suddenly decreed that full-time private sector workers should have their names removed from the waiting list for government employment, several hundred workers resigned from their jobs in protest, asking to be rehired as temporary employees so they could remain on the list.

Significantly, the enterprises in 10th of Ramadan offered higher wages than government jobs, and complied with all the insurance laws often evaded by other private sector entrepreneurs; in seeking reclassification as temporary employees the workers sacrificed these benefits. Asked to explain their actions in this context, some workers mentioned the fact that government positions enable workers to take prolonged leaves of absence for employment abroad, a sentiment seized upon by privatization proponents as evidence of widespread redundancies and moonlighting in the public sector. However, most of the workers cited the harsh conditions and remote location of their employment.

Among public sector workers, there have been five types of entitlement protests related to privatization: (1) struggles against prospective sales or liquidation, often intertwined with (2) struggles over deteriorating pay and working conditions in existing SOEs, as public sector managers try to make their firms more attractive for sale; (3) protests over reductions in pay, benefits, or employment levels after SOEs have been sold; (4) struggles over the failure of companies to live up to the negotiated early retirement packages; and (5) distributional protests over inequalities in the treatment of workers deemed to be redundant.

Protests against Sales and Closures The holding companies formed under the auspices of Law 203 are empowered to decide to liquidate all or part of the SOEs they manage, or to fully or partially privatize them through the stock market or direct sales.[14] In the late 1990s, announcements of intended sales or closures of plants precipitated numerous protests. The list includes: occupation of the Sitka Rubber factory in Tanta, June 1998, versus plant closing; occupation of the Nasr Co. for Pharmaceutical Manufacturing and Services, which won reconsideration of the intended closure of two branches; a sit-in and brief strike at the Janaklis plant, versus intended sale; a December 1998 strike of 1600 workers at a Jute factory in Shubra, protesting impending closure; and a sit-in by 800 workers at the Egyptian Co. for Synthetics in the Tabin area of Helwan during November 1998, versus preparations for closure.

Protests against Pre-sale Take-Aways Public sector managers have been under pressure to improve the financial performance of their firms so that they will be more attractive for sale. This has often resulted in attacks on workers' pay and benefits, in dismissals of temporary employees, and/or in harsh disciplinary actions intended to encourage workers to leave voluntarily. An early job action in response to such measures occurred at the General Battery Company, where workers occupied company headquarters in April 1992, protesting the sudden curtailment of their incentives. This change resulted in a 50% decline in their take-home pay. Workers also complained of an end to compensation for work clothes and an increase in occupational diseases as a result of cutbacks in protective apparatus.

The most severe incident of the decade occurred in 1994 in the historically militant mill town of Kafr al-Dawwar, near Alexandria. Its roots date from May 1993, when a new manager began to lay off temporary workers, and to implement a series of policies designed to drive wages down. After a year of sending urgent appeals to various union and government officials, the workers occupied the plant on 30 September 1994, when the new manager refused to rescind measures that included a three-month loss of incentives for workers taking one day of sick leave or being caught sleeping or absent from their work site. The workers demanded the removal of the manager, the reinstatement of the laid-off temporary personnel, the return of all workers who had been transferred, and the nullification of all the policy decisions of the previous months, with back pay to all workers who had suffered losses as a result of them.

The most sustained protest of this type in recent years has occurred at the Misr-Helwan Spinning and Weaving plant (known in the area as *Harir*) in Helwan, another factory with a history of leftist presence and activism. After several unsuccessful attempts to rent the plant to a private owner, the management offered workers early retirement in December 1997. Some 2400 of the near-11,000 workforce accepted, but in the spring the remaining workers began a series of bi-weekly (on payday) demonstrations outside the plant protesting the management's intentions to privatize. In July 1998, the company announced that it would halt incentive payments, and one of the demonstrations turned into a two-day strike. The management responded by closing the plant; it was reopened in August but with only 2080 workers who were issued special security passes for admission; of the other workers, an additional 1700 were offered early retirement and the remaining 7000 were put on open holiday with basic wages only. Workers from the latter group have continued their bi-weekly protests, seeking to be re-employed.

Post-sale protests Regime rhetoric notwithstanding, there are numerous reports of setbacks for workers who initially remain employed after privatization.

New owners have resorted to laying off temporary employees, subjecting permanent workers to forced transfers, cutting back on bonuses and incentive pay, forcing workers to sign new contracts with a lower basic wage, and increasing use of monetary penalties for lateness, absence, or poor job performance. Among the more recent job actions sparked by such events, 500 workers at the Kahrumica electrical projects factory occupied the plant protesting declines in their incentive pay and benefits, and some forced transfers; workers at the newly privatized Ideal who demonstrated against forced transfers won a pay-raise as compensation. In addition to the customary forms of protest, workers in such cases have also sought redress through the courts. At the Al-Ahram Beverages Company, one of the first plants to be privatized under Law 203, workers filed a case seeking severance pay. The company claims they resigned voluntarily, but the workers charge that they were forced to quit because of declining pay and frequent harsh disciplinary actions.

Unmet promises There have been numerous cases of companies delaying early retirement payments to workers, or failing to pay them the promised amount. Workers occupied the Misr-Ediko Maritime facility in September 1998 protesting management attempts to lower the agreed-upon lump-sum payments. In Kafr al-Dawwar, workers at the Misr Company for Synthetics opposed a cut in the lump-sum calculation formula that would reduce payments to 2000 workers. Workers who took early retirement demonstrated in late 1998 when they didn't receive the expected stipend from the Delta Ironworks in Shubra al-Khayma, and the expected lump-sum payment from Harir plant in Helwan.

In some agricultural concerns, workers have been offered parcels of land rather than cash payments as an incentive to retire. Company failure to deliver on such promises has also sparked protest. At the Bahira food processing company, workers staged sit-ins and hunger strikes in late summer 1998 when they were told that the company would be sold after they had been led to expect land distribution; during one occupation they held the company manager and several prospective buyers hostage in the plant.

Finally, *distributional norms* have also been evidenced in some of the protests. Some of these cases involve company decisions over which workers will be kept on, and which retired or transferred. Others involve the retirement incentives: during the course of debates over the early retirement program, the regime permitted some firms to negotiate the terms with the local union and its associated federation, and if necessary to sweeten the package beyond the minimum guaranteed by the government. The resulting disparities between packages offered to workers in different plants precipitated struggle in numerous locations.

At the Cairo Prefabricated Housing Company, 30 workers who were getting only basic wages filed a suit seeking equal treatment with colleagues who were reassigned to other branches where supplemental pay was available. Similarly, workers on basic pay only at the Ahaliyya Metallurgy Company demonstrated in October 1998 demanding that they be offered an early retirement option. Siklam Dairy workers occupied their factory seeking equal treatment with other food processing laborers who had been offered better early retirement packages.

At the Southern Company for Land Reclamation, the parity demand was for land. The agricultural ministry issued orders in 1992 to liquidate the company and sell half its land; the remainder would be distributed to employees upon their formal resignation from the company. However, roughly half the workforce had been working under non-permanent employment contracts for periods ranging from two to seven years. Although lacking a formal job grade, they had been receiving all the customary benefits and pay of permanent public sector employees. After the liquidation decision, these 750 workers were terminated and denied pensions, severance pay, and the opportunity to purchase land. Demanding equal treatment with their officially permanent colleagues, they began a hunger strike in January 1993, which lasted at least 10 days and caused several workers to be hospitalized.

Informality, Symbolic Protest, and Repression
With the ETUF's endorsement of Law 203, the draft new labor law and the early retirement program, the confederation leadership signaled that it would not support rank and file struggles to protect public sector firms. As a consequence, the protests against privatization that occurred in the 1990s originated from below, and conform to the pattern of informal actions that characterized labor protest in the preceding decades. In some job actions, workers have targeted unsupportive union leaders in addition to plant managers. At a 1994 plant occupation in Kafr al-Dawwar textile, for example, the workers sought the right to elect a new union local; during the sit-in three local leaders were beaten by workers, and the rest fled.

In the early 1990s symbolism continued to characterize the protests against privatization. The private-sector employees in 10th of Ramadan city resigned, the workers of the Southern Company for Land Reclamation chose a hunger strike. At the General Battery Company, in addition to occupying the company headquarters, the workers twice floored the offices of the prime minister and president with telegrams. There were also numerous paycheck boycotts and other short-lived sit-ins. Even the protest at Kafr al-Dawwar did not involve an actual work stoppage.

Symbolic protests such as these continued in the late 1990s. Significantly, though, the more recent incidents have also included a growing number of actual strikes. According to the Land Center for Human Rights, 33 out of 114 job actions in 1998, or about 29%, were strikes, as were 21 out of 80, or about 25%, of those in the first half of 1999 (LCHR, 1998, 1999).[15]

At the end of 1994, it appeared that the regime was going to deal harshly with even symbolic protests against privatization. At least six workers or their relatives were killed, and hundreds more wounded, in the protest at Kafr al-Dawwar; these are the highest casualties from a single factory protest in Egypt's modern history. During the plant occupation there, the state security police (SSP) were out in full force, and special forces and reinforcements were brought in from neighboring towns. A confrontation at the factory gates began when the SSP tried to turn back families bringing food, then confiscated the food and threw it in a nearby canal. One of those killed was a 9-year-old boy who was shot while his father was leading him home from school, which the police had ordered to be closed early. Some 75 people were hospitalized, including eight individuals who lost one or both eyes, and one who lost the use of his legs; many others were afraid to seek medical treatment for fear of arrest.

At the time, some labor activists felt that the regime was using Kafr al-Dawwar, a historically militant area, as a test-case – to see how far job cuts could go before sparking protest, and how much repression would be needed to subdue it. In the last couple of years, however, it seems that the government has shied away from bloody confrontations with workers. I do not mean to suggest here that repression has been eliminated – decidedly, it has not. Several of the incidents reported here, and some others not described, involved large numbers of arrests. In numerous cases state security was called upon to break up plant occupations, and tear gas was employed. But there were no further reports of either ordinance being used or of mass beating of workers, and only one report of detainees (four) being tortured by police; in most cases it appears that arrested workers were quickly released.

This moderate let-up in repression has occurred in spite of the fact that the new labor law itself has not yet been enacted, and those strikes which did occur were neither sponsored nor encouraged by the union hierarchy. It thus appears that the regime has been somewhat backed into a corner by its own rhetoric surrounding the law and the privatization program more generally. In diminishing its resort to force, the government is implicitly acknowledging that it cannot continue to sharply repress strikes while giving employers a free hand in dismissing workers.

5. Conclusions

Under pressure from its creditors, the Egyptian government committed itself to privatization in the early 1990s, and moved in a serious way to implement this pledge in the latter half of the decade. As it betrayed its 1980s promise to protect the public sector, so too has the regime reneged on its 1990s vow that privatization would not harm Egyptian workers. Many workers have been legitimately enticed into leaving their jobs, but thousands of others have resigned out of fear or near-compulsion. Retired workers report being unable to find other employment, and fear for their future access to housing and medical insurance as well as their ability to meet basic living expenses if their lump-sum payments fail to generate an ongoing income stream. Workers who are still employed, either in the remaining public sector enterprises or in newly privatized firms, face declining incomes, deteriorating conditions, and sharply diminished job security. Private sector workers who previously anticipated an eventual appointment to the public sector can no longer hold out this hope.

At the same time, the government's privatization propaganda does appear to be having an effect upon workers. As the regime increasingly sends the message that public sector workers are inefficient and redundant, more workers appear ready to challenge this claim by halting production. Symbolism continues to characterize most protests, but actual strikes are an increasingly regular occurrence. The government, in turn, appears to be backing off from the brutality with which it has suppressed labor protest in the past. Thus, the moral economy that has characterized Egyptian labor–state relations to date is in a process of evolution. If the government continues with its slow but steady withdrawal from the economy, market rationality could gradually supplant moral economy beliefs as the dominant philosophy informing workers' actions.

The logic of the process suggests that Egypt's corporatist labor system will come under increasing strain in the new millennium. The new labor law is likely to be passed eventually; the government cannot continue indefinitely to withstand external pressures for a more capitalistic labor relations system. But its provisions for greater union centralization contradict the increasing *decentralization* of the economy that privatization entails, and appear unsustainable. When most of the important economic policies affecting workers were made by the national government, having a centralized and hierarchical union system made some sense. In spite of the confederation's neglect of plant-level issues earlier described, corporatism arguably proved more to workers' benefit than not, and could be seen as part of the moral economy. As privatization continues, however, more and more economic decision making will take place at individual plants, making the quality of local union organization at these establishments more important to workers' livelihoods and futures. This will prompt workers to place more emphasis on the struggle for flexible and independent unions.

Notes

1. This section condenses an analysis previously made in Posusney (1997), but originally developed in Posusney (1993). Original sources are cited in these works. Both works contrast the moral economy approach with rational choice and Marxist perspectives.

2. The use of 'labor protest' rather that strikes as an operative category here reflects empirical realities associated with studying collective actions by workers in authoritarian countries where strikes are illegal.

3. My personal favorite was the ironic cable sent by 600 workers at Delta Ironworks to then-President Sadat after his January 1997 removal or lowering of many food subsidies. It read: 'To the President of the Republic: We thank you for increasing prices, and raise the slogan, "more hikes for more hunger and deprivation". May you always be a servant of the toiling workers.'

4. Information in this section covering the period from 1989 through mid-1996 is drawn from Posusney (1997); original sources are cited there.

5. Interview with Niyazi 'Abd al-'Aziz, former president of the Electrical, Engineering, and Metal Workers' Federation, Cairo, January 1999; see also Imam (1997).

6. This discussion of the law is based on the complete draft published in *Al-Ahali*, 30 November 1994. There have been slight alterations since then, but my understanding is that the main thrust of the legislation, as described here, has not been changed.

7. Interview with Niyazi 'Abd al-'Aziz, Cairo, January 1995; *Al-Ahram Weekly*, 23–29 May 1996.

8. See also Assaad (1993, pp. 2, 41–2).

9. I am grateful to Ragui Assaad for calling this to my attention. On employers' objections to the strike/lay-off trade-off, see *Al-'Alim al-Tawm*, 5 June 1993.

10. This discussion draws on Posusney (1999).

11. 'Abd al-'Aziz interview, 1999, and coverage in the Egyptian Arabic press.

12. This discussion is based on interviews with numerous labor activists and social scientists conducted in Cairo in January 1999. See also Center for Workers' and Trade Union Services, n.d.

13. Information in this section on anti-privatization protests through mid-1996 is drawn from Posusney (1997). Discussion of subsequent years is drawn from LCHR reports (1998, 1999), Center for Trade Union and Workers' Services (1998a, b, c), and interviews with labor activists conducted in Cairo in January, 1999.

14. A small number of concerns have been sold fully to workers, and many of the partial privatizations have involved setting aside 10–20% of the shares for newly created 'employee shareholder associations'. On issues raised by the different types of sale, see Posusney (1999).

15. The 1999 report includes actions by professional as well. It is worth noting that one of the first job actions in 1999 was a one-month slowdown by EgyptAir pilots; among their demands was increased insurance for accidents.

References

Assaad, Ragui (1993), 'Structural Adjustment and Labor Reform in Egypt', Paper presented at the 1993 annual meeting of the Middle East Studies Association, Raleigh Durham, North Carolina, 11–14 November 1993.

Assaad, Ragui (1997), 'The Employment Crisis in Egypt: Current Trends and Future Prospects', *Research in Middle East Economics, 2*, 39–66.

Center for Trade Union and Workers' Services (1998a, b, c), *Industrial Talk*, No. 1 (October), No. 2 (November), No. 3 (December). All published in Helwan, Egypt (in Arabic).

Center for Trade Union and Workers' Services (n.d.), 'Early Retirement . . . the Complete Truth', Helwan (in English and Arabic).

el-Shafei, Omar (1993), 'Workers' Struggles in Mubarak's Egypt', MA thesis, The American University in Cairo, Political Science Department.

Imam, Samya Sa'id (1997), 'The Workers' Elections and the 10th Session of the Trade Union Organization', in *Analysis of the Workers' Elections*, Cairo: Friedrich-Ebert-Stiftung (in Arabic).

Land Center for Human Rights (1999), 'Labor Conditions in Egypt during the First Half of 1999', Cairo, 1999.

Land Center for Human Rights (1998), 'Labor Conditions in Egypt in 1998', Cairo, December (in Arabic).

Pfeifer, Karen and Marsha Pripstein Posusney (1997), 'Islam and Labor Law', in Sohrab Behdad and Farhad Nomani (eds), 'Islam and Public Policy', special issue of *International Review of Comparative Public Policy, 9*, 195–223.

Posusney, Marsha Pripstein (1995), 'Egypt's New Labor Law Removes Worker Provisions', *Middle East Report,* No. 194/5 (May–August), 52–3, 64.

Posusney, Marsha Pripstein (1997), *Labor and the State in Egypt: Workers, Unions, and Economic Restructuring,* New York: Columbia University Press.

Posusney, Marsha Pripstein (1999), 'Privatization in Egypt: New Challenges for the Left', *Middle East Report,* **210** (April/May), 38–40.

4. The Political Element in Economic Reform: Labor Institutions and Privatization Patterns in South Asia[1]

Christopher Candland

1. Introduction

Much of the political economy of reform literature views economic change as a process that governments effect upon societies. These studies not only presume that effective reform requires the skillful dislodging of entrenched rent-seekers. They also reflect a preference for examining economic policies and elite political coalitions and for ignoring the societies in which governments and political elites operate. The political element in economic reform runs deeper than acknowledged by the political economy of reform literature. Insufficient attention has been devoted to the influence of social institutions on economic change. Close comparative historical study does not support the conventional political economy of reform scholars' contention that 'the packaging of programs or the manipulation of opposition groups' explains economic reform outcomes better than socio-economic structures (Haggard, 1986, p. 161). The observation that similar government economic policies have widely differing effects in different institutional environments is an invitation to explore the salience of social institutions in economic change.

South Asian governments, with the exception of Sri Lanka's, opted for structural adjustment programs a decade later than did Latin American governments. Bangladesh, owing to a balance of payment crises, initiated structural adjustment measures in the mid-1980s. In the late 1980s and early 1990s, India and Pakistan adopted structural adjustment programs. Privatization was a central feature of these nearly identical International Monetary Fund (IMF) structural adjustment programs. But these privatization programs have had very different results. Why? Why have India and Pakistan had such different experiences in implementing nearly identical privatization programs?

Research on labor institutions and patterns of privatization in South Asia suggests that the structure of social institutions accounts for this variance.[2] Comparative historical analysis can identify both the institutional features that facilitate or obstruct the implementation of privatization policies, on the one hand, and those which help to determine whether privatization involves compensation to displaced workers, creates new employment, and promotes labor productivity, on the other hand. The research reported here focuses on the relationship between labor institutions and patterns of privatization. Labor institutions include relations between trade unions and political parties, mechanisms for the selection of union leaders and recognition of trade unions for the purposes of collective bargaining, and the level – national, industrial, or enterprise - at which collective bargaining is conducted.

In this chapter I first summarize the major features of recent privatization measures in India and Pakistan, and labor responses to them. Then, drawing on the cases of Bangladesh and Sri Lanka as well, I discuss the influence of labor institutions on patterns of privatization. I argue that patterns of privatization can be traced to specific labor institutions.

Privatization patterns involve the speed and method of privatization, the compensation afforded displaced public sector employees, and the effectiveness of privatization in promoting new employment and productivity. I do not define privatization in the broad sense of the promotion of policies to expand the private sector but in the narrower sense of the transfer of tangible public assets to private hands. Opening up new areas to the private sector, repealing legislation that provides for public sector monopolies, franchising, leasing, and sub-contracting also constitute privatization but these techniques do not entail the sale of tangible government assets. There are three principal mechanisms for privatization in this narrower sense. Governments may sell public sector assets to financial institutions, may sell shares of public sector units on the stock market, or may hold public auctions.

I use a method which is under-employed in comparative politics, close comparison of a once unified polity. Countries that are created by partition – India and Pakistan, North and South Korea, Zimbabwe and Zambia, and formerly East and West Germany – provide an unusual opportunity to gauge the impact of different political regimes on once closely similar, if not unified, political, social, and economic structures. The technique is particularly productive for the study of labor in what was British India because Pakistan and India inherited identical labor legislation and national labor organizations but their governments reworked them after independence in distinct ways.

2. Privatization in India and Pakistan

The four South Asia countries considered in this chapter – Bangladesh, India, Pakistan, and Sri Lanka – comprise 20% of the world's official labor force and a far larger share of the world's real (i.e., paid and unpaid) labor force (World

Bank, 2000, pp. 278–9). Within two generations, India and Pakistan are projected to be the first and the fifth most populous countries in the world. Ranked by per capita income, India and Pakistan are squarely in the middle of the lower income economies. Unlike other populous lower income economies, including Brazil and Indonesia, India and Pakistan are resource scarce on a per capita basis. India and Pakistan have closely similar economic structures, with similarly sized industrial, service, and agricultural sectors as a percentage of gross domestic product (GDP). Some of the difference in unionization rates is accounted for by the fact that Pakistani agricultural laborers are prohibited from forming unions. A number of other economic similarities make India and Pakistan apt comparative cases for assessing the impact of labor institutions on patterns of privatization. The textile industry in each country is the largest non-agricultural employer and the largest source of export earnings. Moreover, before the onset of the recent reforms, India and Pakistan had public sectors of roughly equal proportions to their GDP and roughly equally sized organized public sector labor forces as a percentage of their total unionized labor forces. These facts are often disguised by Pakistan's neoclassical economic ideology and India's former socialist economic ideology.

A comparative perspective on economic, social, and labor data for the four countries is provided in Table 4.1. Although Pakistani GDP growth rates have fallen recently, and Indian GDP growth rates have risen, Pakistan has been able to achieve higher growth rates than India since independence. Pakistan has maintained the highest GDP growth rate in South Asia, an average of more than 6% per year since independence. At the same time, it ranks as one of the world's poorest in human development indicators such as adult literacy, female school enrollment, and maternity survival rates. Surprisingly, many development theorists refer to this as a paradox – high growth rates combined with miserable human development. There is no paradox. This is precisely what Pakistani planners and their American advisors intended to accomplish with the principle of 'functional inequality' a strategy devised to concentrate capital and to create inequality, and thereby promote economic growth.[3]

India has had regular elections to parliament and state legislative assemblies even before independence. Pakistan has spent 27 years under military rule. Indian economic development ideology has been socialist. Pakistani economic development ideology has been predominately neoclassical. Despite this variation in political regime type and in professed economic ideology, governments in each country were committed to strong intervention in the service of rapid industrialization.

What are the major features of economic reform in India and Pakistan? In Pakistan, General Zia's 11-year rule created social groups and political constituents which had a significant long-term impact on governance and the

Table 4.1   *Comparative economic, social, and labor data for Pakistan, India, and Sri Lanka*[4]

	Pakistan	India	Sri Lanka
Economic Indicators			
population (millions in 1995)	136.3	929.0	17.9
growth rates of GDP (per annum 1980–95)	5.8	5.3	4.6
purchasing power parity per capita (US$ in 1997)	1590	1650	2460
industrial production (% GDP in 1995)	25	27	25
direct foreign investment as a % of GDP (1994)	0.69	0.45	1.35
foreign assistance as a % of GNP (1996)	1.4	0.6	3.6
external debt as a % of GNP (1996)	39	22	41
exports as a % of GDP (1996 –1998)	15.1	7.7	35.1
Social Indicators			
adult literacy (% of adult population in 1995)	38	52	90
female primary school enrollment (% of age group)	25	76	100
Labor Indicators			
labor for as a % of population	36	43	42
industrial employment as a % of total (1990)	19	16	21
unionization rate (% of labor force)	2.9	5.0*	26.7
official unemployment rate	5.4	4.7	14.0
share of wages in value added (1985–92)	19.9	45.2	17.2

* Union density cannot be reliably established in India because trade unions are not required to submit membership figures. trade unions which do submit figures exaggerate them so that they might secure greater representation in government-labor consultative bodies.

economy. Zia promoted a business class that is well characterized by industrialist and former Prime Minister Nawaz Sharif. General Zia, however, did not effect comprehensive economic reform after he dismissed the populist government of Zulfikar Ali Bhutto. Concerted economic reform began only with the interim government, appointed by General Zia before his death. That military-appointed interim government foisted an IMF agreement upon the subsequently elected government of Benazir Bhutto. In each of their alternating two terms in office, Bhutto and Sharif, and especially the interim governments that ruled during each of the three military-brokered transitions, effected broad-based economic reforms, including comprehensive privatization. Bhutto began the privatization process in December 1988. Sharif announced, when he succeeded Bhutto in 1991, that he would speed up the privatization process, and he did. Nearly all state-owned enterprises have been sold in auction. These include all public sector factories and most banks.[5] The pace of privatization in Pakistan is among the world's quickest.

In India, shortly after the announcement of the new economic policy and an IMF agreement in July 1991, Finance Minister Manmohan Singh announced that within two years subsidies to state-owned enterprises would be eliminated and non-performing public sector enterprises would be privatized. Several years later, not a single central government public sector enterprise had been privatized, despite repeated government attempts. The Indian government has been able to sell shares of state-owned enterprises, but these efforts have largely involved transfers of public sector debt to government financial institutions. Thus, Pakistan has privatized rapidly; India, hardly at all.

Labor's Role

Local and national labor demonstrations, strikes, and threat of strikes organized by political party-affiliated unions, the so-called trade union centers, reversed government privatization decisions in India. Measures by state governments – that is, by provincial-level government – to privatize state government enterprises, where the bulk of Indian public sector employment and value added is concentrated, have also been successfully opposed by political party-affiliated unions. Organized labor has been identified in confidential World Bank documents and by World Bank officials as the single biggest impediment to public sector reform. A senior World Bank economist for India claimed that 'we [pro-reform advocates] can't move until we buy-off labor'.[6]

Nearly eight years after Manmohan Singh's declaration that public sector enterprises would be marketized, Indian labor has yet to be placated. The government's failure to privatize the Indian Iron and Steel Company (IISCO) illustrates how political unionism – wherein unions are allied to political party patrons – can block privatization decisions. In November 1993, the cabinet, under the constraints of IMF budget deficit targets, decided not to finance the modernization of IISCO, but to privatize it. The Communist Party of India (Marxist) government in West Bengal, where IISCO is located, supported that decision. The central government then invited bids and accepted that of an Indian industrialist. The 30,000 workers at the plant objected. The Indian National Trade Union Congress (INTUC), the trade union affiliated to the Indian National Congress party, together with the trade union of the Communist Party of India (Marxist) (CPM) and other party affiliated national unions, organized a national strike throughout the steel sector. A parliamentary committee was thereby convened to review the privatization decision. The committee's report challenged the government's privatization plan and recommended that the cabinet decision be withdrawn and that IISCO be modernized with public funds. Despite the Congress Party's majority in Parliament, the government withdrew the IISCO privatization bill. The Congress could not afford to lose the labor vote. This reversal points to the ability of political party-affiliated unions, even that of the ruling party, to form strategic alliances with other political party-affiliated unions, to oppose government privatization initiatives. One could cite numerous other cases.

In contrast, extensive and rapid privatization in Pakistan was achieved

Table 4.2   Extent, timing, and methods of privatization in South Asia, 1977–97

Pakistan
    extensive and rapid privatization in manufacturing, banking, utilities, and telecommunications through sealed bids, since 1988 public sector labor force reduction through voluntary early retirement, future employment guarantees, lay-off compensation, and worker ownership schemes

India
    no central government unit privatized, limited privatization of state government industries some divestiture through state financial institutions, since 1991 some public sector labor force reduction through involuntary early retirement and lay-offs with compensation

Sri Lanka
    extensive and sustained privatization in manufacturing, banking, utilities, transport, and telecommunications through auctions, stock market divestiture, and privatization of management, since 1977 public sector labor force reduction through voluntary early retirement, future employment guarantees, and lay-off compensation

through labor's political exclusion. In Pakistani enterprises today, labor organizations empowered with collective bargaining rights are found only at the plant level. The few political party organized labor federations that do exist, such as the Pakistan People's Party's People's Labour Bureau, have few members and little credibility. Indeed, the leader of that union was murdered, allegedly by members of the political party to which his union was affiliated, the then-ruling Pakistan People's Party. He opposed the party's decision to privatize the Muslim Commercial Bank.

Pakistani trade unions have been comparatively amenable to privatization. Indeed, public sector unions negotiated an agreement with the Minister of Manpower in 1991 that smoothed the way for privatization. The All Pakistan State Employee Workers Action Committee secured an agreement that gives workers of privatized enterprises severance pay of 25% of the last year's salary for every year worked, a guarantee of one year of future employment, and the option to take shares in the privatized company. Surprisingly, in a society where civic associations have been repressed and destroyed by military and authoritarian civilian governments, nearly 20% of the newly privatized manufacturing enterprises in Pakistan are now under worker management schemes, with varying degrees of managerial control by workers.

The plant-level achievements in a few of Pakistan's privatized enterprises do not make Pakistan a laborer's utopia. Secret ballot elections for trade union officers and clear regulations concerning the recognition of collective bargaining agents, however, do give Pakistani workers more control over their unions and a greater sense of ownership in many industries. A boiler operator at the Pak-China Fertilizer factory conveyed this, when the factory was undergoing privatization. With tears in his eyes he said 'for the past 16 years, I have *loved* my machine because it provides me and my family with our livelihood. But now, why should I not destroy it?' He then added a famous couplet from an Urdu *ghazal* written by Mohammad Iqbal.

> *Jis khet se dekhan ko meyasar na ho rozi,*
> *us khet ke har khosha gundon ko jalado.*
>
> *(The field from which a peasant can not reap a livelihood,*
> *in that field burn every ear of wheat.)*

Labor Institutions Compared
What is the structure of labor institutions in India and Pakistan and what is their impact on the different patterns of privatization in the two countries? Before discussing the mechanics of worker representation and collective bargaining, a comment about institutions is in order. An institution is a custom or

a practice, established by law or by habit. The organizations that preserve and promote these customs and practices, such as government agencies, trade union bodies, non-governmental organizations – not institutions alone – allow individuals to create, articulate, and pursue collective interests. As social organizations change, they transform institutions. Labor legislation, for example, does promote labor practices. But many labor institutions are not established through law, but rather through management practices. In Sri Lanka, for example, members of the Employers Federation of Ceylon only bargain with unions that meet their standards of healthy trade unionism; that is, with non-militant trade unions. Similarly, the federation has sanctioned its own members for failure to pay workers a living wage and failure to pay workers on time. Law mandates neither of these practices.

Despite their common origins in the British colonial legal system, Indian and Pakistani labor institutions – such as relationships between trade unions and political parties, mechanisms for selecting trade union leaders, and collective bargaining arrangements – differ markedly. India has had strong political party-allied trade union federations, or political unionism, since the 1920s. Under the umbrella of the All Indian Trade Union Congress, founded in 1920, and now affiliated to the Communist Party of India, unions in pre-partition India were united by a common anti-imperialist position. Union leaders then became politically prominent with the Provincial Council elections held in 1937, ten years before independence. Organized labor played an important role in the independence movement. After independence, elected governments encouraged the development of politically powerful trade unions that could serve as electoral vehicles for political parties. Many districts are still labor constituencies, where political parties vie for candidates among trade union leaders. Former Labour Minister V.V. Giri, Mrs Gandhi's candidate for President of the country over which the Congress party split, was one such labor constituency unionist. The Home Minister in a recent government, Inderjit Gupta, entered politics through the Communist Party of India's trade union. One of the more contentious recent issues in Indian industrial relations is the government's refusal to admit to government consultative bodies, such as the wage-setting Indian Labour Conference, newer national trade unions that refuse to affiliate with a political party. Such was the case with the National Centre for Labour, which represents informal sector workers who are predominantly women.

Fuzzy rules for trade union recognition are a crucial correlate to political unionism in India. Unlike Pakistan, in India, there is no legal mechanism for trade union recognition, except in the states of Karnataka, Orissa, and West Bengal. Employers must recognize and bargain simultaneously with all unions that possess a credible threat to production. Indian political parties are quite effective in mobilizing labor and providing such a threat. The mobilization of workers is in fact the litmus test of a trade unionist's political skill. George Fernandes, for example, India's current Defence Minister and proponent of India's nuclear option, rose to General Secretary of the Janata Dal-affiliated Hind Mazdoor Sabha because he was able to mobilize railway workers in a national strike against Congress Prime Minister Indira Gandhi in 1974. Fernandes established himself as a successful trade unionist–politician despite the facts that Mrs Gandhi brutally crushed the strike, that paramilitary forces killed workers, and that workers' grievances were not addressed. What was important was that he could mobilize workers.

It should be emphasized, then, that political unionism refers to the influence of political party-affiliated unions within the union movement. Political unionism does not necessarily entail union influence over economic policy. While political unionism can effectively veto government privatization decisions, it is not able to prevent private sector management from illegally shutting down factories, declaring lock outs, or relocating to areas where workers are not unionized. Keeping a factory in the public sector, which political unionism can achieve, does not guarantee workers employment, good working conditions, adequate pay, or even payment for their work. Indeed, political unionism can prevent workers from exercising influence over government policy and has often exacted a high cost from workers. The 1982–83 Bombay textile strike is a clear example. The strike is the world's largest as measured in workdays lost. Hundreds of thousands of mill workers waged the strike because they wanted an amendment to the Bombay Industrial Relations Act – a British colonial legacy – such that the Indian National Congress-affiliated union, the Rashtriya Mills Mazdoor Sangh (National Mill Workers Union), would no longer be the sole collective bargaining agent for all textile workers. The strike, which resulted in the loss of an extimated one hundred thousand jobs and sharp decline in labor standards and in terms of employment throughout the industry, is officially still in force. The leader of the strike, Datta Samant, was murdered, allegedly at the request of the Rashtriya Mills Mazdoor Sangh. The Rashtriya Mills Mazdoor Sangh continues to be the sole collective bargaining agent for workers in the textile industry in the states of Gujarat and Maharashtra, despite strong opposition from workers. Thus, political unionism is not universally liked by Indian workers.

Unions organized in the territory that was to become Pakistan were also political party-allied and predominantly communist before and immediately after independence.[7] But labor occupied no part of the imagined community of the Muslim League, the party that successfully petitioned the British for the creation of a homeland for South Asian Muslims. Thus, organized workers in Pakistan, unlike India, were not incorporated in post-independence development strategies and nationalist ideologies or by Pakistani political parties. The banning of the Communist Party of Pakistan in 1954 further weakened the labor movement. More decisively, at the last gasps of Pakistan's first decade of martial law in 1968, new labor laws were promulgated to limit political unionism and to promote enterprise unionism, that is, factory-based unions without political party affiliation.[8]

The military's Industrial Relations Ordinance of 1969 requires workers to elect other workers to be their exclusive, legally empowered collective bargaining agents. Deputy Martial Law Administrator Air Marshal Noor Khan reported that he wanted to apply to the entire country a model that he had developed when managing Pakistan International Airlines, the military-owned national airline.[9] Instead of jailing union organizers, as his predecessor had done, Noor Khan allowed PIA employees to form a union provided that politicians and lawyers were prohibited from involvement. Noor Khan's Industrial Relations Ordinance fundamentally reconfigured labor institutions in Pakistan and remains in force today. Pakistan's martial law government, facing sustained labor protest in late 1968, devised worker representation and collective bargaining institutions that would de-politicize labor. The martial law govern-

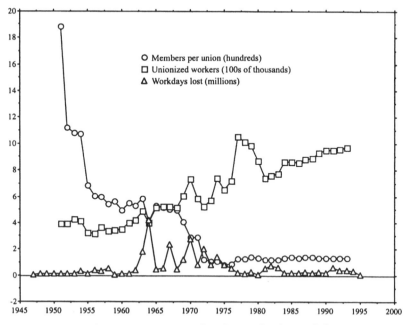

Figure 4.1   Pakistan: unions, membership and industrial disputes, 1947–95

ment prepared the way for Pakistan's first general election 23 years after independence by imposing legal hurdles to strikes, by requiring workers to represent themselves, and by removing from unions labor lawyers and political aspirants, who constitute the bulk of labor leaders in India.

Thus, in contrast to India, labor has had little political voice in Pakistan since the late 1960s. Figure 4.1, especially in comparison with Figure 4.2, suggests that the institutional arrangements devised by Pakistan's military government in 1969 were effective in minimizing the influence of organized labor over economic policy decisions. In Pakistan, after 1969,[10] labor unrest, measured in workdays lost in industrial disputes, decreased, while the number of members per union dropped dramatically. In India, the number of workdays lost in industrial disputes climbed through the mid-1980s, when the number of lockouts began to exceed strikes.

This comparative historical perspective on Indian and Pakistani labor institutions indicates that social institutions can be traced to regime types. Specific political regimes – Pakistan's exclusionary authoritarian regimes and India's multi-party electoral democratic regimes – promoted specific social institutions that, in turn, affected patterns of industrial change in discernible ways. In

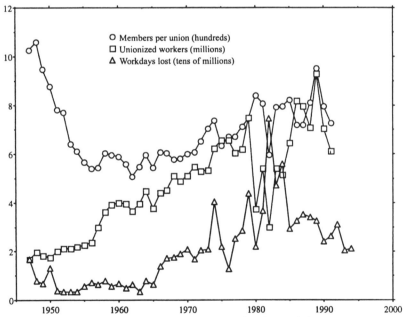

Figure 4.2   *India: unions, membership, and industrial disputes,*
1947–94

particular, political unionism, as the reversal of privatization decisions in India demonstrates, can exercise veto power over economic policies.

3. Labor Institutions and Privatization

The previous section argued that there is clearly a correlation between political unionism and fuzzy institutions for recognizing unions and selecting union leaders, on the one hand, and effective labor resistance to privatization, on the other. Can we extend the model to India's and Pakistan's neighbors, Bangladesh and Sri Lanka?

In Bangladesh and Sri Lanka, too, all major political parties have significant labor wings. Table 4.3 summarizes the differences in political party–trade union relations in all four countries. It should be re-emphasized that political unionism refers to the influence of political party-affiliated unions within the union movement. Its contribution to deflecting privatization in India notwithstanding, political unionism does not necessarily imply the influence of unions over economic policy decisions.

Figure 4.3 provides a relative ranking of the pace of privatization and strength of political unionism in these four South Asian economies. In Pakistan, where political unionism is most restrained and enterprises have only one legally recognized collective bargaining agent, privatization has been most rapid. In

Table 4.3   Trade union – political party relations in South Asia

India
  political incorporation of labor during the 1920–47 independence
    movement
  strong left political tradition
  strong political unionism

Pakistan
  no incorporation of labor during the 1940–47 independence movement
  weak left political tradition (after 1951 Rawalpindi Conspiracy and banning
    of Communist Party of Pakistan in 1954)
  weak political unionism (after 1969 Industrial Relations Ordinanace)

Sri Lanka
  political incorporation of labor during the 1915–48 independence
    movement
  strong left political tradition
  strong political unionism

India, where political unionism is strong and unions establish employers' recognition through threats, unions have effectively halted formal privatization. In Sri Lanka and Bangladesh, which have strong political party-affiliated unions but clear procedures for trade union recognition, privatization has been steady.

The structure of labor institutions, of course, does not explain all privatization outcomes in all places. Interviews with trade unionists and government officials and collection of economic data in Bangladesh and Sri Lanka help to complicate what has, until this point, been a relatively parsimonious comparative historical institutionalist's argument. Sri Lankan workers in enterprises undergoing privatization have received more handsome severance packages and employment guarantees and have faced less overt brutality than have their counterparts in Bangladesh or Pakistan. And, Sri Lanka has not seen the recent increase in the incidence of child labor that India, Pakistan, and Bangladesh have.

The Sri Lankan government was the first in the region, and one of the first in the developing world, to implement a program designed to build an open trade regime and to achieve export-led growth. In response to economic stagnation, high inflation, and high unemployment in the 1970s, the United National Party of Julius Richard Jayawardene promoted, beginning in 1977, currency devaluation, trade liberalization, foreign investment and exports, reduction of government expenditure and the money supply, and privatization. The shift toward a more open economic regime coincided with a shift toward a decidedly less liberal political regime. The 1978 constitution replaced Sri Lanka's Westminster-styled parliamentary democracy with an executive President who appoints the Prime Minister and can remove members of the judiciary and parliament.[11] A referendum in December 1982 – involving widespread vote rigging – extended the term of the parliament elected in 1977 to 1989. Under Jayawardene and his successor, President Ranasinghe Premadasa, political violence, replete with death squads, and election fraud were widespread.

In this environment of democratic decay, the Sri Lankan economy went further toward international economic interdependence than all other South Asian economies. The Sri Lankan public sector has been extensively privatized. Despite a very high unemployment rate, privatization in Sri Lanka involved voluntary retirement schemes, comparatively generous compensation packages, and future employment guarantees. The export-led industrialization strategy also generated significant new employment, most of it in export- processing zones (Rodrigo, 1998, pp. 159–200).[12]

How do we explain the willingness of Sri Lanka's political party-affiliated trade unions to allow privatization and negotiate concessions? The centrality of the public sector to economic development ideology does not explain the difference. In Sri Lanka, as in India, the public sector was intended to guide and even progressively absorb the private economy. The fact that employers – in the case of the public sector, government agencies – negotiate with a single, recognized union helps to explain why Sri Lanka's privatization measures could be extensive, effective at increasing productivity and new employment, and yet be relatively generous to displaced workers.

The degree of international economic interdependence and influence of international financial institutions and donor governments also helps to explain Sri Lanka's privatization pattern. Indicators relating to the external economy, reported in Table 4.1, suggest that Sri Lanka's so-called modern sector is more strongly linked to the international economy than it is to its own traditional, rural sector.

The Role of Female Labor

But well-defined collective bargaining institutions and linkages to the international economy do not tell the whole story. Close examination of employment data and visits to export-processing zones, where the bulk of new employment in Sri Lanka has been created, suggest that the government has been able to promote privatization as well as create new employment because the economy has gone further in the feminization and informalization of labor than other South Asian economies. Five times as many jobs have been assumed by women than by men in the post-adjustment period. More than 80% of the workers in the export-processing zones are female, most of them between the ages of 18 and 25 (Rodrigo, 1998, pp. 186–7). Although surveys find that two-thirds of the employees in the free trade zones are O-level graduates, these women work at low-skill, low-pay, piece-rate jobs without contracts, much less security of employment.

Labor force surveys elsewhere in South Asia suggest a similar trend.[13] Bangladesh too has seen a movement of women from unpaid family work to paid informal work, especially in the garment industry. In both Bangladesh and Pakistan, however, social restrictions on women's activities outside the home have kept female participation in the official labor force to under 10%. India's more gradual adjustment is accompanied by increased women's casual and contract-based employment and decreased women's formal salaried employment, approximately 1% per year (Deshpande and Deshpande, 1998, L31–L39). The trend is toward feminization and informalization, but the pace of change, like the pace of adjustment, has been far less rapid than in many so-called developing economies. South Asia, in which female participation in the official labor force is 28%, is beginning to look more like Southeast Asia, where it is 42% (Moghadam, 1995, p. 129). As one labor economist put it with reference to Bangladesh, apparently without intended irony, 'the next phase of industrialization may ... reap the benefits of the "reserve of surplus female labour"'(Rahman, 1998, p. 61).

In all of South Asia, public sector workers and trade unionists who negotiate privatization bargain from a position of legally protected, formal employment. The concessions that these trade unionists – who represent formal sector workers – have been able to extract from government during the privatization process fall only to these few formal sector, predominantly male workers, not to the general labor force.

Given the segmentation of organized workers in the formal sector, who are overwhelmingly male, from unorganized, informal sector workers, who are increasingly female, the most interesting development in South Asian trade unionism is the formation in 1995 of the Indian National Centre for Labour. The Centre represents two dozen unions of informal sector workers, workers who are predominantly female. These workers include fish workers, *bidi* (handmade cigarette) rollers, home-based garment stitchers, domestic servants, and forest product collectors. The Self-Employed Women's Association or SEWA, which was expelled from the Congress Party-affiliated Textile Labour Association and is now a leading member of the National Centre for Labour, was the principal agent in the adoption of one of the International Labour Organization's latest conventions, a convention extending the coverage of national labor legislation, which in most of South Asia is quite progressive on paper, to home-based informal sector workers.

4. Conclusions

I have argued here that variance in patterns of privatization and in the manner in which structural adjustment programs are implemented can be traced to the structure of social institutions. The focus on labor institutions – that is, on relationships between trade union and political parties, on mechanisms for the selection of union leaders, and on levels of collective bargaining – institutions that are politically embedded yet wield enormous influence over economic performance, allows us to return the social element to the politics of economic reform. If scholars working with the conventional concepts and methodologies of comparative politics are to understand and explain emerging labor organization and the changing nature of work, then they must develop a theory of labor that can see segmentation of jobs by class, caste, ethnicity, and gender, that can see work sites as shifting and employers as changing, that can see workers not as isolated but as socially embedded, not as individuals, but as communities, conditioned by history and politics.

Notes

1. Author's note: This chapter originated as a presentation to the Department of Political Science at Wellesley College in March, 1999. I am grateful to the Council of Overseas American Research Centers for support for my latest research on the subject. That research was conducted in Bangalore, Colombo, Dhaka, Karachi, Mumbai, and New Delhi from June through August 1998.

2. It should be noted that in the economies of South Asia, as in other so-called 'developing economies', governments possess a substantial stake in 'private' enterprises. There are hundreds of private firms, including India's largest business houses, in which central government financial institutions hold significant shares. According to the Public Interest Research Group, 'there are 297 private sector companies in which public financial institutions along with state level indictrial development corporations, central and state governments, jointly held 25 percent of more of equity capital'. See Public Interest Research Group (1992). Similar lavels of public investment in private firms can be found in Bangladesh, Pakistan and Sri Lanka.

3. On the human costs of Pakistan's early development strategies, see Candland (2000, pp. 256–72).

4. Sources: Population for UNDP, *Human Development Report 1998*, New York: Oxford University Press, 1998, 176–7. Growth rates of GDP (1980–95) are from *Human Development Report 1998*, 184–5. Labor force as a % of population and employment in industry as a % of total employment from *Human Development Report 1998*, 164–5. Purchasing power parity per capita from World Bank, *World Development Report 1998–99*, New York: Oxford University Press, 1999, 190. Adult literacy rates and female primary school enrollment from Mahbub ul Haq and Khandija Haq, *Human Development in South Asia 1998*, Oxford: Human Development Centre, 1998, 166 and 87. Pakistan's unionization rate is for 1993 and calculated from Ministry of Labour, *Pakistan Labour Gazette* (July 1993 to June 1994), Karachi: Manager of Publications, n.d., 166 and 170. Sri Lanka's unionization rate is calculated from Ministry of Finance and Planning, *Statistical Abstract of the Democratic Socialist Republic of Sri Lanka 1996*, Colombo: Department of Census and Statistics, 1996, 58 and 77. Pakistan unemployment rate is from the Ministry of Finance, *Economic Survey 1997–98*, cited in Economic Intelligence Unit (EIU), *Pakistan Afghanistan Country Report 1998*, London: EIU, 1998, 33. India's unemployment rate is for 1993–94 and is from National Sample Survey Organization, *Savekshana*, 50th round, Delhi. Sri Lanka's unemployment rate is for 1993–94 and is from *Statistical Abstract of the Democratic Republic of Sri Lanka 1996*, 105, 113. Shares of wages in value added and direct foreign investment are from International Labour Office, *World Employment Report 1996/7*, Geneva: International Labour Office, 1996, 152 and 167. Foreign assistance and external debt are from *World Development Report 1998–99*, 231. Pakistan's exports are for 1997–98 and is from *Pakistan Afghanistan Country Report 1998–99*, 31. India's exports are for 1996 and is from EIU, *India Country Report 1998–99*, London: EIU, 1998, 71 and 73. Sri Lanka's exports are for 1996 and from EIU, *Sri Lanka Country Report 1998–99*, London: EIU, 1998, 40.

5. It should be noted that Pakistan, like Bangladesh, was undergoing a transition from military rule while initiating privatization. India had already established a firm electoral regime. Sri Lanka saw a decay of electoral democracy.

6. Senior World Bank Economist for India (anonymous), World Bank, interview, Washington, DC, 17 June 1992.

7. Bashir Bakhtiar's *Pakistan Mazdoor Terik aur Mai* (The Pakistan Labor Movement and Me), a pamphlet, is one of the very few sources on the period. Written by a leading Pakistani trade unionist, it is an engaging memoir of efforts to organize unions in the face of British colonial and upper caste repression. I am translating the pamphlet from Urdu into English. Also important is Zafar Shaheed (1977) and Amjad and Mahmood (1982).

8. The laws related to students organizations, the other social force that spearheaded the street

protests against the military government, were also written by the outgoing martial law government of Yahya Khan so as to limit the influence of political parties in student activism.

9. Air Marshal (retired) Noor Khan, interview, Karachi, 28 and 29 March 1995.

10. Workdays lost in the preferred indicator of labor unrest because it combines the number of
workers involved with the duration and, of course, the number of strikes.

11. The latter power falls to the Prime Minister in her capacity as head of the ruling party.

12. Earlier estimates suggested that it would not. See Kelegam and Wignaraja (1988).

13. For Bangladesh, see Bhattacharya (1997, pp. 37–8).

References

Amjad, Rashid and Khalid Mahmood (1982), *Industrial Relations and the Political
Process in Pakistan, 1947–1977*, Geneva: International Institute for Labour
Studies.

Bhattacharya, Debapriya (1997), 'Export processing zones in Bangladesh: Economic Impact and Social Issues', ILO Multinational Enterprise Programme,
Working Paper 80, Geneva: ILO.

Candland, Christopher (2001), 'Institutional Impediments to Human Development
in Pakistan', in Amita Shastri and A. Jeyaratnam Wilson (eds), *The Post-Colonial
States of South Asia: Democracy, Development, and Identity*, London: Curzon
Press.

Deshpande, Sudha, and L.K. Deshpande (1998), 'Impact of Liberalisation on
Labour Market in India: What Do Facts from NSSO's 50th Round Show?',
Economic and Political Weekly, **33** (22), (30 May), L31–L39.

Haggard, Stephan (1986), 'The Politics of Adjustment: Lessons from the IMF's
Extended Fund Facility', in Miles Kahler (ed.), *The Politics of International
Debt*, Ithaca: Cornell University Press.

Kelegam, Saman and Ganeshan Wignaraja (1988), 'Labour Absorption in the
Manufacturing Sector in Sri Lanka: With Special Reference to the Post-1977
Period', mimeograph, February.

Moghadam, Valentine (1995), 'Gender Aspects of Employment and Unemployment
in a Global Perspective', in Mihaly Simai, with Valentine Moghadam and Arvo
Kuddo (eds), *An International Investigation into Global Employment and the
Future of Work*, volume 1, Tokyo: The United Nations University.

Public Interest Research Group (1992), 'Structural Adjustment: Who Really Pays?',
Delhi: Public Interest Research Group.

Rahman, Rushidan Islam (1998), 'Structural of the Labour Market, Unemployment and Poverty in Bangladesh', in Ashok Chandra, Horst Mund, Tripurai Sharan and C.T. Thakur (eds), *Labour, Employment and Human Development in South Asia*, New Delhi: B.R. Publishing Corporation.

Rodrigo, Chandra (1998), 'Structural Reforms and Labour Market in Sri Lanka', in Ashok Chandra, Horst Mund, Tripurai Sharan, and C. P. Thakur (eds), *Labour, Employment and Human Development in South Asia*, New Delhi: B.R. Publishing Corporation.

Shaheed, Zafar (1977), 'The Organization and Leadership of Industrial Labour in Pakistan (Karachi), unpublished PhD dissertation, Department of Politics, University of Leeds.

World Bank (2001), *World Development Report 2000/2001*, New York: Oxford University Press.

5. Enterprise Reform and Labor in North Africa

Chris Alexander

1. Introduction

Structural adjustment has been a painful experience for much of Eastern Europe and the developing world. But it is hard to deny that these reforms also have been a boon to comparative scholars in many disciplines. The past two decades have provided valuable opportunities to observe a relatively similar set of policy changes, affecting virtually every social constituency, across countries that vary dramatically in terms of their cultures, histories, economic and political institutions.

Some of the most intriguing and dramatic reform issues involve organized labor. Scholars generally count trade unions and their members among the 'losers' in the reform process. Privatization, subsidy reduction, labor code reform and other adjustment policies eliminate jobs, erode purchasing power, and weaken established union and bargaining institutions. Particularly in the early period of reform scholarship, analysts suggested that the ability of unions to mobilize workers in strategic sectors of the economy could make them effective reform opponents.

On the whole, organized labor has not undermined structural adjustment to the extent that some had hoped and others feared. But the passage of time now allows us to assess the impact of these reforms on organized labor and on state–labor relations more generally. Most countries are several years into their reform programs. Some governments even talk of entering the 'post-adjustment' period. Thus, we are in a better position to address the following sorts of questions: did the reform process generate an identical set of challenges for workers and their organizations across the developing world? Have workers' organizations adopted similar strategies in response to these reforms? Are reforms changing the structures of worker organization in similar ways? In sum, has structural adjustment had a homogenizing effect on worker organization and state–labor relations?

The three core countries of the Maghreb – Tunisia, Algeria, and Morocco – provide interesting cases for exploring these questions. Beyond their broad cultural affinity, these cases share a number of important similarities. In all three countries, 'indigenous' trade unions broke away from French labor organizations as part of the independence struggles in the 1940s and 1950s. Following independence, all three governments pursued development strategies that spawned large public sectors. Unions built their strongest bases in these sectors and played important political opposition roles despite efforts by all three governments to control them. Indeed, the literature on social protest movements is often more useful for analyzing state–labor relations in the Maghreb than the literature on trade unions and corporatism. Finally, all three governments began to implement economic reform programs in the 1980s that they hoped would reduce government expenditures and lay the foundations for market-driven growth.

At the same time, important differences distinguish these three cases. Algeria and Tunisia developed republican governments with strong presidents who sought to control politics by coopting all factions into single parties and single trade union confederations. The Moroccan monarchy encouraged a multi-party and multi-union system that divided the country's *classe politique* and protected the king's role as the ultimate arbiter. Algeria's hydrocarbon resources fueled the region's most explicitly socialist development strategy while Tunisia's socialism left more room for private sector activity. Morocco's development strategy was always explicitly capitalist, though it, too, spawned a large public sector in the 1970s.

State–labor relationships also developed particular characteristics in each of the three cases. Morocco developed three major union confederations, two with strong ties to political parties. Competition between rival unions and their party sponsors weakened labor's unity but generated high levels of worker militancy in the structural adjustment era. Tunisia's *Union Générale des Travailleurs Tunisiens* (UGTT) emerged as the country's most important political opposition force in the early 1970s and maintained that role until the government cracked down and coopted it again just as structural adjustment was getting under way in the late 1980s. At the same time in neighboring Algeria, the *Union Générale des Travailleurs Algériens* (UGTA) – an organization that had never enjoyed the UGTT's degree of influence – found new independence and became one of the most important players in that country's deepening economic and political crisis.

These differing patterns of union activity and state–labor relations make the Maghreb an interesting context for analyzing the effects of economic reform on organized labor. This chapter argues that privatization and enterprise reform have not produced identical outcomes across the Maghreb. Differences in economic and political conditions have shaped the ways in which governments have approached these reforms. These differences, along with others related to how labor is organized in the three countries and differences in the history of state–labor interaction, have shaped labor's response to these reforms. At the same time, however, we can also point to important similarities in the ways that enterprise reform and other adjustment policies have affected worker organizations and their relations with reforming governments.

2. Privatization: The Maghreb's Non-Issue – So Far

Of all the elements in the standard structural adjustment package, none should incite more intense labor opposition than privatization. In countries where organized labor is concentrated heavily in the public sector, privatization threatens the jobs of large numbers of rank and file union members. It also weakens the public sector union structures upon which labor leaders' influence depends. Marsha Pripstein Posusney argues persuasively that the leaders of centralized union organizations are more likely to take up policy issues like privatization that affect large numbers of workers and that are decided at the national level (Posusney, 1997).

In light of these considerations, the relatively low level of labor opposition to privatization in Tunisia, Algeria, and Morocco deserves explanation. All of the major labor confederations have denounced privatization as socially and economically irresponsible. And workers have protested against the privatization of their individual plants or sectors. But these cases have been sporadic and generally organized at the plant level. In none of these countries has privatization provoked the kind of broad-based, peak-led opposition campaign that one might expect. In fact, privatization seems not to command much serious attention from most peak labor leaders in the Maghreb. It rarely comes up in conversations with them, and it makes only sporadic appearances in media coverage of labor issues or on the agendas of major union congresses.

Three broad factors account for this tepid reaction. First, all three Maghrebi governments have talked about privatization more than they have actually done it. While all of them launched structural adjustment programs in the mid-1980s, the privatization process did not gain substantial momentum until the mid-1990s. Even Tunisia, the country that many analysts consider the Maghreb's most successful reformer, has been chastised by the IMF and the World Bank for the slow pace of its privatization effort. There, and in Morocco, privatization delays stemmed largely from difficulties finding buyers and from fears that job losses would generate recruits for Islamist movements. In Algeria, the delay had more to do with opposition from powerful interests inside the government and from the hope that oil and gas prices would rebound and restore the country's economic health without negotiating an adjustment deal with the IMF and the World Bank.

The way in which governments have implemented privatization also helps to explain labor's timid opposition. Thus far, most privatization exercises have occurred in sectors like tourism, textiles, and food processing. These sectors are labor-intensive but not heavily unionized in the Maghreb, where labor movements have long enjoyed their strongest bases among civil servants, teachers, university professors, and workers in 'strategic' enterprises that governments pledged not to touch. Additionally, the Moroccan and Tunisian governments have made job maintenance a central part of their privatization policies.

All things considered, then, it seems reasonable to suggest that peak labor leaders have not opposed privatization more aggressively because it has not threatened their organizations. This could change in the near future. In the very late 1990s privatization expanded in all three countries, even encroaching on some of the 'strategic' enterprises that governments had promised not to sell off. If this continues, and it very likely will, stronger opposition could develop.

Finally, it is hard to avoid the sense that labor leaders have not opposed privatization more aggressively because they simply feel that they cannot stop it. In each of these countries, the decision to privatize was made without labor's involvement and at a time when unions were not in a position to reverse that choice. Privatization policy has been designed and implemented by teams of insulated technocrats who are accountable to no one other than the king or the president. In this environment, union leaders have opted to focus their resources on issues such as labor code reform that will help them adapt to economies in which privatization is a given.

If privatization has not sparked serious opposition from peak labor leaders, the following country overviews demonstrate that it has done so more often among affected workers. So, too, has enterprise 'restructuring' – efforts by current owners, public or private, to reform their firms in ways that they believe will make them more efficient. It is important to note, however, that these conflicts over privatization, restructuring, and their consequences have not followed the same trajectory in all three cases. Each country's experience reflects its own economic, political and institutional environment.

Algeria

Algeria developed the Maghreb's largest public industrial sector in the 1960s and 1970s and its most severe economic crisis in the late 1980s. Consequently, Algeria has experienced the region's sharpest conflicts over privatization and restructuring. These conflicts, in turn, have affected modes of worker organization in Algeria much more dramatically than in Tunisia or Morocco.

To a much greater extent than its neighbors, Algeria's industrialization strategy from the late 1960s through the late 1970s created huge operations that incorporated engineering, manufacturing, and distribution functions under one state-appointed director. Beyond their productive functions, these enterprises also played a critical social role, providing workers and their families with an extensive array of social services.

In the early 1980s, President Chadli Benjadid initiated a controversial program aimed at reducing enterprise expenditures and boosting their efficiency without resorting to privatization. The government reduced the enterprises' social functions, lengthened the work week, tied a larger portion of worker pay to productivity, imposed more direct party rule over union officials, and took a much harder line against worker militancy. But the core of the reform plan involved breaking the enterprises into smaller, still public, firms that specialized in only one specific part of the production process. In 1982–83, the government divided 85 public corporations and industrial enterprises into more than 500 individual units. Benjadid hoped that these reforms would force public enterprises to become more productive and efficient without ceding them to the private sector.[1]

When opponents inside the government stymied these reforms, and after the 1985–86 oil price collapse made it clear that Algeria could not count on rising oil export revenues to solve its economic crisis, Benjadid's reform team developed a more aggressive enterprise reform plan. In late 1987, the government unveiled a plan to free public enterprises from the state's administrative and financial control. Under this new plan, passed by the National Assembly as law 88-01, the government would no longer determine investment levels, foreign exchange allocations, or prices for public enterprises. The state would help the plants settle their debts and would provide an initial dose of operating capital. After that, each enterprise would have to manage its own affairs and survive according to market standards of efficiency or close down.

In order for decentralized plant management to succeed, reform proponents argued that wage policy had to follow suit. Managers needed the freedom to develop wages appropriate to their particular markets and economic conditions. Toward this end, law 88-01 also called for a new wage bargaining regime that would allow unions and directors to negotiate plant-level wage accords. But this was as far as the law went. New wage bargaining institutions might be desirable over the long term. In the short term, however, reform architects wanted to give plant managers great latitude to make their enterprises more efficient as quickly as possible. Consequently, the government talked about new bargaining institutions while it actually expanded directors' powers to define their own management plans, to replace permanent workers with temporaries, and to link pay and promotions to productivity.

Along with the deepening economic crisis, law 88-01 had a powerful impact on the labor movement from the shop floor to the top of the UGTA. From the late 1960s through the mid-1980s, Algeria's public industrial workforce remained deeply divided between low-paid manual workers and better-paid administrative workers. Plant-level institutions played an important role in creating and nurturing these tensions. Algeria's labor laws mandated base unions and worker assemblies for all public enterprises with at least 35 workers. These institutions enjoyed considerable influence over promotions and pay scales. But plant directors regularly manipulated worker elections and loaded the base unions and worker assemblies with skilled technical and administrative workers. These workers used their positions to give themselves pay raises and promotions while they neglected the demands of the more numerous manual workers in lower pay categories. Tensions between these 'classes' within the workplace undermined the UGTA's credibility and stunted the development of a broad-based worker identity.[2]

Economic crisis and law 88-01 changed all of this. Although they regarded most plant directors as incompetent bureaucrats, better-paid technical and administrative workers had no reason to care about managerial competency in the 1970s and early 1980s. Hydrocarbon rent covered enterprise deficits. Skilled workers could migrate from plant to plant in search of the best deal. In the face of rampant unemployment and public sector layoffs, skilled workers dared not leave their positions. Turnover plummeted and workforces became more stable (see Said Chikhi (1994), 'Question ouvrière et rapports sociaux', *Naqd: Revue d'études et de critique socials*, **6**, p. 10). Trapped in firms where directors could ignore worker assemblies, fire at will, and where job security and future incomes would depend on productivity and efficiency, better-paid workers suddenly faced the same uncertainties as their colleagues down the pay scale. All workers feared that incompetent directors would resort to layoffs as the fastest way to cut costs and compensate for their own inexperience. Higher-paid workers, in particular, feared that directors seeking to cut costs would target them first.

Along with deteriorating purchasing power, these concerns laid the foundation for a new surge in militancy that united workers across the pay scale. Previously privileged workers wanted to get rid of incompetent directors and establish bargaining institutions that allowed them to defend their interests before the government cut their firms loose. To press these demands effectively, however, technicians and administrative workers needed the cooperation of the more numerous workers in lower pay categories. To purchase this support, white-collar and skilled workers accepted the need for more democratic unions that would represent all segments of the workforce. Between 1988 and 1991, this new worker coalition launched a wave of strike activity that freed the UGTA from FLN control and forced the government to accept wage increases and to begin developing early retirement and unemployment insurance programs. In a very real way, then, the enterprise reforms that the government laid out in 1988 actually enhanced worker organization, unity, and influence. By 1991, the UGTA had become the single most important non-party organization on Algeria's socio-political landscape. Even though the new 1989 constitution ended the UGTA's monopoly on worker representation and allowed other unions, few workers felt compelled to exercise this new freedom. Building a new union organization would require substantial investments of time and money. The UGTA already had a well-established national structure, and that structure was becoming more militant and independent. Moreover, most workers and labor leaders still believed that unity within a single organization offered the best strategy for defending their interests.

Through most of the 1990s, the UGTA defined those interests in terms of salary increases to counteract inflation, job protection and union rights guarantees, and greater union involvement in reform planning. While the union consistently opposed privatization, the issue did not begin to pose a serious threat until the very end of the decade. Privatization has been a much more contested policy choice in Algeria than in either Tunisia or Morocco. Opponents have been much better placed to challenge it in public debate and to delay its actual implementation. This opposition, combined with a lack of clarity about which government agency exercised real authority over privatization, meant that very little of it got done. Successive governments continued trying to reform public enterprises by converting them into holding companies that would function according to market standards. But these companies continued to struggle under the state's financial and administrative control. In late 1999 and early 2000, Prime Minister Benbitour pledged to speed up the privatization process. In the first half of the year, the government floated plans to privatize the post and telecommunications sector, the social security system, the national airline, and the industrial vehicle complex Rouiba. Government officials even suggested that they might open SONATRACH, the national petroleum company and second largest employer, to private investment. In cases where reform architects have allowed their input, UGTA leaders have supported some of these privatization plans. The post and telecommunications sector provides the best example. The government consulted UGTA officials and provided them with strong assurances about job protection. The union leadership, in turn, publicly supported the plan.

Unfortunately, cases like this have become the exception rather than the rule in recent months. At the same time that it developed more ambitious privatization plans, the government also seemed to become even less interested than its predecessors in a dialogue with the UGTA. Tripartite negotiations between the union, the government, and representatives of private capital – talks that UGTA pressure initiated in 1991 – have not resumed since they broke off in September, 1998. When asked recently about the UGTA's role in privatization decisions, the Minister of Participation and Reform Coordination, a convoluted title designed to avoid the term 'privatization', said proudly that government officials would happily meet with labor leaders at the national, sectoral, or plant levels to 'inform them about the way in which the government intends to conduct privatization'.

These more ambitious privatization plans, combined with the government's unwillingness to involve labor in the process, generated mounting unrest through the spring of 2000. Social security workers struck for two hours on 8 May to protest the Minister of Labor and Social Affairs' announcement that the government planned to open the fund to private investment. The UGTA central supported the workers and their threat to call a general strike if the government persisted in its plans to privatize the social security fund without worker involvement. Workers at the industrial vehicle plant in Rouiba, an enterprise with a long history of labor militancy, made similar threats when they learned that the government might sell the facility to Renault. These actions, along with strikes over wage demands in several plants, have prompted dire predictions from some UGTA officials about serious unrest in coming months. As ominous as it sounds, this rhetoric is not new. Neither is the feeling that the government does not involve the union in economic policy-making. The UGTA leveled the same criticism at the previous government and offered the same predictions about a general strike and a breakdown in public order.[4]

When government officials take these threats seriously, they do so not only because the UGTA can cripple strategic sectors of the economy. They also know that there are just as many workers, perhaps more, that the UGTA cannot control. Over the course of the 1990s, changes in political institutions and continued economic and political deterioration frayed this new-found worker unity. Throughout this period, the UGTA tried to walk a very thin line. On the one hand, the union became the most aggressive opponent of the government's economic reform program. On the other hand, the union also became one of the government's most ardent supporters in the fight against the Islamists. As the economic crisis deepened, neither the union's economic resistance nor its political support seemed able to force the government to keep its promises. The government failed to honor its wage commitments and it began simply to close plants without any prior consultation with unions.

In this environment, workers in many sectors began to lose confidence in the UGTA. Some of these workers broke with the UGTA entirely and formed new, autonomous unions. Some of the most significant new organizations formed among mechanical and metallurgy workers, pharmacists, airline pilots, and teachers. These unions represented constituencies that had been hardest hit by plant restructurings and closure in the early and mid-1990s (mechanical and metallurgy workers), or smaller professional constituencies who felt that the UGTA remained too focused on blue-collar issues to deal with their particular concerns (pilots, pharmacists, and teachers). Eight of these autonomous unions tried to establish a new confederation in 1994. The organization collapsed fairly quickly when a group of political parties asserted control over it.

A similar, but more formidable, union is currently fighting for recognition. The Syndicat National des Travailleurs Algériens (SNATA) applied for legal recognition in the spring of 1999. Claiming 320,000 members in public administration and 120,000 across other sectors, SNATA has criticized the UGTA for negotiating on behalf of workers it does not truly represent and for being too willing to accept the government's propositions for resolving workplace conflicts. To date, the government still has not granted SNATA legal recognition. The union has vowed to launch a grass-roots campaign to form base unions and to press for authorization and the subsidies that would come with it.[5]

Other workers broke with the UGTA and joined 'Islamic leagues'. Descendants of the dissolved Syndicat Islamique de Travail (SIT), a union created by the Islamic Salvation Front in 1989–90, the leagues built support across a diverse range of sectors. Although the government has renewed suspension orders every six months since 1992, most observers believe that the leagues continue to operate clandestinely in a number of sectors.[6]

Finally, many workers have stayed with the UGTA because they know that it remains the only union with which the government negotiates wages and other issues. But these workers have begun using their base unions to pursue their own strategies. They organize strikes and demonstrations that will force their grievances to the top of the UGTA's agenda or that will force the government to intervene directly. Recent strikes by rail workers in the central and eastern parts of the country and by workers in portions of the al-Hadjar steelworks plant provide two examples of grass-roots strikes that have bedeviled the UGTA leadership's effort to improve relations with the government.

In light of these developments, it is fair to say that the UGTA's control over the rank and file of Algeria's labor movement is considerably weaker today than it was in the early 1990s. The union still can mobilize workers for strikes and marches. But it has lost much of its ability to reign in workers who now have alternative organizations for pressing their own demands. Consequently, as privatization makes deeper inroads into the industrial sector, it likely will provoke serious worker opposition.

Tunisia

Of the three countries, enterprise reform – and structural adjustment in general – have generated the least conflict and change in Tunisia. This is not to say that there has been no labor conflict in Tunisia. But Tunisia has not witnessed the sustained unrest that has shut down whole sectors from time to time in Algeria and Morocco.

Several factors account for this relative quiescence. Unlike Algeria, where state-owned enterprises accounted for over 90% of the country's industrial production and at least 70% of industrial employment, Tunisia's state enterprises in the early 1980s accounted for only a quarter of non-agricultural employment.[7] Despite its smaller size, however, subsidies for the state-owned enterprise sector consumed 30% of the state budget in the early 1980s (Ferchiou, 1991). Because the government borrowed to cover these transfers, public enterprise deficits became 'the central cause of the growth of the country's external debt' (Grissa, 1991). In early 1985, these rising costs prompted the government's decision to begin privatizing non-strategic state enterprises.

From 1985 through the mid-1990s, Tunisia's privatization effort progressed very slowly. In the early part of this period, the political turmoil that dominated President Habib Bourguiba's last two years in office prevented any kind of dramatic economic reform. Zine al-Abidine Ben Ali breathed new life into the structural adjustment process after he deposed Bourguiba in late 1987. But privatization still lagged far behind other components of the reform process. The government sold off only 48 enterprises between 1987 and 1994.

While some union officials have tried to take credit for this slow pace, the UGTT was in no shape to seriously contest privatization. We will return to this matter presently. Instead, the slow pace was the product of a deliberate choice by the new president and his reform architects. Though he wore a suit rather than a uniform, Ben Ali was a military man, not a career politician. He had no real constituency inside or out of the government. Challenging vested interests in the public sector did not make sense for a man who needed to make powerful friends. And he needed to make them quickly. Aided by the country's economic and political deterioration in the mid-1980s, Tunisia's Islamist movement had emerged as the single most powerful opposition force.

The fight against the Islamists dominated Ben Ali's first decade in power. And although this struggle culminated in a wave of vicious repression in the early 1990s, Ben Ali's political strategy always contained a strong social component. Convinced that unemployment and economic hardship generated Islamist recruits, he never allowed the drive for economic reform to subvert that strategy. Moving slowly with privatization was an integral part of the plan. So, too, was a firm commitment to a broad range of social expenditures. Buoyed by a rapid economic recovery in the late 1980s and early 1990s, the government maintained investments in consumer subsidies, education, expanded health care, severance indemnities, and new employment programs that seemed out of character for a government committed to structural adjustment.[8] The government even continued to hire new civil servants and to increase the budget for state offices and enterprises deep into the 1990s.[9]

Concern for political stability and the quick return to economic health also shaped choices about the first privatizations. The government intentionally began with deeply troubled firms like the Confort appliance company and some state-owned hotels (Mehdi, 1994). Because these firms had difficulty paying wages regularly, Ben Ali and other privatization architects reckoned that workers would actually welcome new ownership. Starting with troubled enterprises would give the new government an opportunity to demonstrate its commitment to social concerns and dispense with tough cases that would have a hard time finding buyers. In some cases, particularly in the hotels sector, Ben Ali personally forbade new buyers to lay off workers. In others, the government paid generous severance indemnities to workers who lost their jobs. One study of Tunisia's early privatizations found only one enterprise, the STIA auto plant in Sousse, that had to close its doors because of financial difficulties. Even in this case, the government continued to pay all 2200 workers (Harik, 1992, p. 220).

This sensitivity to the social repercussions of economic reform did much to mute worker opposition to privatization. But authoritarianism has been just as important. To a greater extent than anywhere else in the Maghreb, state–labor relations have been a central issue in Tunisia's post-independence politics. For the first decade after its birth in 1946, the UGTT launched strikes and other protest measures in support of the nationalist party's effort to negotiate Tunisia's independence. The union actually ran the nationalist struggle for a brief period in the early 1950s when the party's leaders were in jail or exile.

Because of its role in the independence struggle, and because it supported Bourguiba's wing of the nationalist party after independence in 1956, the UGTT entered post-independence politics with considerable influence. The government succeeded in coopting the union in the 1960s, but the UGTT re-emerged as the country's most important political opposition movement from the early 1970s through the mid-1980s. In 1978, and again in 1985–86, fierce government repression divided and nearly destroyed the UGTT. The union remained in that condition when Ben Ali seized power in 1987.

Rather than allow the UGTT to languish, Ben Ali believed that using the government's resources to resuscitate the union would help his effort to create both an image of democratic reform and a social counterweight to the Islamist movement. It also allowed him to rebuild the union on his own terms, loading its peak leadership with coopted leaders who owed their positions to him more than to the rank and file. Through the early and mid-1990s, the new UGTT leadership worked – with the government's support – to purge the union of leftists, Islamists, and anyone else who wanted the union to become a more independent organization. While Ben Ali restored many of the rights that the UGTT lost in the mid-1980s, he deliberately refused to restore the 1% check-off that would have given the union an independent income. Instead, the UGTT became wholly dependent on government funds.

These conditions made it impossible for the union to take an aggressive stand against privatization or anything else that the government did. Even the few independent individuals who managed to win election to the UGTT's Executive Bureau in the late 1980s and early 1990s acknowledged that the union simply did not have the strength to contest the regime. Responding to a journalist's question about the UGTT's position on privatization, Tahar Chaieb, the most outspoken privatization critic on the Executive Bureau in the early 1990s said, 'We cannot challenge this policy, which is a choice of the government. We are working to ensure that it does not have terrible consequences for workers.'[10] After the crackdown of the mid-1980s, most union activists, even those who opposed the government's policy, felt that it was more important to focus on rebuilding the UGTT as an organization.

The conflict between the government and the Islamists in the early 1990s also encouraged union leaders to mute their criticism and to crack down on rank and file activists. Unlike Morocco, Tunisia developed a relatively unified and well-organized Islamist movement. But unlike Algeria, the conflict between that movement and the Tunisian government never erupted into a full-blown civil war. It simmered at a high temperature, creating the impression that Tunisia could go the way of Algeria if Tunisians did not manage the conflict very carefully. The government exploited this fear to convince many trade unionists that they should avoid any unrest that might ignite an open conflict, force the government to clamp down on the union, and/or result in a victory by Islamists hostile to the union.[11]

Finally, new collective bargaining institutions have helped to reduce labor unrest in Tunisia. In 1988–89, the Tunisian government created new wage bargaining arrangements. These new procedures replaced annual wage talks with three-year accords. They also created a bit more latitude for sectoral-level negotiations. Having observed this new bargaining framework over the past decade, it is clear that the process has not changed as much as the government and UGTT officials suggest that it has. In reality, wage negotiations remain highly centralized and the Ministry of Social Affairs remains deeply involved in them. Moreover, most observers agree that the resulting accords have not allowed wages to keep pace with the real cost of living. Nevertheless, these accords give workers greater assurances that their wages will increase over a longer period of time. Those increases may not be as substantial as they would like. But the old system gave them no guarantees beyond the current year. In an environment where many believe – rightly or wrongly – that dramatic wage increases could cost jobs, Tunisian workers have been willing to trade wage moderation for greater certainty over a longer time horizon. Negotiating three-year accords also has prevented wage bargaining from becoming the annual battle between the government and the UGTT that it was in the 1970s and 1980s.[12]

If worker organization and state–labor relations in Tunisia have shown unusual resilience over the past decade, recent developments suggest that this could change in the near future. In the mid-1990s, the Tunisian government launched a second wave of privatizations. This wave is considerably larger than the first. The government sold off 45 enterprises in 1995 alone. In 1999, 73 more firms went on the block (Mokni, 2000). This second wave also involves plants that are more profitable, located in more strategic sectors, and that contain more unionized workers.

While the Tunisian press remains less inclined to cover strikes and other forms of worker protest than its Algerian and Moroccan counterparts, there is clear evidence that grass-roots unrest has increased in recent years. Through the late 1990s, workers in a handful of enterprises and public offices struck to protest violations of union rights or the failure of plant mangers to implement wage accords. In the past year, the privatization of state-owned cement companies and of textile enterprises in Ben Arous and Moknine sparked protests by workers concerned about their jobs.

Dissension also has increased inside the UGTT. In April, 1997, police arrested a number of union activists who signed a petition criticizing the lack of democracy inside the UGTT and its failure to defend workers' interests more aggressively. In recent months, rumors have circulated about an effort by some disgruntled UGTT officials to break away and form a new union. As in Algeria, this discussion is often couched in terms of broader democratic change: how can a political system that allows multiple parties oppose multiple unions?

A new union organization would certainly attract some level of rank and file support. But we should treat these rumors with some circumspection. Recall that Algeria's new unions are sectoral organizations, the products of real work-related grievances in particular industries. Thus far, rumors of a new union in Tunisia do not appear to grow directly out of the grievances of workers in specific sectors who feel that the UGTT no longer serves their needs. The talk is of a new organization that would be more internally democratic than the UGTT. This, combined with the fact that talk of a new union increased after last year's UGTT congress, when the general secretary completed his purge of the leadership, suggests that the rumors have more to do with political ambitions than with rank and file worker concerns.

Then there is the matter of historical precedent to consider. The Tunisian government has never expressed any serious interest in multiple trade unions. The general assumption has been that a single confederation is easier to coopt while competition between multiple unions generates greater militancy. As we shall see, Morocco's experience offers little to challenge these assumptions. On two occasions, however, in 1957 and again in 1985, government officials encouraged and manipulated breakaway unions as part of an elaborate strategy for pulling a wayward UGTT back into the government's orbit. On both occasions, President Bourguiba encouraged disgruntled UGTT officials to leave the union and to form a new confederation with government support. In so doing, the government weakened the UGTT and bolstered the reputations of unionists who were more willing to do Bourguiba's bidding. Some months later, the government brokered 'reunifications' that dissolved the newer unions, reintegrated their members back into the UGTT, and established peak union leaders more to the president's liking.

These machinations allowed the government to reassert control over the UGTT while presenting itself as a protector of worker unity. They also justify speculation that the government would be deeply involved in any future effort to form a new union in Tunisia. In any event, it is hard to see how a new union could pursue a strategy that differs substantially from the UGTT's. To an even greater extent than in Algeria or Morocco, periods of well-organized union militancy in Tunisia correspond to periods of more general political conflict and uncertainty. Immediately after independence in 1956, and again from the mid-1970s through the mid-1980s, inter-elite conflict generated new opportunities for the UGTT to find powerful allies and to influence policy. Given Tunisia's current economic health, President Ben Ali's effective control of the political system, and the current UGTT leadership's control the union's structures, conditions conducive to a more assertive labor movement will not develop anytime soon.

Morocco

Robert Bianchi has described state–labor relations in Egypt as unruly corporatism. But with 21 unions and some of the region's highest sustained levels of worker unrest, Morocco may qualify as the Arab world's unruliest corporatist (Bianchi, 1989).

Two broad sets of factors account for this state of affairs. The first is economic. The Moroccan government never developed the sort of populist development strategy that the Algerian and Tunisian governments pursued in the 1960s and 1970s. It never invested comparable resources into education, health care, wages, and other social expenditures. As a result, Moroccan workers faced more difficult living and working conditions than their Algerian and Tunisian counterparts. These conditions, in turn, generated more profound grievances (Berrada, 1986; Labzour, 1982).

Political and institutional factors played an equally important role in creating Morocco's unruly corporatism. As in Tunisia, a nationalist trade union movement – the Union Marocaine du Travail (UMT) – played a vital role in Morocco's struggle for independence. But unlike Tunisia, where the UGTT helped a popular nationalist movement establish an effective government, Morocco's nationalist party and union moved immediately into the opposition against a monarchy that enjoyed a less organized support base. Hoping to expand that base, King Mohammed V reached out to the UMT. The government involved the union in social and economic policy-making and in the design of a new labor code and new bargaining institutions at the national and plant levels.

This mutually beneficial relationship began to break down in 1958–60, when tensions between the UMT and the government, and within the UMT itself, produced a new trade union, the *Union Générale des Travailleurs Marocains* (UGTM). In part, the UGTM reflected growing disenchantment with the bureaucratization and authoritarianism inside the UMT. More importantly, it signaled a rebellion against the UMT's apolitical brand of trade unionism that focused solely on workers' material interests. Tied to the old nationalist party, the Istiqlal, UGTM leaders argued that workers could no more separate their interests from the political process in the early 1960s than they could separate them from colonialism prior to independence. Government would respond to workers' demands only when it was democratically elected and contained workers' representatives.

The end of the UMT's honeymoon with the monarchy and the founding of the UGTM coincided with the ascension of a young new king, Hassan II. It also opened a new period in state–labor relations. Concerned that labor posed a threat to the monarchy, Hassan II opted for a decidedly less populist strategy than his father. The government stopped enforcing much of the social legislation adopted in the late 1950s and stopped convening many of the institutions for worker participation and negotiation. Across the economy, especially in the private sector, many owners and managers paid below minimum wages, fired workers at will, refused to declare all of their workers to the social security fund, and refused to negotiate with unions. The government rewarded the UMT's non-political unionism with preferential treatment.[13] But it also repressed labor activists and played the UMT, the UGTM, and smaller unions against one another in order to keep labor divided and weak.

This game became more complicated in 1978 when leftist activists affiliated with the Union Socialiste des Forces Populaires (USFP) established a third national labor organization, the Confederation Démocratique du Travail (CDT). Like the UGTM, the CDT espoused an explicitly political philosophy. From the beginning, the CDT was more than a labor organization. It acted as the striking arm of the USFP's campaign for democratic political and social reform. Most CDT leaders held positions in the USFP, and the union depended heavily on the party for money. Also like the UGTM, the CDT drew most of its support from civil servants and workers in large public enterprises. The UMT maintained its dominant position in the private sector.

Workplace institutions fueled a fierce competition for worker support between these three confederations. In the late 1950s and early 1960s, the government adopted rules that called for elected personnel delegates in public and private enterprises and in the civil service. Under pressure for democratic reform, the monarchy supported a new constitution in 1972 that allowed these elected worker delegates to select ten of their members to sit in parliament.[14] Unions did not have a legal role in either of these elections because unions did not have a strong legal presence in the workplace. The constitution proclaimed a general right to join unions and to strike. But the government never supplemented these vague declarations with additional legislation that guaranteed and regulated the exercise of these rights in individual plants or offices. National unions and strikes were perfectly legal in the abstract. But individual workers in individual firms had no clearly defined laws to defend them when owners and managers fired them for organizing unions or strikes. Owners and managers routinely ignored labor laws, and the government lacked the will to enforce those laws or to establish any kind of meaningful concertation at the national, sectoral, or plant levels.

Because of their ambiguous legal status at the plant level, unions used the personnel delegate elections as a vehicle for building worker support, forcing owners and managers to negotiate with them, and gaining access to parliament. This was especially important for the CDT. The other two unions had been organizing workers for two decades, and the government and private owners openly opposed the CDT's militant socialism. To combat this opposition, the CDT launched a wave of strikes in the late 1970s and 1980s. The union could easily justify the strikes by calling attention to Morocco's deteriorating social conditions. But everyone understood that the strikes had more to do with the CDT's effort to build worker support, to win personnel delegate elections, to force the government and owners to recognize the new union, and to support the USFP's campaign for political reform. These strikes, in turn, forced the UMT and the UGTM to become more militant in order to protect their own bases of support. The result was a rolling barrage of strikes through the 1980s, always launched over violations of union rights or demands for pay raises, but always driven by party politics and union competition.

This environment makes it difficult to decode labor unrest in the period since the Moroccan government launched its structural adjustment program in 1983. On the one hand, structural adjustment only increased workers' and unions' grievances. Unlike Tunisia, Morocco did not benefit from a rapid economic recovery in the early phase of the reform period. The government did not have the resources to implement programs that could mitigate the effects of structural adjustment. And since Morocco lacked a unified opposition movement – Islamist or secular – the government felt less political pressure to take such measures in the first place. Over the course of the mid-1980s and early 1990s, the government froze wages, cut subsidies, and drastically reduced public sector hiring at the very time that universities turned out record numbers of graduates who had expected public sector employment. In the face of rapidly deteriorating living and working conditions, the government paid little more than lip service to the idea of union involvement in the reform process.

On the other hand, Morocco's two most militant unions in the 1980s and 1990s, the CDT and the UGTM, maintained close ties to parties that sought first and foremost to turn up the pressure for political reform. In the early 1990s the UGTM and the CDT forged an alliance that launched a wave of coordinated strikes that most observers agree was driven by political rather than professional concerns. The UMT launched strikes, too, but not as part of any coordinated effort with the UGTM and the CDT. Indeed, competition between the UMT and the CDT for rank and file support continued to motivate a considerable number of strikes. Through the 1980s and the early 1990s, it is difficult to distinguish strikes motivated by workers' material grievances from strikes motivated by union competition and party strategies.

Then, in 1995, a new spirit of union coordination began to develop. In the spring, the three confederations worked together in a national rail strike that protested against low pay, violations of union rights, and a restructuring plan that the government developed without union consultation. This strike brought the secretaries-general of the CDT and the UMT together for their first meeting since the CDT's founding in 1978. More recently, the UMT publically supported – but did not join – the CDT's and the UGTM's call for a general strike on 25 April 2000 (Naanaa, 2000).

This willingness to coordinate positions has extended to other issues. One of the most important concerns labor code reform. As elsewhere, international financial institutions, private business owners, and pro-reform government officials have pressed for changes in the code that would give business owners more freedom to hire and fire workers. The protracted negotiations over code reform have given the three unions opportunities to exchange ideas and to develop shared positions concerning union rights in the workplace, the right to strike, and job protections. Securing these rights is critical for all three unions, and their leaders know that they must sustain a united bargaining front in order to prevail (Naanaa, 1999).

Recently, the three unions have coordinated their activities on two additional issues that traditionally have inspired some of their fiercest competition: the administration of the national social security fund (CNSS), long under the control of the UMT, and the conduct of plant-level worker elections. The latter deserves mention because it could have important long-term implications for worker organization in Morocco. We noted earlier that although the law makes a distinction between union delegates and personnel delegates, the unions have taken over the personnel delegate elections. Under the current system, workers vote for lists of candidates – most sponsored by the unions – to a body that then selects the worker representatives who will sit in parliament. The distinction between union delegates and personnel delegates, and the two-step process for electing worker parliamentarians, provides ample opportunities for plant managers and owners to pit the unions against one another and to prevent a united worker front from developing in their plant. In an effort to overcome these divisions, the UMT, UGTM, and CDT proposed in 1997 to abolish the distinction between personnel and union delegates and to allow the direct election of worker parliamentarians. It is interesting to note that the government, which has expressed interest in seeing the labor movement overcome some of the divisions that fuel strikes, rejected this proposition. But the fact that all three unions supported it suggests that each sees greater unity as vital to its own interests.

Privatization and enterprise reform play a central role in this new spirit of cooperation. Although government officials discussed privatization from the beginning of the reform process, parliament did not pass legislation authorizing it until 1989. Evaluating and auditing the first set of firms delayed their actual sales until November 1992. This first wave of privatizations provoked little opposition, in part because there was not much to it. Between 1993 and 1996, the government privatized only 27 companies and 18 hotels. As in Tunisia, the financial resources at the government's disposal influenced its choices about the first firms to go on sale. But unlike Tunisia, these considerations prompted the Moroccan government to begin with healthy firms. Since the government did not have the resources to provide large severance indemnities and other social programs, it needed to make job maintenance a condition of sale without alienating buyers. The best way to do this was to begin with healthy firms that would not need to fire large numbers of workers in order to become more efficient.

Additionally, the unions had good reason to believe that privatization did not pose a serious threat to their organizations. The 1989 privatization law called for the government to draw up a list of 'privatizable' firms and to finish the process by 1995. The CDT and UGTM relied heavily on civil servants and workers in strategic sectors that the government promised not to touch. The UMT's base was already concentrated in the private sector, so privatization posed an even lesser threat to its leaders.

All of this began to change in 1995, the year in which privatization was supposed to stop and the year in which union cooperation began to increase. Continued economic crisis forced the government to consider relying more heavily on privatization receipts to generate revenue. This meant extending privatization beyond 1995 and beyond the established list of firms. It also meant cleaning up some deeply troubled enterprises in order to make them attractive enough for sale. After parliament passed the necessary legislation, the government expanded the privatization list to include more strategic firms and firms in more difficulty (el-Anouari, 1995).

These are the privatization cases that have sparked the fiercest labor opposition. The *Industrie cotonnière de Oued Zem* (ICOZ) has become a sort of reference case for discussions of these conflicts. In June 1995 the government sold 97% of ICOZ to a consortium of Moroccan and international buyers. These buyers agreed to help pay off the firms' outstanding financial obligations and to invest new capital in it. The Ministry of Privatization also agreed to pay off some of the firm's debts. One month after the sale, ICOZ's right to import materials needed for production was suspended because the government had not released the funds necessary to cover its portion of the firm's debt. Unable to produce, the owners had little choice but to close their doors and put 1000 workers at the plants in Oued Zem and Tadla out of work. These workers sustained a nine-month strike that culminated in a sit-in. Ultimately, however, they were forced to seek work elsewhere in an economy with 30% unemployment.

A similar scenario sparked labor unrest at the *Société des industries mécaniques et électroniques de Fès* (SIMEF). The government sold SIMEF to a consortium of the plant's suppliers and clients in the summer of 1995. Like ICOZ, SIMEF promptly slid into economic and social crisis. The buyers did not pay debts owed to the treasury. They did not make the new investments required by the sale agreement. They did not pay the backlog of contributions owed to the national social security fund. Workers never received 10% of the shares as promised in the sale plan, and the firm simply stopped paying wages in October 1997. Three hundred workers and their families were left without income.

It is important to note that protests like these have erupted post fact, when new owners violated the terms of purchase. They have not been protests against privatization as a policy. Nevertheless, poorly executed privatizations and deteriorating purchasing power generated a surge in grass-roots militancy in the late 1990s. Particularly after the USFP and Istiqlal took control of the government in the mid-1990s, rank and file labor activists wanted to ensure that the parties' union allies continued to defend workers' interests. Since 1998, strikes organized at the plant level have lasted longer and workers have adopted new forms of protest, like sit-ins and plant occupations, that resemble those adopted by Algerian workers since the late 1980s.

This pressure from below has forced the labor centrals to take up individual cases like ICOZ, SIMEF, or the restructuring of the rail sector. But it is still extremely rare for labor leaders to challenge privatization or restructuring in general. Part of this stems from the simple belief that privatization as a policy is unchangeable. Ultimately, however, privatization receives relatively little attention from union leaders because a much larger problem both dwarfs and subsumes it. That problem is the unwillingness of successive governments to engage the unions in a meaningful, institutionalized dialogue about the country's economic and social future. Unions have not opposed privatization as much as they have opposed the government's attempts to do it without their input.

This brings us back to Bianchi's unruly corporatism. State–labor–capital relations in Morocco certainly have been unruly. But the unruliness stems in large part from the fact that these relations have not really been very corporatist. Corporatism involves more than the mere presence of professional interest groups. It also involves a set of clear institutions that mediate the relations between those groups. In sharp contrast to Tunisia and Algeria, the Moroccan government never led the way in establishing these kinds of institutional arrangements.

Since the early 1990s, the government has pledged repeatedly to join the unions and the private owners organization (CGEM) in a 'social dialogue'. But these highly centralized meetings have taken place only sporadically and the government frequently has failed to follow through on promises that it makes in them. Beyond giving muscle to demands for political reform, the vast majority of the sectoral and general strikes called by the UMT, UGTM, and CDT in the 1990s were designed to force the government back to the bargaining table. The fact that the government continued to drag its feet about the social dialogue even after the CDT's and the UGTM's party allies took over has been a driving force behind the new spirit of union cooperation. All three confederations expected the USFP–Istiqlal government to be more responsive to labor than it has been. Frustration with the CDT's inability to force the USFP-led government to be more solicitous has prompted some unions in the education and banking sectors – long-time CDT strongholds – to talk openly about breaking away and forming autonomous unions. University professors set the example when they left the CDT in the 1980s over concerns that the union concentrated on politics and blue-collar workers while structural adjustment steadily eroded salaries, promotions, and hiring in the universities.

Moreover, the social dialogue has done nothing to establish stronger bargaining institutions at the sectoral and plant levels. From both the unions' and the owners' perspective, this is where new institutions are needed most. Faced with more intense competition at home and in the region, workers' and owners' unions all talk about being in the same boat. The welfare of both labor and capital increasingly depends on the creation of productive firms that can attract investors and generate new jobs. Peaceful workplaces play an important role in this effort. The unions want new bargaining institutions that give them a clear legal status in the private sector and that give them a fair chance to win benefits for their members at the bargaining table. Owners want more peaceful enterprises and a regularized bargaining system that gives them more certainty about their wage bills over a longer period of time. Thus, at the very time that government leaders in Algeria and Tunisia denounce 'corporatism' as encouraging class conflict, Moroccan officials have actually called for more corporatism – a stronger commitment to professional interest representation that is not contaminated by partisan competition.

3. Conclusion

Privatization and enterprise reform have not followed a universal trajectory across the Maghreb. Differences in macroeconomic and political conditions exerted powerful influences over the choices that governments made about how to proceed with enterprise reform. Nor have these reforms affected organized labor across the region in the same way. Labor organization and state–labor relations in Algeria have changed substantially since 1988. Union structures and strategies have changed much less dramatically in Morocco and Tunisia.

At the same time, though, enterprise reform and privatization have generated important challenges and consequences for organized labor in all three countries. In light of this volume's interest in comparisons across regions, we conclude by highlighting these similarities between the Maghrebi cases rather than trying to explain the differences between them.

The most significant similarity involves the degree to which governments in all three countries have excluded organized labor from the policy-making process. Even in Algeria, where privatization faces its staunchest opposition and where the government makes the most promises about worker participation, organized labor has not been able to influence privatization policy in a direct way.

This exclusion, combined with the other effects of economic reform, has produced two important developments at the grass-roots level. First, worker militancy has become more intense. Particularly in Algeria and Morocco, strikes last longer and often generate additional forms of protest such as marches and workplace occupations. The patterns of state–labor interaction in the two countries over the past decade betray a striking similarity: workers organize strikes and other protests at the plant or sectoral level over material grievances; peak labor leaders exploit this militancy, which they do not control, to press governments to the bargaining table; governments promise to address workers' material grievances and to give their leaders a more substantial role in the policy-making process; governments renege on these promises and the strikes begin again.

This increased militancy conforms to widely held expectations about workers' reactions to enterprise reform, privatization, and other adjustment policies. Perhaps more surprising is the effect that these reforms have had on worker unity. As the Moroccan case best illustrates, peak labor leaders may recognize the need to coordinate positions on important issues. At the grass-roots level, however, adjustment reforms have generated powerful fragmentary pressures. One of the fault lines is as old as the unions themselves. Rank and file workers have steadily lost confidence in peak union leaders who preach moderation for the sake of protecting their relations with other political elites. The exclusion of labor leaders from the policy-making process, including decisions about privatization, has made it more difficult for them to deliver benefits and protections necessary to sustain rank and file support.

A second fault line cuts between sectors. These tensions also are not new. But concerns about privatization and enterprise reform have made them more pronounced. As breakaway unions in Algeria and Morocco demonstrate, workers in sectors hit hard by restructuring or by talk of impending privatization have begun to leave established unions and to form new organizations when they believe that peak union leaders either cannot or will not defend their specific interests. Thus, enterprise reform and other adjustment policies seem to have eroded worker unity rather than strengthened it. Instead of enhancing a sense of shared class solidarity, these reforms generate high levels of uncertainty that encourage an 'every worker for herself' mentality.

These trends toward increased militancy and fragmentation have been less pronounced in Tunisia, where a healthier economy and stronger authoritarian control have muted worker protest. But there have been more instances of worker protest and more rumors of divisions inside the UGTT in the past two years. These developments suggest that Tunisia is not immune to the dynamics affecting labor elsewhere in the region.

These internal divisions make it more difficult for organized labor in the

Maghreb to address the three central challenges that confront it as privatization creeps deeper into the public industrial sector. The first challenge is institutional. In all three cases, the shift to more market-oriented, outward-looking economies has generated pressure for new institutions to regulate state–labor–capital relations. In all three countries, governments, unions, and private owners have been negotiating new labor codes that strike a balance between employers' demands for more 'flexibility' and the unions' desire to preserve as many worker and union protections as possible.

Then there is the issue of wage bargaining institutions. Across the Maghreb, most economic policy-makers argue that more liberal, outward-looking economies demand more decentralized bargaining procedures. Different firms and sectors confront different conditions in their specific markets. To be competitive, firms need wage policies that reflect these particular conditions. In Morocco, the challenge simply is to construct some uniform set of bargaining institutions where none exists. In Algeria and Tunisia, the challenge is to reform highly centralized bargaining procedures established in the 1970s. Both governments have made decentralizing reforms on paper. In reality, however, peak union leaders still control most of the wage bargaining and conflict resolution. This *de facto* centralization keeps labor leaders in a difficult position, caught between the demands of their own members and the governments with which they must do business.

Resolving these institutional issues is central to the welfare of all unions. And as the Moroccan case illustrates, peak labor leaders understand that they must go into negotiations over new labor codes and bargaining institutions with a unified strategy. But the financial and organizational challenges that unions confront in all three countries have always made it easy for governments to coopt some labor leaders and divide the movement. The reform-driven tensions discussed above can make this divide and conquer strategy even easier to play.

The second common challenge concerns the relationship between union work and politics. Tension between these two is not new in any of these cases. But the political and economic reforms of the past decade have given it new importance. Prior to the late 1980s, 'political unionism' generally referred to activists allied with leftist parties who wanted to use the UGTA, the UGTT, or the CDT as battering rams against authoritarian regimes. Others in the labor movement argued that this kind of politicized unionism produced nothing but repression that undermined wages and union rights. It also disempowered workers by turning the strike into an act of political treason rather than a legal and accepted bargaining strategy. Better, they argued, to keep the union free of opposition politics and to focus on improving wages and working conditions. In the late 1980s and early 1990s, leaders espousing this 'pure corporatism' doctrine took control of both the UGTA and the UGTT. With the economic reform process gaining speed, peak union leaders in both countries pledged to free their unions from government control and to concentrate on defending jobs and purchasing power. In Morocco, pressure for unions to depoliticize increased after opposition parties took power in the mid-1990s.

Two developments complicated this effort to depoliticize union activity. First, intensifying conflicts between governments and Islamists forced union leaders to draw closer to their respective regimes than many unionists wanted. Especially in Algeria and Tunisia, union leaders who wanted their organizations to be independent defenders of workers' interests felt compelled to moderate their rhetoric and their positions for fear of undermining governments and playing into the Islamists' hands. Among more militant segments of the rank and file, this moderation reignited talk of coopted peak union leaders who cared more about protecting their relations with the government than about defending workers' interests.

The development of more meaningful parliamentary politics in the mid-1990s has also complicated the effort to depoliticize union activity. Union leaders remain keenly aware that electoral systems in their countries are far from democratic and that government officials still do not involve them in basic economic policy design. Nevertheless, union officials also realize that parliaments are debating, and even legislating, a growing number of issues that concern workers. As a result, the distinction between 'politics' and 'union work' is not nearly as clear as it used to be. Participating in parliamentary life – a quintessentially political activity – is becoming more critical for serving workers' interests. Navigating this entry into parliamentary life has generated considerable debate. Some have suggested that unions should contribute to democratic reform by forming new parties. Others argue that serving workers' interests in such a difficult and threatening economic environment leaves unions with little choice but to support the parties that control the policy-making process and the state bureaucracy.

The prospect of greater parliamentary involvement brings us to the final and greatest challenge confronting organized labor in the Maghreb. Like them or not, and regardless of whether they work or not, structural adjustment reforms – at least in theory – constitute an internally consistent program. At the level of ideas, they involve a package of mutually reinforcing policies, grounded in a set of propositions that link institutional arrangements, micro-level choices, and macro-level outcomes. Opposing these programs, or defending workers' interests in economies dominated by them, requires the kind of coherent, pro-active strategy that Maghrebi trade unions have yet to develop. Across the region, officials in government, the private sector, and even the unions themselves, complain that unions lack the data and the skilled personnel necessary for formulating coherent agendas and well-supported bargaining positions. Labor and its allies have yet to develop and articulate an alternative vision of development that challenges the dominant market-driven paradigm and holds its own in a meaningful debate about the Maghreb's economic and social future. This state of affairs has made it easy for governments and private sector officials to write labor off as a romantic defender of an outdated ideology instead of treating it as a credible bargaining partner.

Notes

1. For a detailed description of Algeria's economic reform process, see Dahmani (1999). For briefer discussions, see Dillman (1998) and Pfeifer (1992).

2. For detailed discussions of these divisions within the Algerian workforce and the role that plant-level institutions played in creating them, see Allouache, et al. (1987), Saadi (1985), and Hatmi (1983).

3. Interview with Hamid Temmar, Minister of Participation and Reform Coordination, in *El Watan*, 6 May 2000.

4. See Dévoluy (1998).

5. See Temouche (2000).

6. A list of the sectors in which the Islamic leagues enjoyed their strongest support includes: the health and social affairs ministries, agriculture, tourism, transport, post and telecommunications, chemical and petrochemical industries, construction and public works, energy and public adminsitration. See *El Watan*, 3 May 2000.

7. See Dillman (1998, pp.17–18), and Akre (1988). See also Nellis (1983).

8. Much of this social investment has been supported by a program called the National Solidarity Fund, known popularly as the 26-26 fund. Officially, 26-26 is a purely voluntary fund to which Tunisians may contribute. But considerable anecdotal evidence suggests that 26-26 operated as a state-run extortion racket. Business owners and other wealthy or influential Tunisians understand that they must give generously to it if they want their dealings with the government to go smoothly and to avoid zealous investigation by tax officials.

9. See then Prime Minister Hamed Karoui's comments to public sector leaders in *Réalités*, 455 (1–7 July 1994).

10. 'Je propose la participation des travailleurs à la gestion des enterprises', *Réalités*, 412 (27 August–2 September 1993). See also, 'L'UGTT, cautionne-t-elle la politique de la privatisation?', *Réalités*, 428 (17–23 December 1993).

11. For a more detailed analysis of the relationship between the labor and Islamist movements in Tunisia and Algeria, see Alexander (2000).

12. In conversations with the author, many goverment and union officials suggested that the government's desire to eliminate the tension surrounding annual wage talks was one of the primary reasons for its support of three-year accords. More militant union officials admitted that they lamented this change precisely because anual wage battles helped them to energize and mobilize rank and file support. For a more detailed discussion of the changes in Tunisia's collective bargaining institutions, see Alexander (2000).

13. In addition to financial support, control of the national social security funds and Morocco's

representation at the International Labor Organization were two of the noteworthy perks that the UMT enjoyed.

14. The number of seats reserved for worker representatives in the lower chamber has since been raised to 27. Currently, the lower chamber has a total of 285 seats.

15. 'Des élections musclées', *Maroc-Hebdo*, 289 (20–25 September 1997).

References

Akre, Philip J. (1998), 'Industrialization in Algeria: The State and the Role of U.S. Capital, 1970–1980', in Cal Clark and Jonathan Lemco (eds), *State and Development*, Leiden: The Netherlands, 22–37.

Alexander, Christopher (1996), 'State, Labor, and the New Global Economy in Tunisia', in Dirk Vandewalle (ed.), *North Africa: Development and Reform in a Changing Global Economy*, New York: St Martin's Press, 177–202.

Alexander, Christopher (2000), 'Opportunities, Organizations, and Ideas: Islamists and Workers in Tunisia and Algeria', *International Journal of Middle East Studies*, **32** (4), (November).

Alloache, Anissa, André Angsthelm and Salah Seddik (1987), 'Les Rapports de Travail Saisis par le Droit Algérien: Contribution á l'Étude du Discours Juridique en Algérie', *Annuaire de l'Afrique du Nord, 1986*, Paris: Éditions CNRS, 531–80.

Barkey, Henri (1992), *The Politics of Economic Reform in the Middle East*, New York: St Martin's Press.

Berrada, Abdelkader (1986), 'La politique de bas salaires au Maroc: èbauche d'analyse', *Bulletin économique et sociale du Maroc*, 157, 11–65.

Bianchi, Robert (1989), *Unruly Corporatism: Associational Life in Twentieth Century Egypt*, Oxford: Oxford University Press.

Dahmani, Ahmed (1999), *L'Algérie à l'Épreuve: Économie Politique des Réformes 1980–1997*, Paris: L'Harmattan.

'Des élections musclées' (1997), *Maroc-Hebdo*, 20–25 September.

Dévoluy, Pierre (1008), 'Algérie: La Facture Sociale', *Jeune Afrique*, 1977 (1–7 December), 24–5.

Dillman, Bradford (1008), 'The Political Economy of Structural Adjustment in Tunisia and Algeria', *The Journal of North African Studies* **3** (3), (Autumn), 1–24.

el-Anouari, Omar (1995), 'A conjoncture novelle, concepts nouveau', *Maroc Économie*, 10 April.

Ferchiou, Ridha (1991), 'The Social Pressure on Economic Development in Tunisia', in I. William Zartman (ed.), *Tunisia: The Political Economy of Reform*, Boulder: Lynne Rienner Publishers, 101–8.

Grissa, Abdelsatar (1991), 'The Tunisian State Enterprises and Privatization Policy', in I. William Zartman (ed.), *Tunisia: The Political Economy of Reform*, Boulder: Lynne Rienner Publishers, 109–127.

Harik, Ilya (1992), 'Privatization and Development in Tunisia', in Ilya Harik and Dennis J. Sullivan (eds), *Privatization and Liberalization in the Middle East*, Bloomington: Indiana University Press, 210–32.

Harik, Ilya and Denis J. Sullivan (eds) (1992), *Privatization and Liberalization in the Middle East*. Bloomington: Indiana University Press.

Hatmi, Mohamed (1983), 'Une Approche Théorique et Pratique de la Grève en Algérie: Témoignage sur le Conflit du Complexe de Véhicules Industriels de Rouiba', *Annuaire de l'Afrique du Nord, 1982*, Paris: Éditions CNRS.

'Je propose la participation des travailleurs à la Gestion des Entreprises' (1993), *Réalités*, 412, (27 August–2 September).

Labzour, Mohamed Kamal Tazi (1982), 'État, Salaire, et Reproduction de la Force du Travail au Maroc', *Revue Juridique, Politique, et Économique du Maroc*, 11.

'L'UGTT, Cautionne-t-elle la Politique de la Privatisation?' (1993), *Réalités*, 428, (17–23 December).

Mehdi, Abou (1994), 'Privatisations, Mode d'Emploi', *Réalités*, 433 (28 January–3 February).

Mokni, Naceur (2000), 'Bilan de la Privatisation (1987–2000)', *Réalités*, 744 (23–29 March).

Naanaa, Abdellah (2000), 'Les Griefs des Syndicats Rapprochent les Centrales', *La Vie Économique*, (21–27 April).

Nellis, John (1983), 'A Comparative Assessment of the Development Performances of Algeria and Tunisia', *Middle East Journal,* **37** (3), 370–93.

Pfeifer, Karen (1992), 'Algeria's Implicit Stabilization Program', in Henri Barkey (ed.), *The Politics of Economic Reform in the Middle East*, New York: St Martin's Press.

Posusney, Marsha Pripstein (1997), *Labor and the State in Egypt: Workers, Unions, and Economic Restructuring*, New York: Columbia University Press.

Saadi, Nourredine (1983), 'Syndicat et Relations du Travail dans les Entreprises Socialistes en Algérie', *Annuaire de l'Afrique du Nord, 1982*, Paris: Éditions CNRS, 95–121.

Temouche, Ali (2000), 'Des Syndicats Autonomes en Quête d'Agrément/Le SNATA et les Autres', *El Watan*, 6 May.

Zartman, I. William (ed.) (1991), *Tunisia: The Political Economy of Reform*, Boulder: Lynne Rienner Publishers.

6. Public Sector Downsizing: An Introduction

Martín Rama

1. Introduction

Public sector downsizing is not a final goal of economic policy, but economic reforms may require mass layoffs. State-led development strategies left a legacy of bloated bureaucracies and overstaffed public enterprises. Severe labor redundancies characterize transition economies, where the shift from plan to market requires millions of workers to be relocated out of the public sector. In Latin America and South Asia, decades of protective policies led to the proliferation of white elephants and sick industries. All over the world, technological progress is making natural monopolies disappear, thus confronting formerly somnolent utilities with harsh competition. Increasingly, authorities are correcting the employment excesses from past patronage and cronyism as more modern and democratic ways replace traditional and authoritarian ones.

The extent of labor redundancies could make politically unfeasible any serious downsizing, especially based on involuntary dismissals. Hence, a voluntary approach to reductions in public sector employment is increasingly popular among developing-country governments, multilateral organizations, and donor countries. The voluntary approach offers severance pay to encourage the redundant workers to quit, thus overcoming their resistance to downsizing, restructuring, and privatization. In many developing countries, buying out the redundant workers is in fact the only way to bypass the legal obstacles to the dismissal of public sector employees. In addition, it seems fair to compensate those who may suffer from a change in the rules of the game. In this respect, severance pay resembles the lump-sum transfers that characterize textbook analyses of economic policy. If public sector downsizing increases efficiency, it should be possible to compensate redundant workers in the public sector and still make a net gain for the economy. Public sector downsizing could thus qualify as a Pareto-optimal reform.

Until recently, one of the main obstacles to the implementation of the voluntary approach to public sector downsizing was its cost. Sometimes downsizing requires the relocation of hundreds of thousands of workers to the private sector, with the average compensation, retraining, and redeployment package amounting to several thousand dollars per worker. A single downsizing operation may therefore cost hundreds of millions of dollars. However, some of the countries that most desperately need public sector downsizing are strapped for cash. Recent changes in the attitude of multilateral organizations toward mass retrenchment have significantly softened this constraint. In March 1996 the World Bank modified its operational rules to allow lending for severance pay aimed at restructuring the public sector. The International Monetary Fund also favors public sector downsizing because it could allow a more durable reduction in government expenditures than cuts in the wages of civil servants, which are not sustainable in the long run. And regional organizations such as the Inter-American Development Bank will lend for severance pay. As a result, many developing countries and transition economies have plans for public sector downsizing in preparation or already in execution.

While the gains from downsizing are potentially large, the chances of mishandling it are considerable, too. It is quite obvious that many workers in the public sectors of developing countries contribute little to aggregate output or welfare, if anything at all. The issue is whether the use of severance pay packages really helps to relocate these workers to more productive activities. The frequently observed 'revolving door' syndrome, whereby separated workers are subsequently rehired, suggests that some downsizing operations lead to the departure of the few who make the public sector work.

The amount and nature of the assistance provided to separated workers may be inadequate. The authorities usually set up severance pay packages in an arbitrary way. Typically, they use a rule of thumb involving salary and perhaps seniority in the public sector (see Nunberg, 1994; Kikeri, 1997; and Kouamé, 1997). For instance, separated workers receive two years of salary, one month of salary per year of service, or some other combination of these two variables. But the resulting amount may bear little relation to the loss these workers experience as a result of their separation. Some of them clearly suffer, whereas others become net winners. Moreover, the authorities may spend large amounts of resources on ineffective retraining and redeployment programs. Thus, in practice, public sector downsizing may diverge a lot from the envisioned Pareto optimality.

Assessing the returns to downsizing operations is also difficult. The typical assessment compares the savings in terms of public sector wages with the cost in terms of severance pay packages, retraining, and redeployment programs. Overstaffing is only one among several distortions characterizing the public sector, however, so the analysis should not use financial returns to measure economic returns. Public sector wages usually differ from private sector wages and therefore are not a good indicator of the opportunity cost of labor. Furthermore, the analysis should not ignore the externalities from mass retrenchment.

The most obvious externalities arise in the context of one-company towns, which may easily become ghost towns after downsizing takes place. Public sector downsizing leads to fiscal externalities, too, because it reduces the equilibrium level of government expenditures and hence the burden from distortionary taxes.

This chapter provides a conceptual framework for analyzing the effects of downsizing operations. It presents the lessons from a recently completed World Bank research project on Public Sector Retrenchment and Efficient Compensation Schemes.[1] It also draws lessons from other studies on public sector downsizing, including the studies by Svejnar and Terrell (1991), Diwan (1994), Fiszbein (1994), Kikeri (1997), and Lindauer and Nunberg (1994). Most of the previous research dealt with relatively narrow downsizing issues. The Public Sector Retrenchment project represents the first systematic attempt to address downsizing from a variety of perspectives, ranging from public economics to labor economics to mechanism design.

2. A Mixed Record

The World Bank indirectly supported more than 40 attempts to downsize the public sector in developing countries between early 1991 and late 1993. The units targeted included government administration, state-owned enterprises, and, in the context of post-conflict demobilization, the military. The average downsizing operation led to the separation of 125,000 workers at a cost of $400 million, including $87 million in severance pay. The downsizing operations varied considerably. For instance, the smallest one affected 247 public sector workers, compared with more than 1.6 million workers for the largest one (Haltiwanger and Singh, 1999).

Downsizing reduces public sector expenditures, particularly the public sector wage bill. When the present value of this reduction is higher than the upfront cost in terms of severance pay and enhanced safety nets, downsizing has positive financial returns. A more precise assessment has to be based on economic returns. Downsizing also reallocates workers across sectors. When aggregate welfare increases as a result of this reallocation, downsizing has positive economic returns. Haltiwanger and Singh (1999) evaluate the financial returns of 15 of the surveyed operations based on the number of years it would take to recover their direct financial costs, using a 10% annual discount rate. This indicator is called the break-even period. Measured by this indicator, the downsizing operations performed remarkably well. The average break-even period was two years and four months, and it exceeded four years in only one case. Few investment projects display such high financial returns.

As an indirect measure of economic returns, Haltiwanger and Singh calculate the percentage of the displaced workers who were subsequently rehired by the restructured units. Rehires indicate a poorly handled downsizing process. In the best case, they imply that workers who were essential to the operation of the restructured units were mistakenly considered redundant. In the worst case, they suggest that workers who had no intention of leaving the public sector were able to cash in golden handshakes.

Rehiring occurred in 40% of the operations for which the required information was available. More than 10% of the separated workers were rehired in half of these cases. If anything, these results underestimate the extent of labor misallocation. The fact that 60% of the operations display no rehiring does not imply that essential workers did not leave. Moreover, rehiring provides no information on another type of error, which consists of retaining redundant public sector workers.

Haltiwanger and Singh find that for every dollar spent on severance pay, on average more than two dollars were spent on safety net enhancements. Almost two-thirds of the downsizing operations surveyed included some enhancement of the safety net, such as early retirement programs, counseling and placement services, or wage subsidies. Retraining was a feature in more than half of the operations. Are these programs worth their cost? Probably not, based on previous assessments of the effectiveness of vocational education programs in developing countries (see Middleton et al., 1993). Usually, the same government agencies that get low grades in the evaluations of vocational education programs end up in charge of the retraining component of downsizing operations. In the context of public sector downsizing, a more relevant assessment is provided by a microeconometric study of the effects of active labor market programs on employment and earnings in the Czech Republic, Hungary, Poland, and Turkey (Fretwell et al., 1998). This study finds that some of the active labor market programs made it more likely for subsets of workers to find jobs after separation. But others did not, and the programs do not appear to have a significant impact on the labor earnings of those who did find jobs.

Two of the studies prepared for the Public Sector Retrenchment project suggest that a considerable amount of resources has been wasted on active labor market programs. An evaluation of the public sector downsizing operation implemented by Spain in the 1980s showed its limited ability to relocate workers to alternative industries, in spite of its extremely large retraining program (Campa, 1996). This failure was partly due to retraining being focused on the update of previous skills, rather than on the acquisition of new ones. A case study of downsizing in the Central Bank of Ecuador found that only 12% of the displaced workers took the retraining courses that were offered, in spite of these courses being free of charge (Rama and MacIsaac, 1999).

3. Adverse Selection

Some of the difference in productivity among public sector workers is associated with observable worker characteristics, such as educational attainment or occupation. But part of it is unobservable. Although productivity differences also exist in the private sector, they seem to be exacerbated in the public sector. Jeon and Laffont (1999) analyze how policy-makers should take into account these unobservable differences when deciding the extent and composition of public sector downsizing. They apply the tools of mechanism design to examine the optimal manner for reducing public sector employment. They show that the optimal composition of the layoffs depends on the nature of the public sector unit and on the prospects workers face after separation. For instance, the public sector unit could produce a socially valuable service, such as basic health or economic management, and the labor market could be tight, so that the prospects for workers with low productivity would be relatively good. In this case, the optimal downsizing policy would be to retain all of the workers with high productivity and to retrench some of those with low productivity. Conversely, the public sector unit could produce a service with little social value, such as steel or direct credit allocation, and the unemployment rate could be high, leaving little hope of finding a job for workers with low productivity. In this case, the optimal downsizing policy would retrench all of the workers with high productivity and retain those with low productivity.

Standard voluntary separation programs usually lead to the departure of the workers with high productivity, because those workers have the best prospects outside the public sector. It follows that standard voluntary separation programs are not appropriate in all circumstances. For instance, these programs would lead to the wrong composition of layoffs when applied to public sector units that produce valuable services and operate in a tight labor market. The fact that these programs were used quite systematically in the past could be one of the reasons why so many separated workers were rehired in the aftermath of downsizing operations.

Before the use of voluntary separation programs became common, governments used other methods to cut expenditures. Several analysts have criticized those efforts, saying that they had an adverse impact on the effectiveness of governments (see Van Ginneken, 1991 and Colclough, 1997). By compressing the pay scale, the argument goes, budget cuts encouraged skilled workers to leave, thus jeopardizing the ability of governments to deliver on basic services. There is little doubt that better outcomes could have been achieved by getting rid of genuinely redundant public sector workers and offering better wages and working conditions to the others. However, standard voluntary separation programs can lead to the departure of skilled public sector workers, too, much the same as budget cuts did in the past, and in substantially larger numbers.

Several alternatives have been proposed to standard voluntary separation programs for cases where adverse selection is a serious concern. In a study prepared for the Public Sector Retrenchment project, Levy and McLean (1997) analyze the merits and demerits of some of those alternatives. Randomization is one of them. Each public sector worker would face a probability of losing the job equal to the estimated percentage of redundant workers. This alternative would make the composition of separated workers resemble that of those who remain in the public sector (Diwan, 1994). For units producing socially valuable services in a tight labor market, randomization thus represents an unambiguous improvement compared with standard voluntary separation programs. However, Levy and McLean show that closing down those units, or leaving them untouched, could be preferable to a randomized downsizing and that, in general, randomization is not an efficient mechanism for downsizing the public sector.

In the presence of unobservable information, the efficient mechanism for downsizing has to lead the workers to reveal their productivity. Jeon and Laffont (1999) show how to implement this mechanism by means of a menu of wage and severance pay pairs. Each pair is associated with a different probability of separation. If the probability of separation is equal to one, the pair can be interpreted as a standard severance pay offer. If it is equal to zero, it can be viewed as a typical, open-ended public sector contract. All of the workers choosing the first pair are retrenched, whereas all those choosing the second one are retained. For pairs in between these two extremes, some of the workers are retrenched whereas others keep their jobs. If the menu is appropriately designed, workers should choose the pairs associated with their socially optimal probability of separation. For instance, if the overstaffed public sector unit produces a valuable service and operates in a tight labor market, workers with low productivity should choose a pair associated with a strictly positive probability of separation.

However, setting up the right menu might be difficult in practice, so that other, simpler devices for identifying workers with low productivity in the public sector should be used as well. In their cross-country survey of downsizing operations, Haltiwanger and Singh (1999) find that the targeting of separations significantly reduces the probability of subsequent rehiring. The targeting mechanism can include such simple devices as chasing ghost workers (workers on the payroll, but not working). The experience of the Central Bank of Ecuador, analyzed by Rama and MacIsaac (1999), is also interesting in this respect. After a first, disastrous attempt to downsize using voluntary separation programs, the Central Bank decided to classify all of its personnel in three categories: those who were essential for its functioning, those who were clearly redundant, and those for whom it was difficult to tell. The classification was based on the nature of the worker's unit and on the worker's occupation and educational attainment. Essential workers did not have the option to leave, clearly redundant workers did not have the option to stay, and the rest of the workers were offered a voluntary separation program. In light of the article by Jeon and Laffont, the menu approach has potentially higher payoffs for the third group of workers.

4. Losses from Separation

The welfare loss a separated public sector worker experiences can be disaggregated into three components. The first one is the present value of the resulting change in earnings, including bonuses and other cash benefits. Except for highly skilled workers, salaries in the public sector tend to be higher than labor earnings out of it. Moreover, it may take a long time for some of the separated workers to find a new job, and earnings can be close to zero during that period. For simplicity, it is assumed here that displaced workers do not withdraw from the labor force after separation. The logic would be similar in case of withdrawal, except that reservation wages (rather than labor earnings out of the public sector) should be considered when assessing the present value of the earnings loss. The second component is the present value of the loss in non-wage benefits. Public sector jobs usually provide health coverage and old-age pension, among other benefits. In most developing countries, the jobs available to separated public sector workers do not carry such benefits. The third component is other, more intangible losses from separation. For instance, effort levels tend to be lower in the public sector than out of it, whereas job security is almost invariably higher. The possibility of taking bribes or using government facilities for private purposes also falls into this category.

In preparation for a downsizing operation, policy-makers should assess the welfare loss that separated workers might experience. This assessment may help predict the cost of the downsizing operation in terms of severance pay, if workers are fully compensated, or the harshness of their resistance to downsizing, if they are not. The Public Sector Retrenchment project used three empirical strategies to assess the workers' welfare loss and to link it to a variety of observable characteristics of the workers. These characteristics include salary and seniority in the public sector, which are the two variables most commonly used when designing severance pay packages. But they also include gender, age, education level, and province of residence, among others.

The first and more direct strategy is to interview separated workers, and to ask them to evaluate subjectively the change in their well-being. Rama and MacIsaac (1999) apply this strategy to the study of downsizing in the Central Bank of Ecuador. The subjective evaluation of well-being depends on the amount of compensation received at the time of separation. Rama and MacIsaac use information on the subjective change in well-being and the amount of compensation received to infer the welfare loss from separation.

A second empirical strategy relies on the welfare loss predicted by public sector workers before separation. Robbins (1996) applies this strategy to voluntary separation programs in several banks and government agencies in Argentina. Some of the workers in these banks and agencies accepted the severance pay package they were offered, whereas others rejected it. Robbins uses this information to infer the amount of severance pay that would have made workers with specific individual characteristics indifferent between accepting or rejecting the offer. That amount is an indicator of the welfare loss expected by each worker.

The third empirical strategy assumes that there is a stable relationship between the welfare loss and the earnings loss. Assaad (1999) applies this strategy to the case of workers in Egyptian public sector enterprises. Using data from a national household survey, Assaad compares the present value of earnings for workers in and out of the public sector. This comparison shows that some public sector workers earn less, over their work life, than similar workers out of the public sector. If these workers do not voluntarily quit, it is probably because they derive other benefits from their jobs. The gap in earnings observed for the most disadvantaged group of public sector workers can thus be used to infer the value of nonwage and other intangible benefits from public sector jobs. Assaad assumes that the loss of non-wage and intangible benefits is the same proportion of the salary for other public sector workers.

Under the hypothesis that a stable relationship exists between welfare losses and earnings losses from displacement, studies dealing with the latter can be expected to provide information on the former. Several articles have analyzed the impact of observable characteristics of separated public sector workers on their earnings losses. Some of the studies use data on earnings out of the public sector from surveys of separated workers. For example, Rama and MacIsaac (1999) refer to Central Bank employees in Ecuador. In another study prepared for the Public Sector Retrenchment project, Tansel (1997) assesses the welfare losses of blue-collar workers in cement and petrochemical factories in Turkey. Alderman et al. (1996) and Younger (1996) look at the case of civil servants in Ghana. Orazem et al. (1995) analyze how earnings changed in Slovenia with the transition to a market economy.[2]

Table 6.1 summarizes the findings of the available studies on the determinants of welfare and earnings losses from displacement in developing countries and transition economies. The table reports the signs of the impact of workers' characteristics on their welfare and earnings losses. Several regularities emerge. First, it appears that the wage level in the public sector is a poor predictor of welfare losses, at least as long as other observable characteristics of the workers are taken into account. Secondly, with the exception of Egypt, where government hiring and compensation policies strongly distort the payoffs to schooling, the loss from displacement is usually smaller the higher the educational level of the workers. Thirdly, while higher seniority in a public sector job may lead to larger losses from displacement, there is no clear link between total work experience and losses from displacement. And fourthly, female workers and those with bigger families may suffer more from displacement.

5. Compensation

The rationale for compensating displaced workers stems from the welfare loss they may experience as a result of separation. However, compensation may contradict the broader objectives of economic policy reform in developing countries and transition economies. Many efforts by multilateral organizations and donor countries focus on reorienting public expenditures toward the most needy. Efforts to tilt the budgetary process in favor of the poor may conflict with the willingness to lend generous amounts of money to finance severance pay packages for workers who are not poor, even after separation (see London Economics, 1996). This perspective would justify full compensation only when legal or political constraints make it absolutely necessary. This conclusion may not be valid, however, when public sector workers share a significant portion of their earnings with their extended families, as is the case in some Sub-Saharan African countries. Private transfers imply that for each public sector job suppressed, several households are bound to experience a welfare loss. And some of those households were probably poor even before downsizing. Private transfers also suggest that the displaced public sector workers are likely to share the compensation they receive with their less fortunate relatives. In the extended family setting, compensating the displaced workers may therefore reduce the adverse impact of downsizing on poverty.

While the decision to fully compensate displaced workers should be made on a case-by-case basis, there are clearly no circumstances that would justify overcompensation. This is, however, a bias of downsizing operations based on voluntary separations. Workers who are offered less than full compensation will prefer to stay in the public sector, whereas those who are offered more than full compensation will accept the offer and leave. Therefore mistakes in

Table 6.1 *Determinants of losses from separation*

Worker Characteristics	Welfare Loss				Earnings Loss			
	Argentina, white-collar employees	Ecuador, central bank employees	Egypt, public sector workers	Turkey, cement and oil workers	Ecuador, central bank employees	Ghana, civil servants	Slovenia, formal labor force	Turkey, cement and oil workers
Public sector wage	+[a]	0	n.a.	0	0	0	n.a.	+
Seniority in the job	n.a.	+	?	0	+	0	+[b]	0
Educational level	0	–	+	–	–	0	0	–
Total work experience	?	+	–	+	0	0	+[b]	–
Female	n.a.	0	+	0	+	+	–	0
Married	–	0	n.a.	0	+	0	n.a.	0
Number of dependents	?	+	n.a.	+	0	0	n.a.	0
Source	Robbins (1996)	Rama and MacIsaac (1999)	Assaad (1999)	Tansel (1997)	Rama and MacIsaac (1999)	Alderman et al (1996)	Orazem et al (1995)	Tansel (1997)

Note: Statistically significant signs are indicated by a + or –, while 0 indicates a non significant coefficient and ? indicates a change in sign across specifications or groups of workers. When the variable was not included in the analysis, n.a. is reported.
a. The coefficient is positive as a result of an implicit restriction imposed by the chosen specifications.
b. Almost all work experience was under the self-management system that characterized Yugoslavia until the late 1980s.

the direction of excessively low compensation will not reduce severance pay costs, whereas mistakes in the direction of excessively high compensation will materialize. A poor tailoring of compensation packages may exacerbate this second type of mistake.

The Public Sector Retrenchment project leads to a five-step procedure to tailor assistance to the displaced workers when full compensation is needed. This procedure relies on the third empirical strategy used to estimate losses from displacement because this is the only one that can be applied before any retrenchment has taken place. Fiszbein (1994) used a simpler version of this procedure for Sri Lanka. Assaad (1999) refined it in his analysis of downsizing in the Egyptian public sector. The five-step proposal in this section also draws from lessons of experience in several countries.

The first step estimates an earnings function for workers who are out of the public sector. The data should come from individual records in labor force or living standards surveys. The right-hand-side variables in the earnings function include individual characteristics that are also observable for workers in the public sector. Ideally, the variables should be exactly the same as those in the records the public sector has about its own employees. The left-hand-side variable measures the labor earnings of all individuals working out of the public sector, including the self-employed and those in the informal sector. More sophisticated analyses of earnings out of the public sector could also try to infer the reservation wage of unemployed or economically inactive individuals. Whatever the sophistication of the analysis, this first step aims to predict the value of earnings for the public sector workers who are bound to be separated.

The second step calculates the present value of the earnings loss that public sector workers experience when they lose their jobs. This calculation compares, for each worker to be separated, his or her public sector salary with the earnings (or reservation wages) estimated in step one. The difference between the two is discounted over the duration of the contract the worker has with the public sector. In most cases this duration is the number of years to retirement.

The third step assesses the loss in benefits. In many developing countries, the most important component of this loss concerns old-age pension. An actuarial calculation of the present value of the forgone old-age benefits can be used to quantify this loss. As a simpler alternative, the calculation could rely on the present value of past contributions to social security, plus accrued interest when applicable. Whatever the chosen approach, previous experience with downsizing suggests that the loss in benefits needs to be dealt with separately. Explicitly canceling outstanding social security obligations is important to avoid misunderstandings (or opportunistic behavior) that can eventually lead to legal and political wrestling.

The fourth step evaluates workers' loss of other, more intangible benefits. This analysis focuses on groups of public sector workers for whom the sum of the earnings loss estimated in step two and the benefits loss estimated in step three is substantially negative. If these workers stay in the public sector, it is because they derive some other benefits from their jobs. The monetary value of these other benefits is at least equal to the sum of the earnings and benefits losses. The ratio between this monetary value and the public sector salary can be used to infer the intangible benefits enjoyed by other, less disadvantaged public sector workers.

Finally, the fifth step develops a simple formula to calculate compensation based on a few observable characteristics of public sector workers. Under the assumption that the losses related to old-age pension are settled separately, the problem is to identify a relatively small set of information that can be used to predict the loss of earnings and intangible benefits in a convenient and non-controversial way. For instance, making compensation depend on individual characteristics such as gender would not be legally or socially admissible in some countries. Other characteristics, such as marital status or the number of dependents, may be subject to manipulation in countries where common law marriages and extended families are widespread.

The compensation formula developed in step five differs from the typical rules of thumb used to design severance pay packages in two important ways. First, the information set may or may not include salary and seniority in the public sector, depending on how useful these two variables are to predict the loss of earnings and intangible benefits. Secondly, the coefficients multiplying these two variables, as well as the other variables in the relevant information set, are not arbitrary. They are the coefficients of a regression explaining the predicted loss of earnings and intangible benefits as a function of observable characteristics of public sector workers.

For state-owned enterprises in Egypt, Assaad (1999) finds that a well-tailored package could reduce the total compensation cost by 31%, compared with the best performing rule of thumb. In the case of the Central Bank of Ecuador, Rama and MacIsaac (1999) find that well-tailored compensation could have reduced the cost of voluntary separations by 19%. Given that the average downsizing operation surveyed by Haltiwanger and Singh (1999) spent $87 million in compensation payments, the potential savings from the proposed procedure could be substantial. Moreover, the procedure would be more fair, because it would provide more assistance to those who lose more.

6. Returns to Downsizing

Downsizing operations involve spending a considerable amount of resources in the short run in order to reap some gain in the longer run. Consequently, the decision to undertake a downsizing operation should consider its payoff, in much the same way as an investment decision. The most common approach focuses on financial returns, that is, on the impact of downsizing on the budget deficit. This approach can be justified when downsizing is part of a broader adjustment program. However, the decision should also consider the economic returns to downsizing – that is, its impact on aggregate output or welfare.

The first and most obvious financial gain from downsizing results from the cut in the wage bill. In government administration, this cut directly reduces budget expenditures. The budgetary impact may be smaller in state-owned enterprises if their wage bill is only partially subsidized by the budget. A second financial gain results from the reduction in long-term liabilities as separated workers lose all or some of their entitlement to old-age pensions. A third potential gain is the increase in privatization prices when downsizing is done in preparation for privatization and contributes to its success. The upfront cost is the amount of resources spent in compensation, retraining, and other redeployment programs for separated workers.

An assessment of financial returns should focus on the consolidated budget, not just on the budget of the overstaffed unit. Examples abound where redeployment programs simply shift the fiscal burden to another government body. Consider, for instance, the social services provided by state-owned enterprises in many transition economies. Often taxpayers pay for the cost of these services under the form of explicit or implicit subsidies. When downsizing reduces the number of beneficiaries of these services, it also reduces the burden to taxpayers. However, there is no such reduction if downsizing leads to a mere transfer of these services to central or local governments. Another example is provided by redeployment programs that allow the redundant workers to take another public sector job elsewhere.

This fiscal illusion may be particularly severe when downsizing affects entitlements to old-age pension and other social security benefits. For example, Carneiro and Gill (1997) show that in Brazil the savings from downsizing are substantially smaller for the consolidated government than for the individual states. The pension benefits granted to the displaced workers increase the long-term liabilities of the federal government. As a result of the implicit transfer of obligations, budget savings are 15 to 25% lower than it appears at first glance.

Economic returns focus on aggregate output or welfare, rather than on budget revenue and expenditures. Downsizing affects aggregate output or welfare in two different ways: it reduces the equilibrium level of taxes, and it relocates public sector workers to activities where they are supposedly more productive.

The value to society of a lower taxation level should not be confused with the financial returns to downsizing. If transfers were costless, financial returns would be totally irrelevant when assessing economic returns. In practice, however, when the government raises one additional dollar of revenue, there is a net loss to society due to the inefficiencies created by distortionary taxation. This loss, known as the marginal tax burden, can be quite large in developing countries. In India, for example, it was estimated at around 0.8, which means that 80 cents of output are lost per dollar of revenue raised (Ahmad and Stern, 1987).

The overall assessment of a downsizing operation depends on whether it uses financial or economic returns. As an example, consider a downsized unit that cannot be privatized and whose wage bill is entirely paid for by the budget. Assume that public sector jobs entail no intangible benefits and that compensation is tailored so as exactly to offset the loss in salaries and benefits that the separated workers are bound to experience. Because the potential earnings of at least some of the separated workers are positive, the government spends less in compensation than it saves in salaries and benefits. Financial returns are thus positive. But this conclusion is not warranted on economic grounds. If many separated workers end up unemployed, downsizing may reduce aggregate output. More specifically, economic returns to downsizing are more likely to be positive when productivity in the public sector is low, when potential earnings out of it are high, and when the marginal tax burden is large.

Adverse selection can dramatically affect the economic returns to downsizing, without modifying its financial returns much. If the retrenched workers were genuinely redundant, their productivity in the public sector would probably be very low. In the limit, if productivity in the public sector were equal to zero, the economic returns would just be a multiple of the financial returns, so that financial returns and economic returns would be perfectly correlated. However, if the retrenched workers were essential for the operation of a unit producing a socially valuable service, productivity in the public sector could actually be quite large. Good civil servants can contribute to society more than they cost. If they leave, public sector downsizing may have negative economic returns, in spite of positive (and possibly high) financial returns.

There have been several attempts to evaluate the economic returns to the public and private sector retrenchment, including those by Jenkins and Montmarquette (1979), Svejnar and Terrell (1991), and Brander and Spencer (1994). Ruppert (1999) estimates the financial and economic returns to the downsizing of state-owned enterprises in Algeria. She shows that the program is financially sound under a wide range of assumptions; however, its impact on aggregate output depends very much on the efficiency or inefficiency of these state-owned enterprises.

Ruppert considers two extreme cases. In one of them, the public sector productivity of the retrenched workers is equal to zero, and economic returns are high. At the other extreme, state-owned enterprises are on their labor demand curve, so that the marginal productivity of labor is equal to the public sector salary. But the public sector salary is probably much higher than labor earnings in the private sector in Algeria. The unemployment rate there is 28%, which suggests that searching for a good job (mainly in the public sector) is much more attractive than taking a bad job (mainly in the informal sector). As a result of this earnings gap, there is a tradeoff between the reduction in distortionary taxation from downsizing and the fall in aggregate output. Ruppert shows that under plausible assumptions, economic returns can be either positive or negative.

The possible discrepancy between financial returns and economic returns illustrates the second-best principle. The initial situation of the public sector unit to be downsized is one where several distortions and imperfections prevail, including overstaffing. Most likely the public sector unit is also characterized by a distorted pay scale, compared with the private sector. And the public sector unit is at least partially financed out of taxes that create distortions and reduce aggregate output. Downsizing operations usually only tackle one of these distortions and imperfections, namely overstaffing. Thus downsizing may not result in improved economic efficiency.

7. One Company Towns

Public sector downsizing may affect the rest of the economy not only through its fiscal impact, but also through its direct impact on private sector output. The one-company town setting provides an illustration of this productive externality. The main feature of this setting is the large share of jobs in a particular region (the town, for short) provided by the public sector unit to be downsized (the company). As a result, many of the other jobs in the town also depend on employment and wage levels in the company. For instance, the company's employees are probably the most important customers of the town's private shops. A drastic reduction in employment in the company is therefore likely to depress private sector activity in the town in a very Keynesian way. It follows that the level of earnings and productivity out of the public sector cannot be taken as given.

Productive externalities from downsizing may also occur at the national level. Mass retrenchment programs, affecting a substantial fraction of the urban labor force, can increase unemployment rates over long periods of time. For instance, in some Sub-Saharan African countries, where the public sector represents a large share of the modern economy, downsizing may depress economic activity in the short run.

Externalities like those arising in the one-company-town setting provide a justification for retaining some of the redundant workers. Limiting the extent of downsizing certainly entails a cost to the rest of society, which has to pay for these redundancies in the form of higher taxes or lower social expenditures. But retrenching the redundant workers entails a cost to the population that depends on the company. The optimal extent of downsizing involves a tradeoff between these two costs.

Rama and Scott (1999) evaluate the potential externalities from downsizing in the one-company towns of Kazakhstan, a country that has dozens of them. Admittedly, their estimates represent an upper bound for other countries, where labor mobility between towns is probably higher. The one-company towns of Kazakhstan are quite isolated, both for geographic and for institutional reasons. On the geographic side, Kazakhstan has a relatively small population but is the ninth largest country on earth. On the institutional side, the housing market is poorly developed, and the unemployed need to hold a local passport to draw their benefits. Consequently, the externalities from downsizing could be stronger in Kazakhstan than elsewhere.

Rama and Scott's results suggest that the externality from downsizing can be substantial: retrenching the equivalent of 1% of the town's population would reduce the average labor earnings of the town by roughly 1.5%. Completely shutting down the average company, in turn, would reduce those earnings by more than 11%. These results imply that compensation should not be restricted to the retrenched workers and that transfers of resources to the community as a whole are justified. Whatever the compensation strategy adopted, the calculation of the economic returns to downsizing needs to take this productive externality into account.

8. A Practical Guide to Downsizing

Many things can go wrong in a downsizing operation, as the discussion in the previous sections shows. But these warnings should not be seen as an encouragement for inaction. One of the studies prepared for the Public Sector Retrenchment project, by Basu et al. (1996), deals with the consequences of not addressing the overstaffing problem. In India firms employing more than 100 workers may seek government permission for any retrenchments they wish to make. But these applications seldom succeed, and in the end the firms are often declared sick and are required to continue functioning on the basis of government subsidies. Basu et al. show that this seemingly protective legislation not only reduces economic efficiency but also may harm the workers it aims to protect. This is because it reduces labor demand, thus lowering the equilibrium wage level.

This section integrates the main lessons about downsizing into a simple blueprint for action. Figure 6.1 presents the blueprint in the form of a decision tree, intended to assist policy-makers in developing countries and task managers in multilateral organizations and donor countries. For simplicity, Figure 6.1 assumes that there are no productive externalities from downsizing, like those foreseeable in one-company towns.

Question 1 in this decision tree refers to the appropriate private sector counterfactual to public sector downsizing (see Devarajan et al., 1995). In some cases, the choice is not whether to downsize, but whether to have the government or the private sector manage the downsizing operation. Discussing whether an agency or enterprise should be privatized (Question 1 in Figure 6.1) is clearly beyond the scope of this chapter. The answer involves efficiency considerations and public interest issues that policy-makers need to evaluate carefully in each case. This section addresses whether downsizing should precede privatization when the latter is advisable (see Question 2).

If the government does not downsize prior to privatization, the new private owners have to deal with labor redundancies. Because of the ensuing differences in the extent of labor shedding, in the amount of compensation, and in the privatization price of the enterprise, assessing the net gains from downsizing prior to privatization may be difficult. But a net loss is likely.

The total number of displaced workers may be larger when downsizing is managed by the government prior to privatization than when it is left to the new owners. Kikeri (1997) reports examples from various countries where the new owners kept the labor force more or less intact. Based on a more systematic comparison of employment patterns across Polish firms during the transition to a market economy, Frydman et al. (1999) show that employment cuts were larger in state-owned enterprises than in otherwise similar privatized firms. Furthermore, when the government is in charge of downsizing, it may separate the wrong workers from their jobs at an excessively high cost. A wrong composition of the separations is possible because governments usually are not good at managing human resources. If they could make the right decisions regarding whom to retain and whom to lay off and, in addition, if they were able to deliver on those decisions, the rationale for privatization would be seriously weakened. An excessively high cost of separation is likely because governments can shift part of the downsizing costs to the taxpayer, for instance in the form of early retirement programs, while in principle the new

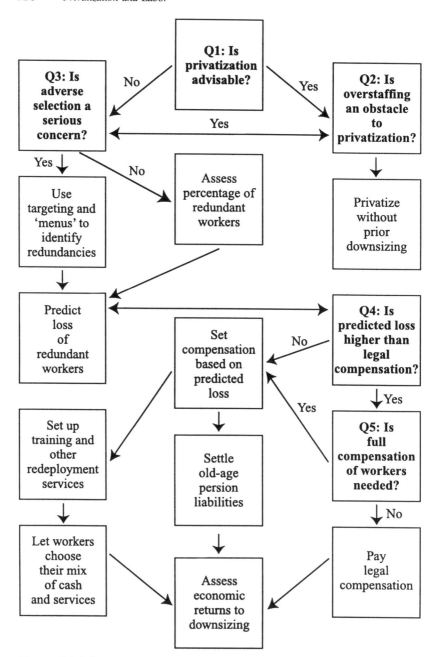

Figure 6.1 A downsizing decision tree

owners cannot. The temptation to resort to golden handshakes should therefore be stronger when downsizing takes place prior to privatization. Case studies suggest that this has happened in practice (see Galal et al., 1994).

Unnecessary downsizing costs cannot be recovered through a higher privatization price of the state-owned enterprise. At the theoretical level, the privatization price would of course increase every time a redundant worker is separated from his or her job. But getting rid of workers who are not redundant would not increase that price. And even for the genuinely redundant workers, the increase would be equal to the amount of resources the new owners would have spent to secure their separation, not to the amount of resources actually spent (directly and indirectly) by the government. Therefore, the net proceeds from downsizing prior to privatization can be expected to be negative.

At the empirical level, some evidence suggests that the increase in privatization prices resulting from downsizing prior to privatization may not be worth its cost. In a study of the determinants of auction prices for 263 Mexican enterprises privatized between 1983 and 1992, López-de-Silanes (1997) finds that downsizing had a marginal impact on privatization prices. The effect was actually insignificant in one specification and only weakly significant in another. If the significant estimate is taken literally, a 5% reduction in employment prior to privatization increases the price of the enterprise by 6%. Given the substantial cost of prior restructuring policies, López-de-Silanes draws the key lesson that governments should not do too much: they should simply sell.

Financial returns to downsizing prior to privatization are most likely negative, but what about economic returns? Most likely, aggregate welfare would increase if the new managers of the privatized firms made the downsizing decisions. Discrepancies arise between financial and economic returns because of the presence of several distortions and imperfections, in addition to overstaffing, including distorted pay scales in the public sector and deadweight losses from taxation. The new management has no interest in keeping distorted pay scales, so wages in the privatized enterprise should move closer to the alternative earnings of the workers. And privatization usually eliminates the soft budget constraint, so the fiscal externality disappears, too.

Downsizing may be justified prior to privatization, however, if it enhances the credibility of the reform process (see Vickers and Yarrow, 1991 and World Bank, 1995). The ability to overcome labor resistance and trim employment could signal the government's commitment to privatization. This signal, in turn, would reduce the uncertainty faced by potential investors, thus making privatization possible. If the government took no action to overcome the opposition of those who stand to lose from privatization, the chances are there would be no bids for the enterprise to be privatized.

Question 3 in Figure 6.1 concerns the adverse selection problem. The willingness of multilateral organizations and donor countries to lend substantial amounts of money for severance pay may create a bias in favor of voluntary separation schemes. Moreover, buying out the workers is a simple and convenient way to defuse the opposition to public sector reform. But severance pay creates an incentive for the most productive workers to leave the public sector and for the least productive ones to stay. This may not be socially desirable in the case of public sector units producing valuable services. In this case, it is better to target separations based on the observable characteristics of the workers and to use a menu approach to deal with their unobservable differences.

Questions 4 and 5 in Figure 6.1 concern assistance for separated workers. Whatever the combination of cash, retraining, and redeployment services, the government should not spend more than the amount needed to buy out the redundant workers. The expected losses from separation thus provide a benchmark against which to judge both the existing laws on compensation and the ad hoc packages proposed in the context of downsizing. Analysts can use labor market data to predict the expected losses based on observable characteristics of the workers, such as education, seniority, and gender.

Workers' predicted losses may be higher than their legal compensation. In this case, given that public sector workers are rarely poor, even after separation, it is preferable to apply the law. Alternatively, the predicted losses may be lower than legal compensation. In Guinea-Bissau, for instance, severance pay for civil servants was set at 10 months of salary per year of service. The average compensation package thus amounted to 9.6 years of salary. Using the procedure proposed in Section 5, the average loss from separation would be 4.2 years of salary (Chong and Rama, 2001). In a case like this, it is advisable to try to modify the laws governing severance pay.

Retraining and other redeployment programs deserve special attention when assessing the cost of the assistance to be provided to separated workers. More resources may be spent on this component than on direct compensation. However, the evidence on the effectiveness of retraining and other redeployment programs is mixed at best. If these programs are to be part of the downsizing operation, a safeguard should be introduced to minimize the potential waste of resources. Basically, separated workers should be allowed to choose between enrolling in any of the programs offered and cashing in the equivalent of their marginal cost. This demand-driven approach would make it more difficult for vocational training programs and other (often ailing) government agencies to divert resources from the downsizing operation.

9. Concluding Remarks

Public sector downsizing may become a major reform endeavor in developing countries in the coming years, in much the same way as trade liberalization and financial liberalization were in the past two decades. These reform efforts can substantially improve economic efficiency. But the risks are considerable, too. The comparison between the successful experience with trade liberalization and the more mixed record with financial liberalization shows the importance of a well-designed reform protocol.

This chapter and, more generally, the Public Sector Retrenchment project represent an attempt to sketch a protocol for public sector downsizing. This attempt should be interpreted with great caution. Some of the findings and policy recommendations may need to be adjusted, and some are possibly wrong. More research and experimentation are certainly needed to move in the direction of a more comprehensive and reliable protocol. Forthcoming downsizing operations provide an ideal opportunity to test and evaluate some of the hypotheses and recommendations. A strong interaction of policy and research in the immediate future could contribute to the success of public sector downsizing endeavors over the longer run.

But even a carefully designed protocol could prove ineffective if the mechanisms that led to overstaffing in the first place remain unchallenged. The equilibrium level of public sector employment is probably determined by political forces operating in the context of a particular institutional setting. Temporary incentives to downsize, such as financing for severance pay packages, will probably fail to modify that equilibrium. The institutional setting itself would need to evolve in the direction of increased professionalism and efficiency. Downsizing operations should therefore be part of a broader effort to reform and modernize the public sector, not just isolated endeavors.

Notes

1. For more information see http://www.worldbank.org/research/projects/downsize. A complete version of most of the resarch papers produced for the project can be downloaded from this website.

2. Other empirical studies on public sector downsizing in developing countries, such as the one by Mills and Sahn (1996) for Guinea, or the one by London Economics (1996) for Zambia, do not estimate the impact of individual characteristics on displacement losses. For a comparison with losses from job displacement in industrial countries, see Hamermesh (1989); Topel (1990); Jacobson et al. (1993); and Fallick (1996).

References

The word "processed" describes informally reproduced works that may not be commonly available through library systems.

Ahmad, Ehtisham and Nicholas Stern (1987), 'Alternative Sources of Government Revenue: Illustrations from India, 1979–80', in David Newbery and Nicholas Stern (eds), *The Theory of Taxation for Developing Countries*, New York: Oxford University Press.

Alderman, Harold, Sudharshan Canagarajah and Stephen Younger (1996), 'A Comparison of Ghanaian Civil Servants' Earnings before and after Retrenchment', *Journal of African Economies*, 4 (2), 259–88.

Assaad, Ragui (1999), 'Matching Severance Payments with Worker Losses in the Egyptian Public Sector', *World Bank Economic Review,* 13 (1), (January).

Basu, Kaushik, Gary S. Fields and Shub Debgupta (1996), 'Retrenchment, Labor Laws, and Government Policy: An Analysis with Special Reference to India', Presented at the conference on Public Sector Retrenchment and Efficient Compensation Schemes, World Bank, Washington, DC. Processed.

Brander, James A. and Barbara J. Spencer (1994), 'Trade Adjustment Assistance: Welfare and Incentive Effects of Payments to Displaced Workers', *Journal of International Economics*, 36 (May), 239–61.

Campa, José Manuel (1996), 'Public Sector Retrenchment: Spain in the 1980s', Stern School of Business, New York University, New York. Processed.

Carneiro, Francisco and Indermit Gill (1997), 'Effectiveness and Financial Costs of Voluntary Separation Programs in Brazil: 1995–1997', Economic Notes 25. Country Department I, Latin America and the Caribbean Regional Office, World Bank, Washington, DC. Processed.

Chong, Alberto and Martín Rama (2001), 'Do Separation Packages Need to be that Generous? Simulations for Government Employees in Guinea–Bissau', in Devarajan Shantayanan, F. Halsey Rogers and Lyn Squire (eds), *World Bank Economists' Forum*, World Bank, Washington, DC, 169–94.

Colclough, Christopher (ed.) (1997), *Public Sector Pay and Adjustment: Lessons from Five Countries*, London: Routledge.

Devarajan, Shantayanan, Lyn Squire and Sethaput Suthiwart-Narueput (1995), 'Reviving Project Appraisal at the World Bank', Policy Research Working Paper, 1496, Policy Research Department, World Bank, Washington, DC. Processed.

Diwan, Ishac (1994), 'Public Sector Retrenchment and Severance Pay: Nine Propositions', in Shahid A. Chaudhry, Gary J. Reid and Waleed H. Malik (eds), *Civil Service Reform in Latin America and the Caribbean: Proceedings of a Conference*,
Washington, DC: World Bank Technical Paper 259.

Fallick, Bruce (1996), 'A Review of the Recent Empirical Literature on Displaced
Workers', *Industrial and Labor Relations Review*, **50** (4), 5–16.

Fiszbein, Ariel (1994), 'An Opportunity Cost Approach to Redundancy Compensation: An Application to Sri Lanka', *Estudios de Economía: Special Issue on Labor
Economics in Less Developed Countries*, 115–26.

Fretwell, David, Jacob Benus and Christopher J. O'Leary (1999), 'Evaluating the Impact of Active Labor Market Programs: Results of Cross-Country Studies in Europe and Central Asia', Social Protection Discussion Paper, 9915, World Bank,
Washington, DC.

Frydman, Roman, Cheryl W. Gray, Marek Hessel, and Andrzej Rapaczynski (1999),
'When Does Privatization Work? The Impact of Provate Ownership on Corporate
Performance in the Transition Economies', *Quarterly Journal of Economics*, **114**
(4), 1153–91.

Galal, Ahmed, Leroy Jones, Pankaj Tandoon and Ingo Vogelsang (1994), *Welfare Consequences of Selling Public Enterprises: An Empirical Analysis*, New York: Oxford University Press.

Haltiwanger, John and Manisha Singh (1999), 'Cross Country Evidence on Public
Sector Retrenchment', *World Bank Economic Review*, **13** (1), (January).

Hamermesh, Daniel (1989), 'What Do We Know about Worker Displacement in the
U.S.?' *Industrial Relations*, **28** (1), 51–9.

Jacobson, Louis, Robert LaLonde and Daniel Sullivan (1993), 'Earnings Losses of
Displaced Workers', *American Economic Review*, **83** (4), 685–709.

Jenkins, Glenn P. and Claude Montmarquette (1979), 'Estimating the Private and Social Opportunity Cost of Displaced Workers', *Review of Economics and Statistics*,
619 (3), 342–53.

Jeon, Doh-Shin and Jean-Jacques Laffont (1999), 'The Efficient Mechanism for
Downsizing the Public Sector', *World Bank Economic Review*, **13** (1), (January).

Kikeri, Sunita (1997), 'Privatization and Labor: What Happens to Workers When
Governments Divest?', *World Bank Technical Paper*, 396, Washington, DC.

Kouamé, Auguste-Tano (1997), 'Workers' Severance Pay Packages in Privatization of State-Owned Enterprises in Bangladesh, Pakistan, and Sri Lanka: Options for the Future', Internal Discussion Paper, South Asia Regional Office, World Bank, Washington, DC. Processed.

Levy, Anat and Richard McLean (1997), 'Optimal and Sub-optimal Retrenchment Schemes: An Analytical Framework', Policy Research Department, Rutgers University, New Brunswick, NJ. Processed.

Lindauer, David L. and Barbara Nunberg (eds) (1994), 'Rehabilitating Government: Pay and Employment Reform in Africa', A World Bank Regional and Sectoral Study, Washington, DC.

London Economics (1996), 'The Impact of Privatisation on Labour in Africa', Prepared for the Africa Regional Office, World Bank, Washington, DC. Processed.

López-de-Silanes, Florencio (1997), 'Determinants of Privatization Prices', *Quarterly Journal of Economics*, **112** (4), 965–1025.

Middleton, John, Adrian Ziderman and Arvil Van Adams (1993), *Skills for Productivity: Vocational Education and Training in Developing Countries*, New York: Oxford University Press.

Mills, Bradford and David Sahn (1996), 'Life after Public Sector Job Loss in Guinea', in David Sahn (ed.), *Economic Reform and the Poor in Africa*, Oxford: Clarendon Press.

Nunberg, Barbara (1994), 'Experience with Civil Service Pay and Employment Reform: An Overview', in David L. Lindauer and Barbara Nunberg (eds), *Rehabilitating Government: Pay and Employment Reform in Africa*, A World Bank Regional and Sectoral Study, Washington, DC.

Orazem, Peter, Milan Vodopivec and Ruth Wu (1995), 'Worker Displacement during the Transition: Experience from Slovenia', Policy Research Working Paper, 1449, Policy Research Department, World Bank, Washington, DC. Processed.

Rama, Martín (1997), 'Efficient Public Sector Downsizing', Policy Research Working Paper, 1840, Policy Research Department, World Bank, Washington, DC. Processed.

Rama, Martín and Donna MacIsaac (1999), 'Earnings and Welfare after Downsizing: Central Bank Employees in Ecuador', *World Bank Economic Review*, **13** (1) (January).

Rama, Martín and Kinnon Scott (1999), 'Labor Earnings in One-Company Towns: Theory and Evidence from Kazakhstan', *World Bank Economic Review*, **13** (1) (January).

Robbins, Donald (1996), 'Public Sector Retrenchment and Efficient Severance Pay Schemes: A Case Study of Argentina', Harvard Institute for International Development, Cambridge, Mass. Processed.

Ruppert, Elizabeth (1999), 'The Algerian Retrenchment System: A Financial and Economic Evaluation', *World Bank Economic Review*, **13** (1), (January).

Svejnar, Jan and Katherine Terrell (1991), 'Reducing Labor Redundancy in State-Owned Enterprises', Policy Research Working Paper, 792, Policy Research Department, World Bank, Washington, DC. Processed.

Tansel, Aysit (1997), 'Public Sector Retrenchment and the Impact of Labor Shedding Programs on Workers in Turkey', Department of Economics, Middle East Technical University, Ankara. Processed.

Topel, Robert (1990), 'Specific Capital and Unemployment: Measuring the Costs and Consequences of Job Loss', *Carnegie-Rochester Conference Series on Public Policy*, **33** (0), 181–224.

Van Ginneken, Wouter (1991), *Government and Its Employees: Case Studies of Developing Countries*, Aldershot: Avebury.

Vickers, John and George Yarrow (1991), 'Economic Perspectives on Privatization', *Journal of Economic Perspectives*, 5 (spring), 111–32.

World Bank (1995), *Bureaucrats in Business: The Economics and Politics of Government Ownership,* A World Bank Policy Research Report, New York: Oxford University Press.

Younger, Stephen (1996), 'Labor Market Consequences of Retrenchment for Civil Servants in Ghana', in David Sahn (ed.), *Economic Reform and the Poor in Africa*, Oxford: Clarendon Press.

7. Privatization and Employment: Some General Issues

Brendan Martin

1. Introduction

This chapter explores some of the issues associated with the relationship between privatization and labor, mainly through comparative experience in the railways of two West African countries, Ghana and Ivory Coast.

For many labor unionists, it is axiomatic that privatization leads to attacks on employment and on terms and conditions of employment. However, the evidence of cause and effect is less clear cut. Certainly, there are many examples of a close association between privatization and loss of employment. For example:

- Employment in the energy sector in the United Kingdom fell by 42%, or more than 110,000 jobs, from 1990 to 1995, the period of restructuring which followed the privatization of most of the UK's electricity supply industry. During the same period, average decline in European Union energy sector employment was 17.4% (de Luca, 1997, 134).
- In Bulgaria, in the first two years of what was, by regional standards, a modest privatization programme, employment in privatized firms in industrial sectors fell by 75%, to one million (Martin, 1997, 10).
- Aguas Argentinas, the consortium which took over management and operation of water and sewage services in Buenos Aires, reduced its inherited workforce by nearly 50% in the first six months after privatization (de Luca, 1997, 189).

Many more examples could be given, from a variety of sectors and country types, and such numbers certainly tell us a considerable amount about the relationship between privatization and employment levels. However, they do not tell us, necessarily, that privatization *causes* loss of employment, or even that it leads to a loss of employment, even in those cases, much less in general. By interrogating the above facts a little more closely, we shall see difficulties with isolating the relationship between privatization and employment from the context in which privatization takes place and the impact of associated measures.

To return to the UK energy sector case, for example, a number of questions might be asked, including: was the UK energy sector overstaffed in comparison to its Western European neighbours prior to privatization? Was this, indeed, one of the reasons why no restructuring short of privatization was considered sufficient to tackle the scale of the political problem of shedding large numbers of publicly employed workers? How many jobs, if any, have been created – and how many not destroyed – as a result of the increased economic efficiency arising from the energy sector's cost-cutting?

In the Bulgarian case, in order to make serious sense of the social and employment issues around privatization of the enterprises concerned, we would need to know answers to such inquiries as: how many jobs, if any, were created as a result of government or private capital expenditure redirected from subsidizing loss-making enterprises into more productive investment? What social supports and safety nets were put in place to deal with the negative social impacts of the decline in industrial employment, and to what extent were they a part of wider economic development and employment creation strategy in the regions affected?

A similar range of questions, and many more, could and should be asked of the Buenos Aires water experience: was the employment decline in Aguas Argentinas associated to some extent with contracting-out of some functions? If so, to what extent has the decline in the number of people directly employed by Aguas Argentinas been offset by employment growth among firms contracted to Aguas Argentinas? Insofar as new jobs with contractors have been created, how do the terms and conditions of the workers concerned differ from those enjoyed by workers in equivalent positions in Aguas Argentinas' pre-privatization predecessor?

As it happens, Lyonnaise des Eaux, the French-owned transnational which leads the consortium which owns Aguas Argentinas, has offered answers to the first two of those inquiries. The company claims that indirect employment arising from the investment program launched by the privatized utility increased in a proportion of comfortably more than one-to-one in relation to decline in direct employment. That is interesting, but leaves us wondering even more about the comparison between the terms and conditions attached to the new jobs and those enjoyed by the workers whose jobs they replaced.

In short, it is extremely difficult, probably futile and possibly misleading to isolate the impact on labor of privatization per se from its context. It follows that, rather than limiting our analytical focus to a particular privatization project, it makes more sense to broaden and deepen our range of view in accordance with the reality that privatization, where and when it occurs, is one of many factors, planned and unplanned, shaping the consequences for labor. For the purposes of policy and program design, therefore, the issue is the intended and actual impact of a whole package – always assuming that privatization is applied as a means to wider strategic objectives rather than as an end in itself.

That, of course, is an assumption that cannot be safely made. On the contrary, in fact, privatization has been applied in the main within the context of an ideological view that private enterprise and market forces are capable, left to their own devices, of ensuring economic and employment growth.

The range of issues briefly explored above, as well as others, are illustrated through the comparative case study of railways restructuring and privatization in Ghana and Ivory Coast which follows.

2. Railways in Ivory Coast and Ghana: Background

The development of the railways in both Ivory Coast and Ghana, in common with the rest of Sub-Saharan Africa, took place under colonial rule and reflected the priorities of colonial rulers. In both cases, the main purpose of establishing rail infrastructure and operations was to aid exploitation of natural resources by moving primary products from their source to ports, for export to metropolitan markets in Europe, and by moving labor from indigenous locations to plantations and mines.

In both countries, cocoa exportation was an especially important driving force of railways development, and remains of vital importance to their economic development today – Ivory Coast and Ghana are the world's first and second cocoa exporters. Ivory Coast is also Africa's largest coffee producer, while manganese, gold and bauxite are Ghana's other major primary products. As export orientation has been central to the World Bank Structural Adjustment Programs in both countries, the significance of the relationship between rail transport and the export of primary products in which the countries have 'comparative advantage' is as great today in the context of globalization as it was in the context of colonialization. In Ghana, the railway is the sole means by which manganese and bauxite are transported to port.

The Ivory Coast railway was constructed between 1905 and 1954, when the country formed a single French colony with Burkina Faso. The railway enabled Abidjan to become a viable sea port and, today, the 1264 km of line runs from Abidjan in Ivory Coast to Kaya, north of Ougadougou, in Burkina Faso.

Ghana's railway was constructed under British rule. The network of 947 km was built between 1898 and 1956 in three sections forming a triangle linking Kumasi at the apex with the sea ports of Takoradi and Accra at the base.

Until 1989, the Ivory Coast railway was run by Regie Abidjan Niger (RAN), under the supervision of both Ivory Coast and Burkina Faso even following their national separation and independence. In 1989, however, RAN split into two national companies, Societé Ivorienne de Chemin de Fer (SICF) and Societé des Chemins de Fer du Burkina Faso (SCBF).

Ghana's railway and ports were initially run by a single colonial administrative body, the Ghana Railway and Harbour Authority. Following independence, this became the Ghana Railway and Port Authority, but management of the two companies was separated in 1977 and responsibility for the railway handed to the Ghana Railway Corporation (GRC).

The main rail workers union in Ivory Coast is Syndicat des Travailleurs du Rail (SYNTRARAIL), which succeeded the Syndicat National de la SICF (SYNASICF) following railways privatization in 1995. It is affiliated to the Union Général des Syndicats de Côte d'Ivoire (UGTCI). The main rail unions in Ghana, affiliated to the Ghana Trade Union Congress, are the Railway Enginemen's Union and the Railway Workers' Union.

The development of economic crisis in both Ivory Coast and Ghana in the 1980s followed the pattern of many other countries whose governments had borrowed too much in response to policies of international banks to lend too much. A variety of factors conspired to plunge both countries into a downward spiral of debt and state budget deficits. Change in the terms of trade, for cocoa and other products, were among those factors, although opinions differ as to the scale of its significance. In any event, that descent into macroeconomic malaise intertwined with problems specific to the railways – such as the failings of state management, caused by a range of factors including political appointments to key managerial positions, and corruption – to plunge the railways of both countries into decline.

In Ivory Coast, by the beginning of the 1980s, RAN was unable to rehabilitate rolling stock and infrastructure, which in turn drove up operating costs. At the same time, road transport began to benefit from the earlier investment in what remains one of Africa's best road networks, planned and built not to complement rail but in parallel, and, therefore, in competition with it. The combined impact of general economic decline and deteriorating railways found expression in the fact that while, at the peak in the 1970s, RAN was transporting almost 900,000 tons of freight per year, by 1989 that number was down to 260,000 tons.

A similar range of interrelated problems and failings produced a similar level of crisis in Ghana's railway. There is disagreement as to the share of blame deserved by the service's management – one consultants's report held mismanagement to be primarily responsible for the railway's problems, while another, commissioned by the Ghana Trade Union Congress, suggested that poor labor performance was a product of capital decline. 'Whilst it is correct to say that indiscipline of a sort existed at GRC it may however be incorrect to say that such indiscipline is intrinsic', the report stated, adding: 'It is, rather, a response to the deteriorating nature of the GRC basic infrastructure.' Whatever the relationship of chicken and egg, from carrying 1.6 millions tons of freight in 1970, Ghana's railways collapsed to 350,000 tons in 1983. Over the same period passenger traffic fell from 8 million to 3.3 million tickets.

3. Restructuring, Privatization and Labor in Ivory Coast Railways

During its golden age, RAN was employing more than 6000 workers, employed on better terms than most state employees (but average state employee terms were not as good as those of the average worker in the formal private sector). However, after K.J. Budin – formerly with the World Bank – was appointed to head the company, the workforce was reduced by around 600 between 1985 and 1988. The separation of the Ivory Coast and Burkina Faso operations in 1989 was followed in the former by a more commercial approach, under a new managing director, Yao Koukaou, a former car concessionaire with no experience of running a railway.

Under Koukaou, the railway was restructured without consultation with the union, which in any case was unprepared. The employment effect of the restructuring was a further reduction of the workforce, by about a third. It soon became clear, however, that there had been too many redundancies in some key areas – notably signaling and security – and this caused operational difficulties. Moreover, the restructuring did not accomplish another no less important precondition of using labour more productively – namely investment in infrastructure and rolling stock – and because of the labour-intensive nature of making good infrastrucutral deficiencies, the company found itself having to pay some of its remaining workforce for overtime working.

In March 1993, a new stage of restructuring began, the most effective yet, according to the union. The company's 1993 Activity Report highlights changes in commercial attitudes, reduction of fraud by 30% and a 60% increase in availability of locomotives, a good sign of maintenance efficiency. These improvements showed what could be done under state management, but by then the privatization process was under way. In October 1992, a plan to reintegrate and privatize the Ivory Coast and Burkina Faso railways had been announced, and it was followed in December that year by a call for tenders.

There were three bids, but two were soon withdrawn, leaving an uncompetitive field clear for the third application, led by a French/Belgian transnational company called SAGA, in partnership with local investors. The main business of SAGA, a subsidiary of the Bollore group, is freight forwarding – it controls the transportation of more than half of Burkina Faso's imports and exports. After a lengthy period of negotiation, the SAGA-led consortium Société Internationale de Transports Africains par Rail (SITARAIL) was, in August 1995, awarded the concession to run services and rehabilitate the infrastructure on terms rather different from those in the original tender documentation.

The eventual agreement involved leasing to SITARAIL the infrastructure, rolling stock and stations in return for a usage fee related to revenue. Ownership of the infrastructure and responsibility for managing the concession were vested in new state-owned companies, the Société de Gestion du Patrimoine Ferroviaire (SIPF), in Ivory Coast, and Société de Patrimoineroviaire du Burkina Faso (SOPAFER-B). SAGA's stake was 32.65% of the SITARAIL equity. The states of Burkina Faso and Ivory Coast each retained a 15% share, with around 18% purchased by a group of transnational and local companies, namely Maersk, SICC, Transurb and Sofrerail. Sixteen per cent of the company's equity was floated on the Abidjan stock exchange, while 3% was allocated to personnel.[1]

The unions had been unprepared for the workforce reductions imposed upon their members at the end of the 1980s and tried to learn from that experience when it became clear that preparation for privatization would bring further job cuts. The unions set out on this occasion to improve upon the redundancy terms imposed in 1989. They bargained for a program to promote re-employment of as many as possible of those made redundant and to prevent post-privatization job losses. In the event, SITARAIL reduced its combined Ivory Coast and Burkina Faso workforce by more than half, from around 4000 (itself about two-thirds of the mid-1980s level) to 1815. In 1996, the year after privatization, employment numbers increased again, but only slightly.

At the beginning of 1995, the union asked the government for information as to how further labor restructuring would be carried out, but failed to receive a satisfactory response. This led to a strike, and workers displayed such tactics as blocking the center of Abidjan with a locomotive. Negotiations started a few days later, but the union maintained the strike while the talks took place. Eventually, details of the redundancies envisaged were provided and the union argued up the severance terms to the equivalent of 14 months of wages, double the initial offer. In addition, the number of years of contributions required to entitle an employee to an early retirement package was reduced from 20 to 15 years.

There have been no retraining schemes aimed at retrenched workers, although during the negotiations the union proposed a scheme to enable workers to establish their own businesses. However, SITARAIL has agreed in principle to favor companies created by former SICF workers when looking for subcontractors. In practice, track maintenance, company car fleet management and printing of timetables and tickets have been contracted out to firms set up by former SICF workers. SITARAIL has also agreed to give preference to workers made redundant in 1995 when recruiting new staff. However, those workers are treated as new employees for the purposes of pay determination.

The latter is a significant condition, because SITARAIL has abandoned the

Table 7.1   Employment in Ivory Coast and Burkina Faso Railways

Year	Number of Employees	
	Burkina Faso and Ivory Coast	Ivory Coast Only
1980	6600	3800
1981	6600	3800
1982	6600	3800
1983	6600	3800
1984	6600	3800
1985	6450	3725
1986	6300	3650
1987	6150	3575
1988	6000	3500
1989	4000	2350
1990	4000	2350
1991	4000	2350
1992	4000	2350
1993	4000	2350
1994	4000	2350
1995	1815	1000
1996	1850	1020

pay scales in operation before the concession began, replacing them with a new and complicated system in which new recruits are on one scale while employees who transferred from SICF are on another. Over time, the proportion of employees attached to the two systems will shift in favour of the new one; in the meantime, the scheme has enabled the company to honor its commitment not to reduce the pay of employees it inherited with the concession. Under the new system, a 'basic' wage – established by a process of job evaluation – is topped up with various supplements such as accommodation allowances, travel allowances, special payments for working in dirty or hazardous conditions and performance-related bonuses. The overall impact on pay levels is not clear. Average pay has increased, but the sharp increases awarded to managers to raise their salaries to private sector market levels distort the average considerably.

Other terms of employment have also changed. For example, the company health insurance programme enjoyed by the workers before privatization has been privatized through a contract with a separate company. The cost of contributions is shared between the workers and the company. The union wants to increase the percentage paid by the employer. Although on paper it is a worse arrangement for the workers than the social protection provided to them and their families through their employment prior to privatization, in practice the state employees' funds had come to be so heavily in debt in the 1980s (as a result of the government failing to pay its contributions) that most employees no longer even applied to the fund for reimbursement of medical expenses. In practice, therefore, it could be that they are better off under the privatized arrangements which, in theory, are worse for them.

Some other aspects of working conditions have clearly improved since privatization, according to the union, which expects further improvements in the future. For example, workers have been provided with uniforms, and there are plans, dependent on receipt of loans, to upgrade workshops and equipment.

4. Restructuring, Privatization and Labor in Ghana Railways

Efforts to rehabilitate Ghana's railways began in 1983, when the then military government of Jerry Rawlings (later democratically elected) devised a Transport Recovery Program (TRP), part of an Economic Recovery Program (ERP), which went on to involve three Railway Rehabilitation Projects (RRPs). RRP1 ran from 1983 to 1988 and improved important parts of the Western Line, the busiest, at a cost of US$73.7 million, financed by the World Bank. RRP2, 1988–95, again financed by the World Bank, invested US$42.96 million on the Eastern and Central Lines. RRP3, 1995–98, was intended to tackle the chronic problem of lack of rolling stock that has prevented the full potential of the first two RRPs from being realized, and at providing investments in other areas.

According to the Railway Workers' Union, only the tracks that were the most damaged were changed under RRP1, which was undermined by continued problems of deficient signaling, rolling stock and workshops. Both unions and management criticized RRP2 for focusing on the Eastern and Central Lines before the problems of the Western Line had been completely sorted out. Moreover, the Eastern line – vital to cocoa transportation – has continued to have deficient tracks and bridges, and it is difficult to get spares for the maintenance of the radio-based signaling system, because the parts required are either obsolete or too expensive in foreign exchange.

The labor force and its representatives were not invited to contribute to the design and application of the RRPs. The unions emphasize that industrial relations were difficult in the 1980s, before the first multi-party elections in 1992, because of the continuing lack of democracy in the country generally. The unions believe that the tacit knowledge of employees which their greater involvement might have mobilized has been wasted as a result, and that had they been consulted a more holistic approach to the restructuring might have been possible.

Their concerns appear to have substance, although there have been some improvements. By 1995, rolling stock remained in very poor condition, with 24 out of 76 locomotives more than 30 years old. Maintenance was undermined by lack of spares and money to buy them. Although freight traffic increased from 350,000 tons in 1983 to 594,000 tons in 1988, the recovery is modest compared to the 1,600,000 tons carried annually in the mid-1970s. Passenger traffic has increased from 2 to 2.2 million a year over the same five years (having dipped even lower than its 1983 level in the middle of that period). The slower rate of recovery of passenger numbers reflects not only the constant lack of passenger coaches but also the World Bank and government priority of refocusing GRC on the more profitable freight business. The company's losses continued to grow until 1993 but since then have decreased, and, if depreciation costs are taken out of the equation, there was an operating profit in 1996.

The workforce of GRC has more than halved over the last 20 years. In 1978 the company was employing 11,000 people. This figure had reduced to 4500 by 1997, largely by not replacing workers who retired. There has been an embargo on recruitment, which has left labor gaps, especially in track maintenance. In addition, in 1993 more than 1000 workers were made redundant. According to the unions, the severance terms were poor and most of those who lost their jobs joined the burgeoning informal sector, in small-scale trading and crafts, although there have been no small business loans made specially available.

Table 7.2   Employment in Ghana railways

Year	Number of Employees
1978	11,000
1983	6,000
1991	6,204
1992	6,048
1993	4,608
1994	4,558
1995	4,412
1996	5,119
1997	4,500

While the unions view the limited degree of GRC's recovery as a product of the limited character of the RRPs and their effectiveness, the World Bank and the government have argued that they demonstrate the limits of restructuring and the need to privatize the company. In 1995, a study was commissioned from a Danish consultancy, DanRail. The terms of reference involved identifying how GRC could become financially self-sufficient, and included specifically identifying potential areas for private sector involvement. The study was completed in October 1996. Its main recommendations can be summarized as:

1. Employment should be reduced from 4500 to about 1600.
2. The private sector's involvement is a necessary condition of financial self-sufficiency.
3. GRC's functions should be divided into core and non-core activities, and each opened up to private sector participation.
4. The core activities – defined as infrastructure, traffic and workshops – should also be separated from each other and opened up to private sector participation.
5. GRC's management systems, including budgeting, costing and inventory

control, should be reorganized.
6. The government should be committed to the restructuring process.
7. The government should take over debt and finance retrenchments.

The government's view was that the report provided a good identification of the problems but failed to understand fully their origin and consequently did not consistently identify solutions suited to the Ghanaian context. The union commissioned a counter-report, supported by the Ghana Trade Union Congress (GTUC), on the basis of which unions and management went on to cooperate in putting forward a position paper outlining ideas for restructuring without privatization.

While the GRC managers accepted that some further reduction in employment numbers was necessary, they believed the proposed loss of 2900 was too much, and that any reduction should be gradual. The unions shared the view that further job cuts were inevitable, but emphasized that much more attention than in the past should be paid to severance terms and to putting in place a set of accompanying measures designed to cushion the social effects and assist retrenched workers in re-entering the labor market.

Both management and unions also accepted that privatization of non-core activities could reduce costs and thus enable the company to refocus resources on rehabilitation and improvement of GRC's core activities. Activities including coach cleaning and security have already been contracted out, but a scheme to contract out track maintenance failed because it depended on the participation of local communities alongside the railway who were not trained properly or paid regularly.

Unions and management oppose the division of the core activities into separate entities, on the grounds that, while they are functionally distinct from each other, they require vertical integration. Therefore, while supporting some organizational separation, they believe the activities should remain within one overall corporate body and management structure.

The government agreed to give the management–union approach a try, with the proviso that if it failed, a concession along the lines of the Ivory Coast model could follow. This consensus came under strain from strong World Bank pressure on the government to go for a concession more quickly, and there were concerns that the World Bank's opposition could scupper the restructuring approach, since its success could be dependent upon the Bank's financial support. The unions are not opposed in principle to the concession idea, but they do insist that they should be consulted about the way forward and that the more effectively they are consulted, the greater the likelihood of success of future restructuring in whatever form. They are also especially concerned about severance terms, the future of union representation and the rights and conditions of employment of rail employees.

5. Some Lessons of the Comparative Experience

It is striking that, in both Ivory Coast and Ghana, substantial employment reductions occurred without privatization. However, it is also striking that in Ivory Coast, privatization paved the way for a much more drastic reduction, on a scale which, according to one consultants' report, is now required in Ghana. It might be politically more difficult for the Ghana government to impose the employment reduction envisaged while it remains the owner of the enterprise than it would be to privatize the enterprise and pass responsibility for the next stage of anticipated labour reduction to the private sector.

The point of that speculative comment is that rather than viewing employment reduction as a product of privatization, it might be more accurate to view privatization as a political response to a perceived need to reduce employment. The cause and effect relationship between privatization and employment reductions is, therefore, not a straightforward one.

Similarly, privatization in Ivory Coast paved the way for changes in the remuneration system for the railway workers – changes which, while not intrinsically dependent on privatization, might have been trickier (politically and in terms of labor relations) to accomplish without it. It also appears to have led to some improvements in the working conditions of those employees who were retained, an outcome which emphasizes the variable impact of privatization on different groups of employees.

Restructuring and privatization of the railways in both countries have taken place in the context of economic crisis and World Bank Structural Adjustment Programs (SAPs). Those programs were informed by reasoning that sound economic policies would not only overcome problems of debt and state budget deficit but also create the best conditions for economic growth to produce employment expansion. Given that logic, it is not surprising that neither the SAPs in general nor the restructuring of railways in particular incorporated strategic plans aimed concretely at employment creation to soak up loss of employment in either railways or other parts of the economy. Stimulation of market forces and improved transport efficiency were expected to take care of those issues spontaneously.

A weakness with that approach can be seen in what appears to have been inadequate strategic thinking and planning behind employment restructuring in both cases. In both Ivory Coast and Ghana, labor shedding produced skills shortages in key areas, which undermined already inadequate efficiency and capacity to optimize labor productivity. The idea that employment reductions in themselves would necessarily bring improvement in efficiency and productivity appears to have been mistaken to the extent that – in the absence of a strategic approach to the development of an appropriate mix of skills, experience and capacity, allied to continuing capital deficiencies – efficiency and productivity have at times deteriorated as a result of cuts in employment numbers.

Some such negative outcomes might have been avoided had labor been more fully involved in the restructuring processes. Such a participatory approach might not only have strengthened the corporate spirit among employees, but also have enabled a more systematic mobilization of the knowledge and experience of employees, resources which appear to have been undervalued. There is evidence that employees and their unions could have been more effective sources than was realized of information about deficiencies in both capital investment and labor organization, and of solutions to those problems.

A mindset, on the part of those responsible for driving restructuring and privatization, that employees and their unions could be relied upon only to try to protect and advance their own sectional interests appears to have contributed to this neglect of opportunities to engage them more creatively, although there were signs that those lessons were being absorbed in the Ghana case. There, the unions appear to be committed to change, and aware of its necessity, rather than fulfilling the stereotype of public employees' unions as conservative organizations lacking commitment to efficiency, productivity and improving service.

Against that, however, the reluctance of governments and their advisors among international institutions to allow programs of infrastructure and service modernization to become unduly bogged down in discussion among all stakeholders in the search for consensus is also understandable. Evidence of the advantages of pressing decisively ahead might be said to be revealed in the reported financial performance of SITARAIL following privatization, with one report claiming an 11-fold increase in revenues in the first two years (*Financial Times*, June 1997). Moreover, agreements and understandings between the privatized company and the labour unions in Ivory Coast, which appear to have produced new entrepreneurial and employment opportunities for displaced workers, might also serve as evidence of the benefits of combining decisive action with continuing dialogue.

A cautionary note is, however, appropriate. Just as in the case of Aguas Argentinas, while it is clear that some displaced workers have been provided with new employment opportunities as a result of contracting-out decisions of the privatized railway in Ivory Coast, further information about the terms and conditions enjoyed by those contracted workers in comparison with those attached to the jobs replaced through contracting-out would be required before an overall assessment of the social impact could be properly made.

Notes

1. For more detail and discussion on the process which led to SITRAIL winning the concession, see *Structural Adjustment and Railways Privatisation: World Bank Policy and Government Practice in Ivory Coast and Ghana*, by Brendan Martin and Marc Micoud, available from the Information Centre at International Tansport Workers' Federation, 49–60 Borough Road, London, SE1 1DS. Email: mail@itf.org.uk.

References

de Luca, Loretta (ed.) (1997), *Labour and Social Dimensions of Privatization and Restructuring*, Geneva: International Labour Office.

Martin, Brendan (1997), *Privatization in Transition Economies: The Employment and Social Dimensions and the Participatory Approach,* Geneva: International Labour Office.

'The Ivory Coast has Become a World Leader in Privatization' (1997), *Financial Times*, 2 June 1997.

8. Ironies and Obstacles to China's Post-Socialist Housing Privatization

Corinna-Barbara Francis

1. Introduction

The Chinese government has been pursuing urban housing reforms for more than two decades now. A central goal of these reforms has been to alter the structure of production, consumption, and allocation of urban housing so as to shift choice, control, and accountability for this resource from state work units – danwei, to individual consumers. During the Mao era urban housing was primarily produced by state units and allocated directly to their own employees virtually free of charge. The financing, construction, management, and allocation of urban housing was principally the responsibility of individual state work units, not the state or the private sector. One consequence of this was workers' dependence on their bosses for housing, a situation that empowered management vis-à-vis labor and contributed to low labor mobility. It also undercut the role of state and municipal housing agencies, which owned and managed a relatively small portion of China's total urban housing.

A key strategy of China's housing reforms has been the privatization of housing ownership (Liu, 1988). Housing privatization has been expected to achieve many of the goals associated with the reform effort. It was to shift the real costs of housing to individual consumers, improve the efficiency of the housing market, and help improve labor mobility by giving workers greater independence from their employers. For more than two decades the Chinese state has experimented with a variety of privatization strategies, including direct sales of existing housing to individuals, subsidized sales of existing and new housing, and policies encouraging the growth of commercial housing Zhang, 1993; Pudney and Wang, 1995).

Housing reforms appear to have succeeded in some of their broader goals. China's urban housing market appears to operate more efficiently and on a more market-oriented basis than before. There is a growing stock of commercial housing available for direct purchase by individuals, and an increasing proportion of housing has been purchased by individuals. This appears to have significantly shifted the real costs of housing from the state to individual consumers.

However, I argue here that despite the appearance of fundamental change, the substantive goals associated with housing privatization have been blocked and derailed.[1] The reforms have failed to enable the average urban worker to rent or purchase housing independently of his or her employer, a goal that remains beyond the reach of all except for the wealthiest of individuals. The vast majority of urban residents remain dependent on their work units for housing. Housing reforms have furthermore failed to transfer effective housing property rights to individual consumers, despite nominal privatization. State units have retained significant control over this resource through their central role in its production, consumption, and allocation. Neither market reforms nor concerted state effort have succeeded in undoing the institutional pattern established during the Mao era which gave power, privilege, and resources to state units. Despite persistent state efforts, danwei have resisted the usurping of their resources and power.

Two explanatory factors are explored here. First, the state has depended on the very institution that is the prime target of housing reform – the urban work unit – to implement it. Relying on danwei to implement the reforms has not only given them broad discretion and autonomy to act in ways that suit their interests, it has furthermore put them in the position of privatizing their own housing stock through housing sales to their own employees. This has allowed them to retain effective property rights over this nominally 'privatized' housing. And in some ways housing 'privatization' has even intensified the financial leverage that employers may exercise over their employees.

Secondly, China's distinctive approach to market reforms has undercut its housing privatization efforts, as it has other aspects of the privatization of the economy more generally. China's market reforms have been driven largely by the decentralization of financial autonomy and management to individual state entities – including local governments, state enterprises, and other public institutions, a process that has transformed them into increasingly financially self-reliant commercial actors. As a consequence, state units have had steadily increasing extra-budgetary revenues, and they have utilized these to increase their investments in housing and other forms of collective welfare for workers. So just as the state has sought to transfer housing ownership from state units to the private sector, market reforms have enabled these to increase their investments in and ownership of urban housing. As such danwei have continued in their role as allocators of this scarce resource to urban workers.

2. Urban Housing in the Maoist Era

More than other socialist states, the new Chinese socialist regime marginalized private urban housing in favor of public housing. Private housing investment dropped off sharply after 1949, with the founding of the PRC. From its earliest days, the Chinese state discouraged the mobilization of private capital for housing investment. It failed to provide legal protection for private property, gave no property tax breaks for private property, and made it difficult for private builders to obtain the materials and labor necessary for construction (Chao, 1966; Ma, 1982; Howe, 1968). Even in Shanghai, which had one of the highest concentrations of private capital in the country, only 4.6% of all new dwellings built between 1950 and 1956 were constructed with private funds (Howe, 1968, p. 386). According to one estimate, state investment accounted for upwards of 90% of all new urban dwellings built in the 1950s for which there are records (Chao, 1966, p. 391; Zhang, 1998, p. 35). Private investment remained minimal as a portion of total urban housing investment throughout the Maoist era. This contrasts with other socialist regimes, including the Soviet Union and Eastern European countries, that provided relatively greater protection and support for private builders, and where private investment continued to be an important component of total housing investment.[2] Individual investment in housing in these countries was a significant proportion of total investment, as indicated by Table 8.1.

The PRC's (Peoples Republic of China's) urban housing sector was traditionally also distinguished by the predominance of work unit, or danwei, housing – housing owned and managed by individual work units, in contrast to housing owned and managed by the state and municipal governments.[3] Capital resources were budgeted by the state, but work units assumed primary responsibilities for key aspects of the production and distribution of urban housing, including its financing, development, construction, management, repair, and allocation. New urban housing investment was channeled primarily through units of production. Government ministries, state enterprises, universities, and other public institutions were given housing construction budgets that were typically calculated as a proportion of their annual capital construction budgets, having to request these as part of their annual development plans (Wang, 1995; Wu, 1996; Chao, 1966). Urban workers relied heavily on their work units for housing, especially new housing, and work units exercised relative autonomy in allocating housing to their employees. The state provided general guidelines but each unit handled this process with little direct state interference.[4] Municipal housing bureaux sometimes even relied on work units to distribute municipal housing, by assigning groups of municipal housing units to danwei and having them re-assign these to their employees.

By contrast, municipalities were provided wiht few independent sources of revenue for the construction of new housing, whether through property taxes, income taxes, or other channels (Wang, 1995, pp. 63–4; Howe, 1968; Ma,

Table 8.1   *Percentages of state and individual investment in housing construction in the former Soviet Union and Eastern European socialist countries*

	Built by the state		Built by individuals and cooperatives	
	1953	1957	1953	1957
Bulgaria	35	25	65	75
Czechoslovakia	76	50	24	50
Eastern Germany	87	63	13	37
Hungary	55	48	45	52
Poland	77	58	23	42
Romania	23	20	77	80
USSR	50	42	50	58
Yugoslavia	24	48	76	52

Source: The United Nations, *Financing of Housing in Europe* (Geneva, 1958, p. 33). Cited in Chao (1966, pp. 381–96).

1992). The bulk of housing owned by Chinese municipalities came from the nationalization and confiscation of private housing, the high-tide of which occurred in the mid-1950s and continued into the early 1960s. Sporadic efforts on the part of the state to provide municipalities with new sources of housing revenue have not had an impact on the growing dominance of danwei housing.[5] Municipalities relied primarily on housing rents to pay their housing costs. But because of the state's policy of low public housing rents, this typically failed to provide even enough revenue for the upkeep and maintenance of municipal housing stocks, let alone construction of new housing.[6] In Xian, for instance, a rapidly growing city, no new housing construction was carried out by the municipal government during the 1950s, despite the rapid growth of work unit housing (Wang, 1995).

Furthermore, many cities did not even have an independent municipal housing agency, as their housing functions were often divided among a number of different government departments.[7] Municipal housing bureaux were, furthermore, typically understaffed, making it difficult for them to carry out even basic maintenance and repair tasks. Municipal housing, as a consequence, tended to be of lower quality than work unit housing.

Because of this structure of investment, the proportion of danwei housing increased steadily as a proportion of China's total urban housing stock, while that of private and state-owned housing diminished proportionately. By the late 1970s nearly half of China's urban housing was owned by state units, while municipalities owned less than a third, and about 20% continued to be privately held. The growth of danwei housing as a proportion of total housing continued into the early reform era as suggested by Table 8.2.

Table 8.2   *Breakdown of national urban housing stock by ownership (percent)*

Year	Danwei	Municipalities	Private
1979[a]	48.5	31.6	19.9
1982[b]	53.6	28.7	17.7

Sources:
[a] Kirby, (1990).
[b] 'Urban Housing Rental', *Beijing Review*, No. 33, October 11, 1982, pp. 27–28.

Because new urban housing investment was tied to capital investments, danwei housing grew fastest in the cities experiencing the most rapid growth, such as Xian and Nanjing. By 1975 over 64% of Nanjing's urban housing was owned and managed by danwei, while the municipality owned only around 20%, and 15% was still privately held, as illustrated in Table 8.3.

Table 8.3   *Nanjing housing ownership by sector (percent)*

Year	Managed by the housing bureau	Danwei-managed	Private
1949	12.4	20.8	66.8
1958	31.3	40.7	28.0
1962	22.2	55.8	22.0
1975	20.6	64.1	15.3

Source: Yang and Wang (1992, p. 80).

By contrast, cities experiencing slower industrial growth, such as Shanghai, tended to have relatively lower proportions of danwei housing and higher proportions of private and municipally owned housing. Only an estimated 15%

of Shanghai's population lived in new, primarily work unit, housing by 1965, while 85% lived in pre-1949 housing stock, which tended to be either privately owned or owned by the municipal government (Howe, 1968, p. 80). By 1981 the proportion of danwei housing in Shanghai had reached 45.44% – an overall increase but still lower than the national average – compared to 44.23% and 10.33% held respectively by the city government and private individuals.[8] However, nation-wide, danwei housing was increasing as a proportion of total urban housing.

There were important consequences of this unit-based urban housing system. First, it gave effective property rights over a growing portion of China's urban housing to individual institutions and organizations, rather than either central and local government or the private sector. Danwei property rights over 'their' housing derived from their authority to determine the utilization, transfer, and benefits derived from this resource. Danwei managers determined who got to use employee housing, how it was transferred to new users, and it was the danwei community, not the general public, that enjoyed the direct benefits of this good.

Secondly, the danwei's housing responsibilities resulted in the build-up of administrative capacity of danwei and their concentration of institutional and organizational resources. The assumption by danwei of the broad set of functions relating to housing, including financial management, maintenance, repair, and allocation imposed significant financial, administrative, and managerial tasks, especially in the case of large units with tens and hundreds of thousands of employees. The task of processing employee housing applications – evaluating each applicant's qualifications, verifying background information, and assigning housing, presented an enormous administrative challenge. State enterprises, government bureaux, and other units all tended to operate their own housing offices (*ke*) or departments (*chu*). Seen from the national perspective this concentrated significant resources within individual units, while drawing resources away from state housing agencies, causing them to be comparatively underdeveloped relative to danwei.

Finally, this system of public housing contributed to low rates of labor mobility during the Maoist period.[9] Employees who left their work unit were expected to give up their housing and could anticipate a long wait for housing from their new work unit. The role of work units in housing provision further cultivated an orientation of dependence and a sense of expectation among urban workers towards their employers, evident in the fact that individuals often directed their complaints and lobbying efforts for housing towards their employers and not the government.[10]

3. China's Post-Mao Housing Reforms: Goals and Strategies

China's post-Mao urban housing reforms have had a number of goals. One of the most immediate ones was improving housing conditions. State policies of suppressed consumption coupled with low housing rents had effectively inhibited housing investments during the Mao era, while urban housing conditions deteriorated steadily. Chinese urban housing investment averaged only 1.5% of GNP between 1949 to 1978, and in 1978 it dipped as low as 1.3% of GNP, much lower than the international average and lower than other socialist states. Average per capita residential space declined over the Mao years, from 4.5 sq. m in 1949 to 3.6 sq. m in 1978 (Yang and Wang, 1992, p. 72).

A second goal has been to shift the costs of urban housing away from the state and state units to individual users. Although urban workers collectively paid for housing through low wages, individuals did not have to pay for the real costs of their housing consumption as housing was distributed as an employment benefit. Shifting real costs to individuals has been expected not only to give consumers greater choice and discretion but also to improve the efficiency of the housing production (Lim and Lee, 1993).

Thirdly, housing reforms have been seen as a vital component of the effort to free urban workers from their dependence on their work units, thereby facilitating labor mobility. If work units continued to be the primary source of urban housing this could be expected to dampen labor mobility. Housing reforms, finally, have also been seen as a component of the effort to improve China's urban planning and to give municipalities greater control over zoning practices. The system of danwei housing, and the corresponding land allocation system that distributed land for production as well as for housing and other social functions to state units, created obstacles to effective urban zoning (Yeh and Wu, 1995). Urban land tended to be categorized according to the type of unit to which it was attached rather than according to its actual function (Institute of Finance, 1992). By shifting the responsibility for urban housing development out of the hands of individual units, the expectation has been that municipalities would be able to engage in more effective urban planning.

Housing privatization has been a central strategy in the Chinese state's housing reforms. Through a variety of means the state has sought to shift housing ownership from the state and state units to private citizens. These have included direct housing sales, subsidized housing sales, increased rents and housing vouchers, and promotion of commercial housing through housing development corporations. Each is discussed below.

Direct housing sales One of the earliest privatization strategies involved government subsidies for the construction and sale to individuals of new urban housing. Experimental reforms were first launched in Xian and Nanning in 1979 and later extended to over 60 cities (Wang and Murie, 1996; Wang, 1995; Wu, 1996). In Xian the central government provided 1 million yuan to the municipal housing authorities for the construction of new housing. By 1981 6000 housing units had been sold in this way (Wang, 1995). However, this privatization strategy had a number of problems. It placed an excessive financial burden on the state, requiring central and local governments to fully subsidize the construction of new housing. Low public housing rents suppressed worker incentives to purchase housing.[11] And continuing low wages and the lack of long-term individual home mortgages made it difficult for the average worker to pay the high housing costs.[12]

Subsidized housing sales Responding to these problems, the state adopted new privatization strategies beginning in 1983 which focused on providing subsidies to individual home buyers and promoting the sale of existing housing rather than just newly built housing. One of the most actively promoted methods was the 'three one-thirds' method in which individual home buyers, work units, and local governments each subsidized one-third of the total purchase cost. The State Economic Commission approved pilot tests of this approach in the cities of Zhengzhou, Changzhou, Siping, and Shashi in 1983, and it was extended to more than 160 cities in 1984–85 (Wang and Murie, 1996). This approach had the advantage of shifting some of the financial burden for housing subsidies to work units and of incorporating the existing housing stock in the privatization efforts. However, results continued to be plagued by low rents in public sector housing which undercut individual incentives for private home ownership, even with the added subsidies. And despite the additional contributions of work units in providing subsidies, the program was still a major burden on local governments.

Increased rents and housing vouchers In response to these problems, housing reform strategies in the mid to late 1980s focused on the need to raise public housing rents and to devise long-term savings plans in order to increase individual incentives to purchase housing and to help workers accumulate funds for home purchases. The strategy was to raise rents sufficiently to give individuals the incentive to purchase housing while simultaneously introducing long-term savings plans through wage supplements specifically designated for housing purchases (Lu and Wang, 1992; Wang, 1995). Work units and municipalities were expected to raise their housing rents, while providing housing subsidies to workers through wage supplements targeted specifically and solely for the purchase of housing. These housing supplements, or vouchers, were to be fixed at a certain percentage of the wage, with overall guidelines set by the state (Lam, 1996). In principle these funds were to be deposited into individual employee accounts, which would accumulate sufficiently after a number of years to enable workers to purchase their own housing. Housing vouchers were thus an effort to monetarize employee benefits which had previously been distributed to workers in kind. By giving workers monetary compensation and making them responsible for the real costs of housing the idea was to shift from material to monetary distribution and to transform hidden subsidies into open subsidies (Wang, 1995).

Increased rents and housing vouchers were launched experimentally in five cities from 1986 to 1988, most notably Yantai, and were later incorporated into the National Housing Reform Plan of 1988 (Tong and Hays, 1996). The Urban Housing Reform Resolution of 1991 updated and renewed this strategy, pushing for even further increases in rents to the point where they would cover basic housing costs including construction, management, maintenance, and repair, as well as further encourage housing sales (Wang and Murie, 1996).

4. Ironies and Obstacles to China's Housing Privatization

Despite concerted state effort, China's housing privatization strategies during much of this period were repeatedly stalled and derailed. First, these privatization strategies ultimately affected only a small proportion of China's total urban housing. Even in Yantai, an official site of experimental reforms, only 10% of all *new* housing was sold to individuals at the height of the reforms in the 1980s, an equivalent of only 1–2% of the city's total apartment stock (Tolley, 1991, p. 64).[13] A similar situation characterized other cities.[14] Secondly, the housing privatization that did occur generally failed in achieving the kind of substantive change sought by the reforms. It failed to transfer effective property rights and financial choice and accountability to individual home buyers. State work units retained essential property rights over urban housing – even nominally 'privatized' housing, and the average worker has remained highly dependent on his or her work unit to obtain housing. In some ways the process of privatization appears to have even given work units new forms of leverage over their employees.

Two broad explanatory factors are examined below. The first is that China's broader market reforms intensified one of the very conditions targeted by the privatization policy – danwei housing ownership. At the very time that the state was seeking to privatize the urban housing stock, market reforms were contributing to an increase in the proportion of danwei-owned housing. The second is that the implementation process of housing privatization ironically empowered the very institution targeted by the privatization effort – i.e., the state work unit. While housing privatization sought to give employees greater independence from their work units, it ironically empowered this institution by relying on it to implement the reforms. Their role as implementers of housing privatization allowed state work units to distort and derail the policy's principal goals to suit their interests.

5. China's Market Reforms and Danwei Housing Ownership

While China's housing reforms have sought to privatize the urban housing stock and shift ownership from state units to individuals, China's market reforms have, ironically, contributed to the very trend targeted by housing reforms – they have led to a proportional increase in danwei ownership of urban housing relative to the state and private sectors. China's market reforms have decentralized managerial authority to local governments, state enterprises, state agencies, and other public institutions. Consequently, a whole variety of state organizations have been transformed into commercial entities which operate their own for-profit ventures. State policy has encouraged financial self-sufficiency on the part of individual public entities in part by allowing them to retain substantial portions of their self-generated revenue (Blecher, 1991; Duckett, 1996; Francis, 1997; Mueller and Tan, 1997).

One consequence of this is that local governments, state agencies, and public institutions have become financially increasingly self-reliant and have enjoyed expanding extra-budgetary revenues, while state-allocated capital investment has steadily declined. An increasing portion of the total capital investment of state units – the key channel through which the state formerly funded urban housing construction, has been paid through units' self-generated revenue, rather than through state allocations. In 1978 direct state funding accounted for 77.82% of the total capital construction investment of state-owned work units, declining to 22% in 1988 and to 10.22% in 1992 as illustrated in Table 8.4.[15]

The shift towards greater financial self-reliance on the part of state units and institutions has contributed to both an increase in absolute spending on collective worker welfare and benefits, including housing, and to an increase in the portion paid for directly through units' self-generated revenue. Public housing investment, which represented only 1.3% of China's GNP in 1978, more than tripled in less than a decade, reaching 4.2% of GNP in 1988.[16] An increasing proportion of the state allocated budget of state-owned enterprises was spent on worker subsidies, increasing from an average of 39.9% in 1978 to 48.2% by 1986 (Yang and Wang, 1992, pp. 23–4). At the same time state units have steadily increased their spending on collective benefits including

Table 8.4   *Changes in the composition of state revenue and capital construction investment (CCI) in China: 1978–92*

	Budgetary revenue		Extra-budgetary revenue		CCI of state-owned units	
Year	Yuan (bn)	Percentage	Yuan (bn)	Percentage	Yuan (bn)	Percentage
1978	112.11	76.36	34.71	23.64	38.92	77.82
1979	106.80	70.22	45.29	29.78	39.69	75.82
1980	104.22	65.15	55.74	34.85	30.01	53.69
1981	101.64	62.84	60.11	37.16	22.26	50.26
1982	108.39	57.45	80.27	42.55	23.25	41.85
1983	121.12	55.59	96.77	44.41	29.60	49.82
1984	146.71	55.25	118.85	44.75	35.97	48.40
1985	183.72	54.56	153.00	45.44	38.12	35.48
1986	218.45	55.70	173.73	44.30	41.74	35.49
1987	226.24	52.72	202.88	47.28	43.85	32.65
1988	248.94	52.30	227.00	47.40	38.17	24.25
1989	280.38	51.33	265.88	48.67	32.33	20.84
1990	313.43	53.64	270.86	46.36	36.36	21.34
1991	343.08	51.40	324.33	48.60	34.85	16.47
1992	n.a.		n.a.		n.a.	

Source: State Statistical Bureau (1992, 1993). (Cited from Fulong Wu, 1996, p. 1610.)

housing, proportionally outspending state and local governments. Their increasing extra-budgetary revenue, and their discretion in spending it, has contributed to the increase in spending by state units on collective worker benefits, including housing. State enterprise extra-budgetary funds accounted for 60–70% of housing investment during the 1980s (Yang and Wang, 1992, pp. 23–4). As a consequence of these trends, an increased portion of danwei spending on housing is paid for through their extra-budgetary revenue. According to a World Bank investigation, by 1988 state work units were financing 52% of their annual housing investments through retained earnings, a figure that increased steadily in the 1990s.[17] For some especially successful enterprises, retained profits may pay for nearly their entire housing budget.[18]

A further consequence of this shifting pattern of housing investment is that danwei ownership of housing has steadily increased as a proportion of total urban housing, outpacing ownership by both the state and private sectors, as reflected in Table 8.5.

Table 8.5   *Ownership of total urban housing in China by sector (percent)*

	Danwei	City	Private
1979[a]	48.5	31.6	19.9
1982[b]	53.6	28.7	18.7
1984[a]	58.8	24.1	17.1
1985[c]	75.0	9.0	18.7

Sources:
[a] Wu, (1996, p. 1603).
[b] *Beijing Review*, No. 41, October 1982, pp. 26–7.
[c] Based on the first national survey of housing stock conducted in 1985 in 323 cities. See Wu (1996, p. 1603).

The dominant role of danwei in urban housing investment is most striking in new housing. According to one estimate in 1983 80% of all new housing being constructed nation-wide was owned by danwei, while only 8.8% was owned by municipal governments and 11.25% owned by individuals (Yang and Wang, 1992, p. 110).

Increases in the role of danwei in new housing investment has occurred in cities with different types of housing sectors. Cities that have traditionally had high levels of danwei-owned housing, such as Xian and Beijing, as well as cities with traditionally lower rates of danwei ownership such as Shanghai

Table 8.6   *Ownership of total new housing in 1983 (percent)*

Municipal governments	8.8
Enterprises	80.0
Individuals	11.25

have experienced increases in danwei housing ownership. In Xian the proportion of danwei owned housing in total grew 142.1% between 1980 and 1988,
while private housing grew by 77.7%, and city-owned housing grew by 31%
(Wang, 1995, p. 75). The relatively slower growth of state and private housing
has meant that their share of total urban housing fell proportionately throughout the 1980s. By 1988 danwei – universities, enterprises, hospitals, schools,
and other institutions, owned over 88% of all public housing in Xian (Wang,
1995, p. 62). Danwei owned and managed 69% of total public housing in
Beijing in 1989, while 31% was managed by the municipal housing bureau
(Yu, 1992, p. 325). The proportion of privately owned housing in Beijing was
lower than the national average, only 9% in 1991, compared to the national
average of 18%.[19] From 1983 to 1990 the Zhongshan municipality invested a
total of only 60 million yuan in new housing – only twice the amount invested
by *one* municipal enterprise during a comparable period.[20]

Even in Shanghai, where danwei traditionally managed a relatively smaller
portion of total urban housing than in other cities, work units accounted for a
growing portion of all housing investment in the 1980s. In 1980 danwei accounted for 55% of all housing investment in Shanghai, with this increasing to
69.7% in 1986 and to 86% by 1990 (Zhou and Logan, 1996, p. 402).[21] At the
same time the proportion of investment by the Shanghai municipality decreased
from 27.2% of the total in 1986 to 17.3% in 1988 (Yang and Wang, 1992, p.
89).

An irony of China's housing privatization efforts is thus that, while efforts
were being made to shift housing ownership from state units, China's broader
approach to market reforms was contributing to an increase in danwei investment in and ownership of urban housing. This trend not only undercut the
goals of housing privatization, it created facts on the ground that shaped the
nature of the privatization effort, as explored in the following section.

6. The Dilemma of the Danwei Role in Policy Implementation

A second irony of China's housing privatization is that the state has relied on
the very institution to implement the reforms – the danwei, which has been a
key target of the reforms (Lee, 1988).[22] State units have been the key agents of
the PRC's housing privatization efforts. This choice has been driven by two
conditions. First, by the fact that state units have been the owners of the largest, and an increasingly large, proportion of China's urban housing and have
therefore had direct managerial control over it. Secondly, it was driven by the
danwei's traditional role as an agent and implementer of state policy, and the
state's continued reliance on this institution to perform in this manner (Francis,

1999). The danwei's administrative capacity, its concentration of human, institutional, and organizational resources, and its close links to urban workers gives it unique capabilities to implement state policy. By contrast, the under-staffed and resource-poor municipal housing agencies have lacked the administrative capacity to carry out housing reforms, and, as demonstrated above, they had a diminishing portion of China's urban housing under their direct administration. As a growing proportion of China's urban housing was under danwei management, it was natural to make danwei responsible for implementing housing reforms. However, this authority has given danwei broad discretion in interpreting the reforms in ways that serve their own interests and distort and derail the substantive goals of the reforms. This has had important consequences for the process and outcome of housing privatization, as explored below.

7. Housing Privatization as Danwei Housing 'Sales'

The first consequence of the danwei's policy implementation role is that China's housing privatization was, for much of the 1980s and 1990s, a process dominated by the sale by work units of their *own* (danwei) housing to their *own* employees. The fact that state units owned the bulk of the housing being privatized and were in charge of implementing the reforms meant that China's housing privatization was primarily a process of state units 'selling' their own housing to their own employees. All except for the wealthiest of individuals were limited to purchasing housing from their own bosses, not from a commercial market.

A second consequence of the danwei's policy implementation role is that most urban residents were limited to purchasing the housing assigned to them through the traditional, administrative, *fenpei* system controlled by work units. In effect, individual options tended to be limited to purchasing, or not, the housing unit assigned to them largely at the discretion of danwei managers.[23] Most individuals were not even able to choose from among the housing owned by their work unit. China's early housing privatization efforts were thus effectively reduced to being a process by which individuals were given the option, or forced, to purchase the housing unit which had been bureaucratically allocated to them by their employer.

Thirdly, the danwei's role in policy implementation has given them broad discretion in interpreting specific policies in ways that serve their interests and has even given them new sources of leverage over their workers, thereby substantively undercutting the reforms' goals. This is illustrated by the implementation of the housing voucher system. Housing vouchers were introduced as a way to overcome the dilemma of low wages, high housing costs, and the lack of personal mortgage financing through banks. They were to help urban workers accumulate sufficient savings to purchase their own housing through the provision of wage supplements targeted specifically for housing. Monthly wage supplements were to be deposited into individual savings accounts and released only for housing purchases. In principle, in order to satisfy the aim of labor mobility, individual housing accounts should have been designed to be transferable between units, allowing employees to carry the funds accumulated in their accounts to a new job.

However, in practice the danwei's role in the implementation of the housing voucher system has allowed units to interpret this in ways that undermine the ultimate goals of the reform. First, despite the claim of individual housing accounts, these appeared more fictitious than real. In interviews individuals often appeared to have no idea how much they had accumulated in 'their' accounts, they had no records of an actual savings account, an account number, or any other concrete evidence of a real individual account.[24] Rather, the monies appeared largely under the control of danwei managers. Vagaries of state policy have left to the discretion of danwei issues including what should happen to housing funds if an employee leaves prior to being able to recoup these by purchasing housing. Can and should these be returned to the individual when she or he transfers to another job? Such issues have largely been decided in favor of employers. No institutional system has been put in place which enables the transfer of funds between units. Individuals tend to lose the funds docked from their wages when they leave their jobs prior to purchasing housing. Most seemed to write these funds off if they did not intend to remain in their job.

Secondly, employers have enjoyed broad discretion in determining what proportion of employee wages they dock as housing 'supplements'. State policy provided only general guidelines in this matter, allowing considerable local discretion. Municipalities have also set general targets, with 5% of employee wages being most commonly reported. However, individual units exercised considerable discretion in setting their own rates. While Shanghai municipality set a general rate of 5% of wages as the proportion to be placed in housing funds, managers docked up to 25% of their employees' salaries.[25] Thirdly, danwei control over the housing voucher program has allowed employers to place a variety of restrictions on employees' access to and use of these funds. Some enterprises and units have required a certain number of years of employment with the unit before employees can access these funds, in some cases up to five years.

Ironically, then, China's approach to housing privatization has in important ways given work units greater financial leverage over their employees than the traditional housing system. While housing privatization aimed, among other things, to make employees more independent of their work units, danwei's control of the process has given them new forms of leverage over their employees. In the old system the greatest loss that individuals could suffer if they left their work unit was the loss of the *use* of danwei housing. However, since danwei housing was provided virtually free of charge, despite the hidden costs, individual employees did not experience any *direct* financial loss if they left their work unit. However, the new system has given bosses a way to dock significant portions of employees' monetary compensation which can only be recuperated by them through continued employment with the unit and their purchase of danwei housing. This particular strategy of housing privatization has thus provided employers with new mechanisms of financial leverage over employees by enabling them to withhold large proportions – in some cases up to a quarter of potential compensation – and to determine the conditions of how these funds can be utilized. Contrary to the goal of freeing individual workers from dependence on their workplaces for housing and facilitating labor mobility, China's strategies for housing reforms of the 1980s and 1990s in some ways intensified individual dependence on work units, and gave danwei added sources of leverage over employees.[26]

8. Danwei and Restrictions of Private Property Rights

The discretion that state units have enjoyed in their role as agents of China's housing privatization has enabled them to dictate the terms and conditions of housing sales in ways that restrict the private property rights of individuals, seriously compromising the substantive meaning of the reforms. First, danwei have been able to restrict individual rights to transfer or dispose of property by claiming the right to first (re-)purchase of housing sold to their employees. Some danwei write into the housing contracts they sign with their employees that they (the unit) must be given the first chance to re-purchase housing originally bought from them.[27] This limits the individual's rights by restricting to whom they may sell their housing.[28] Secondly, danwei may also prohibit employees who have purchased danwei housing from re-selling it before a certain number of years, in some cases five or more.[29] This effectively ties employees who have purchased danwei housing to their work units for this period of time. Interviews reflect the widespread attitude that one should only purchase danwei housing if one is committed to remaining with one's unit for a long time – if not for life. Some people even spoke in terms of passing their danwei housing onto their children, as the transfer of housing through inheritance and family division seemed more secure than commercial sales.[30]

Thirdly, danwei have further restricted the rights of individual owners to profit from their property, either through sales or rental, a right that was in some cases written into the sale contracts between danwei and employees.[31] State units could claim a portion of, and in some cases the total, capital gains from the re-sale of danwei housing by employees. State units justified this practice by arguing that danwei housing is publicly subsidized, so individuals cannot legitimately claim the full capital gains from this property. The fact that employees most often purchased danwei housing at a subsidized price confirms this logic.[32] However, the difficulty of determining precisely the extent of public housing subsidies, and the further inability of individual home buyers to have any precise knowledge or say in this determination, provides the basis for broad discretion on the part of danwei in limiting individual profits from home ownership.[33] The state, furthermore, has exercised little, if any, oversight over the terms and conditions set by state units in their sale of housing to their own employees, giving units clear autonomy in this process.

Danwei also constrain individual property rights by disqualifying employees who re-sell their danwei housing from ever again being eligible for danwei housing.[34] Employees who re-sell their purchased danwei housing may thus forfeit the chance of ever again being able to purchase danwei housing. Thus, despite the claim that individuals who purchase housing from their danwei are the true owners, and the fact that they are issued an ownership 'certificate' which formally states their ownership rights, private property rights are seriously restricted.

The privatization strategies that dominated during much of the 1980s and 1990s thus failed in important ways to obtain the substantive goals of housing reforms. Housing privatization in many ways was more nominal than real. The private property rights of individual owners were significantly restricted. And state units retained significant rights over housing they nominally 'sold' to their employees. Danwei maintained significant leverage over their employees through their control over the terms and conditions of housing sales. Through their ability to enforce savings programs, and their control over these large sums, bosses even gained new forms of financial leverage over their employees.

9. Commercial Housing and Housing Development Corporations

The most recent effort to tackle the failure of earlier housing privatization efforts has been the state's push for the expansion of commercial housing financed and developed by independent housing and real estate development companies (Wu, 1996; Zhou and Logan, 1996; Wang and Murie, 1996). The expectation has been that the expansion of commercial housing would under-cut the role of danwei in the production, consumption, and allocation of urban housing. Urban residents would be able to purchase directly from commercial markets without having to go through their work units or to rely on the latter for financing (Cai, Yutian, 1990). These market-based companies were ex-pected to be comprehensively involved in the development, financing, con-struction, and distribution of urban housing through market channels.[35]

Housing development corporations first emerged in the early 1980s. Origi-nally, many of these were operated by or closely tied to municipalities and other state agencies (Yeh and Wu, 1995; Wu, 1996). However, over time more independent housing and real estate development companies have prolifer-ated and the number and size of such companies has grown rapidly. Shenyang had 98 housing development corporations by the late 1980s (Tolley, 1991, p. 71). Hangzhou had 19 in the early 1990s (Yang and Wang, 1992, p. 106). Nation-wide, by 1992 China had more than 3700 real estate and housing de-velopment companies (Tong and Hays, 1996, p. 644). Some of these are ex-tremely large companies. In 1998 the China Resources Beijing Land Corpora-tion – one of the largest, built more than 3 million sq. m of housing in Beijing.[36] And there are quite a few that are national-level companies operating across a range of cities.[37]

The push for commercial housing has been accompanied by banking and financial reforms that seek to expand mortgage lending to individual consum-ers.[38] Without the ability to obtain personal bank financing individuals would remain dependent on their employers for subsidies and financing, undercut-ting the goal of freeing labor from their work units. Consequently, the state has been pushing banking and financial reforms throughout the mid to late 1990s that seek to increase the availability of bank credit for individual home mort-gages. Banks have been pushed to increase their lending for personal home mortgages, to extend the repayment periods to 10–20 years, to provide loans that cover at least 70% of total housing costs, and to improve personal mort-gage financing in other ways.[39] Quotas have been set for state banks and mu-nicipalities to force them to increase their mortgage lending to individuals. The city of Shanghai set a target that aimed to increase individual home mort-gages four- to fivefold between 1995 and 1996, from 100 to 500 million yuan.[40] The People's Bank of China announced that it was setting aside $12 billion for individual home mortgages in 1998 – 10 times the amount spent on such loans in 1997. The Agricultural Bank similarly announced an ambitious target – making 20 billion yuan available for real estate loans, half of which would be channeled into individual home mortgages.[41]

The emergence and expansion of commercial housing appears to offer a significant break in China's traditional system of urban housing production and allocation. Commercial housing developed by independent firms potentially pushes state units out of the direct development, financing, and construction of urban housing. Instead of housing investment and development being channeled through individual state units, it would be channeled to profit-oriented corporations through commercial bank loans. Individual consumers in turn could also obtain loans directly from banks for housing purchasing. This scheme offers the potential of cutting state units out of housing production and distribution and increasing direct purchases of commercial housing by individual consumers with the support of bank mortgages. Table 8.7 shows that individual purchase a significant portion of total commercial housing.

As Table 8.7 indicates, in some cities and provinces more than half of all commercially developed housing was sold directly to individuals.

Despite expectations, commercial housing has not brought about the radical change initially anticipated, and this latest approach to housing privatization continues to face significant obstacles. State work units continue to maintain a central position in the financing, consumption, and allocation of urban housing. And in some ways the commercialization of housing has strengthened their position vis-à-vis both the state and the private sector.

First, not surprisingly given their increasingly independent profit-making activities and large extra-budgetary revenues, state entities have emerged as key investors in commercial housing. Real estate and housing development corporations have relied heavily on capital from state enterprises and units to finance their investments (Yang and Wang, 1992, p. 48). The failure of banking reforms to significantly increase mortgage lending to individuals has reinforced the role of institutional investors in this market. In 1997 total bank loans for land and housing development were reported to have totaled only $1.2 billion, far from the large sums set as targets.[42] And while foreign investment in commercial housing has increased significantly in some coastal areas, in 1996 it still represented only 5% of total housing investments nation-wide.[43] As a consequence, state units continue to be the primary investors in urban housing. This trend has even been evident in Shanghai, where state units traditionally accounted for a comparatively small percentage of total housing. While investment by state units accounted for 55% of total housing investment there in 1980, this had increased to 86% in 1990 (Zhou and Logan, 1996, p. 415).

Secondly, state units continue to be key consumers of urban housing, including commercial housing. While there has been an increase in direct purchases of housing by individuals, the largest proportion of commercial housing is still purchased by state units, not individuals or the state. Nation-wide in 1990 individuals purchased 28.7% of total commercial housing, while more than 70% was purchased by units and local governments. Furthermore, the

Table 8.7   *The sale of commercial housing to individuals in provinces and major cities in China, 1990 and 1992*

Provinces (1990)	Percentage of total sold to individuals	Major Cities (1992)	Percentage of total sold to individuals
Beijing	0.6	Beijing	5.9
Tianjin	10.1	Tianjin	18.9
Hebei	23.4	Shanghai	22.3
Shanxi	41.7	Shengyang	12.4
Inner Mongolia	16.8	Dalian	20.8
Liaoning	11.3	Changchun	13.6
Jilin	11.9	Ha'erbin	18.5
Heilongjiang	22.6	Nanjing	5.6
Shanghai	11.4	Ningbo	41.4
Jiangsu	26.4	Xiamen	55.3
Zhejiang	49.4	Qingdao	18.8
Anhui	20.5	Wuhan	16.5
Fujian	61.6	Guangzhou	55.4
Jiangxi	34.4	Shenzhen	36.5
Shandong	10.0	Chengdu	10.2
Henan	36.1	Chongqin	21.4
Hubei	13.5	Xi'an	19.8
Hunan	40.0		
Guangdong	57.6		
Guangxi	13.4		
Hainan	53.4		
Sichuan	19.6		

Table 8.7 (contd.)

Provinces (1990)	Percentage of total sold to individuals	Major Cities (1992)	Percentage of total sold to individuals
Guizhou	18.3		
Yunnan	37.6		
Shaanxi	47.6		
Gansu	12.0		
Quinghai	8.4		
Ningxia	10.0		
Xinjiang	7.6		
National total	28.7	National total	38.2

Source: Wu (1996, p. 1614).

trend in the 1990s pointed to an increase in danwei consumption of commercial housing. In Shanghai – where state units traditionally assumed a comparatively more marginal role – state units purchased 57.28% of all commercial housing units sold from 1980 to 1988. By 1990 this had increased to 85.4% (Wu, 1996, p. 1613). A similar situation has been evident in other cities – even those that are official housing reform sites.

Thirdly, danwei continue to play a key role in the allocation and distribution of housing through the provision of subsidies to employees. The majority of urban workers rely on their work units for subsidies in order to be able to purchase commercial housing, while only a very small proportion of housing is sold directly to individuals at full market prices (Wang and Murie, 1996; Zhou and Logan, 1996). At least three prices for commercial housing have operated in China's urban housing market; the government discounted price; the standard price; and the full market price.[44] The largest proportion of new urban housing is sold to work units at the standard discount price, with small proportions being sold directly to individuals and foreigners at the full market price. Because of continuing low wages and the difficulty of obtaining personal mortgages urban workers have difficulty even buying housing at the government discounted price without additional subsidies from their work units. In Shanghai in 1990, for instance, only 10% of all commercial housing sold in Shanghai in 1990 was sold directly to individuals at discounted prices, and a mere 5.2% was sold to individuals at the full market price (Wu, 1996, p. 1613). The president of the Yantai Real Estate Management Bureau estimated that only 3% of the total sales of housing built by the Yantai City Housing Development Corporation in 1993 was sold directly to individuals at the full price, with the rest being sold to state units and individuals at various subsidized prices.[45] As a consequence of the continuing role of work units in subsidizing employee housing and increases in housing costs, housing subsidies provided by urban work units to their workers have increased over the post-Mao period. While total annual housing subsidies were 4.715 billion yuan in 1978, these increased to 58.37 billion yuan in 1988, representing an average increase from 49.64 yuan per employee in 1978 in 1988.[46]

The danwei's dominant role in financing and allocating housing has been reenforced by continuing attitudes of distrust toward individual consumers and the continuing practice of privileging institutional over individual actors. Anecdotal evidence suggests that engrained attitudes and habit have been important factors explaining this.[47] Bank employees and other financial staff exhibit attitudes of distrust towards individual clients, which appears to have been an important factor blocking increased bank lending for private mortgages. Financial services appear to be enjoyed by a very small number of extremely wealthy individuals. Most people have not been given rights in the financial system and therefore also lack full legal responsibility. These attitudes are re-enforced by the fear on the part of lending institutions that they will have little recourse if an individual fails to pay back his or her loan, as individuals are not given full rights or accountability.[48] As a result, financial assistance for housing development and purchases continues to be primarily channeled through enterprises and institutions rather than to individuals, giving the former continued dominance in this market.

10. Conclusion

For more than two decades the Chinese government has pursued urban housing reforms which have aimed, among other things, to privatize the rights and costs of this resource by shifting ownership and control from state units to individuals. The traditional Maoist housing system which gave a central role in the production, consumption, and allocation of housing to state units has been judged to be inappropriate for the new market economy. It inhibited labor mobility by making workers dependent on their workplace for housing and was inappropriate because it continued to treat housing as an employment benefit rather than a good for which users should pay the real costs. For more than two decades the state adopted a variety of privatization strategies, including direct sales of new housing, subsidized sales of existing danwei housing, and most recently the commercialization of housing through the enhanced role of independent for-profit housing development companies.

Despite important changes that have taken place in China's housing industry, housing privatization has been blocked and derailed in its core goal of shifting control, rights, responsibilities, and ownership from state units to individuals. Despite the significant commercialization of the housing market, state units continue to have a dominant role in the financing, production, consumption, and distribution of urban housing. Through the use of their expanding extra-budgetary revenue, state units are critical to the financing of urban housing. The failure of banking and finance reforms, furthermore, has prevented average workers from being able to buy housing without subsidies provided by their employers. Institutions, not individuals, continue to be privileged in the financial and economic system. As a result, state units have maintained critical property rights over urban housing, even housing that has nominally been privatized.

Two broad explanatory factors are explored here. The first is the fact that China's market reforms have not undercut the traditional pattern of the Maoist era that located resources, staff, capital, privileges, and power in the hands of institutional actors, particularly state work units. China's market reforms and extensive commercialization of the economy have not undercut this pattern, as illustrated by housing reforms. The former power and privileges of institutional actors in terms of resources, staff, capital, and property rights within the housing sector have not been significantly undermined by commercialization. In fact, China's market reforms have been characterized by the dominance of institutions as market actors, and have in many ways enhanced the concentration of resources and power of institutions. Their growing extra-budgetary revenue has allowed state units to build more housing – just as the state has been seeking to privatize this market.

The second explanation is that the state has relied heavily on the very institution that has been a primary target of housing privatization – the state work unit – to implement the reform. In line with its former role, danwei have continued to be principal agents of the state and responsible for implementing its policies. This, however, has allowed them to interpret policies in ways that serve their own interests, ultimately allowing them to obstruct and derail the policy's goals. Their discretion in implementing housing policies has allowed danwei to effectively derail some of their ultimate goals – such as expanding individual ownership and property rights. Danwei have retained significant property rights over nominally 'privatized' housing. And in other ways, housing privatization has even intensified the leverage enjoyed by bosses over their employees, allowing them to retain large portions of employee compensation hostage to the 'purchase' of danwei housing under conditions determined by the unit.

Notes

1. The arguments presented here draw on the author's fieldwork and interviews in China conducted over a period of 31 months between 1986 and 1996, from July 1986 to August 1988, July to September 1993, and May to August 1996. Fifty-seven interviews were conducted from 1986 to 1988 with members of state units ranging from state enterprises, schools, research institutes, hospitals, government bureaus, publishing houses, and other public institutions, the China Youth League, to name the principal categories. Twenty-five interviews were conducted with members and staff of six state-owned enterprises and five semi-public firms. In 1996 24 interviews were conducted with members and staff of eight state units and three subsidiary firms operated by state units. Informants included unit managers, administrators, technical staff, administrative staff, workers, researchers, students, as well as members and staff of local party and government offices.

2. The Soviet Union, for instance, had a 'building right' law that protected private property, and capital, materials and labor were more easily obtained by private builders than in China. See Chao (1966, pp. 390–91).

3. For a general discussion of the danwei's role in urban housing see Whyte and Parish (1984) and Wu (1996).

4. Author's PRC interviews, 1993 and 1996.

5. In the early 1960s the central government adopted a number of policies aimed at expanding municipal sources of housing revenue. In 1962 cities were allowed to raise their own revenue for urban development, including housing, through new commercial and industrial taxes. In 1963 government policy further expanded the sources for city revenue, including a public facility tax, property tax, and a local tax on industrial and commercial activities. See CCP Central Committee Document No. 513 [1962], in Housing and Property Management Department of Xian (ed.) (1984), *Collection of Documents on Housing and Property Management in Xian*, Vol. 2, from Wang (1995, p. 67).

6. Municipalities derived some income from the enterprises they directly managed, but typically little of this was left over to pay for housing maintenance and repair, let alone construction of new housing. See Wu (1996, p. 1606).

7. According to a survey conducted in 1956, of 166 cities surveyed only 83 had municipal housing bureaux. See Wang (1995, p. 63).

8. The World Bank, *Shanghai: Sector Memorandum*, p. 50. Cited in Zhang Jun, *Urban Construction Reconsidered*, p. 8.

9. Barry Naughton has calculated that the total proportion of permanent state workers who left their job in 1978 as a result of individual or managerial choice was less than one-tenth of 1%. See Naughton, 'The economic foundations of a unique institution', p. 173.

10. These lobbying tactics sometimes get extremely personal and hostile, with employees badgering their superiors in their homes. Author's PRC interviews, 1986–88, 1993, and 1996. An indication that this was already the case in the 1950s is suggested by the fact that urban unrest in 1956 and 1957 which was centered on housing conditions targeted factory managers as well as municipal governments. See Howe (1968, p. 94).

11. In 1985 the average monthly rent per square meter was 0.13 yuan (about US$0.02). The typical apartment housing for persons was only 3.2 yuan (US$0.40) in monthly rent, such that average rent consumed only 0.81% of the urban resident's monthly income. See Tong and Hays (1996, p. 638).

12. The average price per square meter of residential housing in the early 1980s was 120–150 yuan, making the price of a middle-sized apartment on 60 sq. m about 9000 yuan, about 10–20 times the average yearly salary. Not surprisingly, a significant number of the individuals who

purchased housing in these early reforms had overseas relatives who helped subsidize their purchase. See Wang and Murie (1996, p. 22).

13. This was despite the fact that 65% of the city's entire housing stock was incorporated into the reform experiments. A total of 1646 housing units were sold in Yantai from August 1987 to February 1989 including 584 new ones and 1062 old ones. See Tolley (1991, p. 64).

14. Shenyang is also reported to have only privatized about 10% of its new housing during the housing reforms of the 1980s, less than 1% of its total municipal housing stock. See Tolley (1991, p. 64).

15. A World Bank study also found that while in 1979 over 90% of total housing investment was financed by the central government, by 1988 this had dropped to 16%, while local governments contributed another 6%. See World Bank (1992).

16. Wang Yuqun, 'Woguo chengzhen zhufang fuli guimode cesuan ji qi yiyi', cited in Yang and Wang (1992, p. 4).

17. Word Bank (1992).

18. The Zhongshan Sugar Refinery, for example, a highly successful state enterprise, is reported to have paid for 90% of its housing costs from 1985 to 1993 from retained profits. Zhou and Logan (1996, p. 413).

19. Reportedly, a relatively large proportion of this was private ownership of old-style single unit housing, not new housing, which indicates that new housing is nearly all unit-owned. Yu (1992, p. 324).

20. One enterprise in Zhongshan was reported to have spent 30 million yuan in the construction of 800 apartments from 1985 to 1993. See Zhou and Logan (1996, p. 413).

21. Zhou and Logan (1996, p. 402).

22. For a more general discussion of this dilemma, see Francis (1996a).

23. Author's PRC interviews, 1993 and 1996.

24. Author's PRC interviews, 1996 and 1996.

25. Work units in Shanghai were reported to have distributed coupons at a rate of 23.5% of the base salary in the late 1980s. See 'Reform goal: ending subsidies: some raise roof as China raises rents for housing', *Los Angeles Times*, 8 December 1987, Part I, p. 1.

26. Interviews with company managers of university-affiliated companies in Beijing suggested that in practice the concept of housing funds being in individual employee accounts was treated loosely by employers. While employees' individual accounts were nominally accumulating finds, companies in the meantime hade access to these funds. Author's PRC interviews, 1993 and 1996.

27. Danwei are interested in this right in order to preserve the integrity of their housing stock, to reserve it for their own employees, to control who resides within their communities, as well as for financial gain.

28. Author's PRC interviews, 1993 and 1996.

29. Author's PRC interviews, 1993 and 1996. For a discussion of this see also 'Survey of China', *Financial Times*, 18 November 1993, p. 11.

30. Author's PRC interviews, 1993 and 1996.

31. Author's PRC interviews, 1993 and 1996. For press accounts of such practices see 'Reforms to bite H-share profits', *South China Morning Post*, 6 May 1996.

32. Author's PRC interviews, 1993 and 1996.

33. For a more general discussion of conflicts over property rights see Francis, 'Bargained prop-

erty rights in China's transition'.

34. 'Survey of China', *Financial Times*, 18 November 1993, p. 11.

35. Wang and Murie (1996).

36. 'Issue get $1.1 billion for Beijing Land', *SCMP*, 26 March 1998.

37. The World Development Corporation, one such company, spent $1.5 billion in the construction of over 16 million sq. ft. of housing in several Chinese cities in 1998.

38. For press accounts of the financial and housing reforms on the late 1990s see 'Housing reform move up a gear', *SCMP*, 29 March 1996; 'Home Economics; private housing program in China', *The Economist*, 18 April 1998, No. 8064, p. 36; 'Reform to spark housing boom', *SCMP*, 8 June 1998; 'China poised for residential mortgage loans', *China Daily*, 15 June 1998; 'The great hope: China is bent on housing reforms but property will not become engine of growth soon', *Asiaweek*, 24 July 1998; 'Jam today? Housing finance in China', *The Economist*, 30 May 1998, No. 8070, p. 71.

39. Commercial banks were called on in the mid and late 1990s to put aside 15% of their total annual loans for private loans. 'The Chinese dream: Beijing's plan to let citizens own their own homes could transform the Middle Kingdom's landscape', *Time International*, 6 April 1998, Vol. 150, No. 32, p. 22, Private home mortgages were supposed to cover 70% of the purchase cost and to be offered on a 20-year repayment schedule. See 'The great hope', *Asiaweek*, 24 July 1998.

40. 'Shanghai mortgage volume rises', *SCMP*, 16 October 1996, p. 5.

41. 'China poised for residential mortgage loans', *China Daily*, 15 July 1998

42. 'Jam today? Housing finance in China', *The Economist*, 30 May 1998, p. 71.

43. In coastal areas foreign investment is put at 25–55% of total housing investments. However, foreign housing investment has been largely restricted to joint ventures with government agencies and sate work units. See Zhou and Logan (1996, p. 415).

44. In 1992 'The Temporary Measure for Pricing Commodities Housing', a government document jointly issued by the Ministry of Commodity Pricing, the Ministry of Construction, and the Ministry of Finance, set out the guidelines for determining housing prices. Cited in Zhou and Logan (1996, p. 410).

45. 'Survey of China', *Financial Times*, 18 November 1993, p. 11.

46. *Zhufang gaige*, p 60.

47. According to Ma Liming, the chief manager of housing and building credit department of the China Construction Bank, 'some Chinese do not have a sense of how they should be using (home mortgage) loans'. According to the manager of the Qianmen branch of the Construction Bank of Chian only the wealthiest of individuals utilize his bank's financial services, estimating that by the end of 1998 his bank had had financial dealings with only four to five individual customers. See 'China poised for residential mortgage loans', *China Daily*, 15 June 1998.

48. According to the manager of the Qianmen branch of the Construction Bank of China mentioned above, is an individual fails to pay back their loan there is little the bank can do, and they cannot confiscate the individual's home. 'Car credit facing uphill battle in China', *Xinhua News Agency*, No. 25, 1998.

References

Blecher, Marc (1991), 'Development State, Entrepreneurial State: The Political Economy of Socialist Reform in Xinju Municipality and Guanghan County', in Gordon White (ed.), *The Chinese State in the Era of Economic Reform: The Road to Crisis*, London: Macmillan.

Cai, Yunlong (1990), 'Land Use and Management in PR China', *Land Use Policy* (October), 337–50.

Cai, Yutian (ed.) (1990), *Fangdi chan shichang*, Shanghai: The Shanghai Social Sciences Publishing House.

Chao, Kang (1966), 'Industrialization and Urban Housing in Communist China', *Journal of Asian Studies*, **25** (3), 381–96.

Duckett, Jane (1996), 'The Emergence of the Entrepreneurial State in Contemporary China', *The Pacific Review*, **9** (2), 180–98.

Francis, Corinna-Barbara (1996a), 'Reproduction of Danwei Institutional Features in the Context of China's Market Economy: The Case of Haidian District's High-Tech Sector', *The China Quarterly*, **147** (September), 839–59.

Francis, Corinna-Barbara (1996b), 'Commercialization without Privatization: Government Spin-offs in China's High-Tech Sector', in Judith Sedaitis (ed.), *Commercializing High Technology: East and West*, Stanford, CA: Center for International Security and Arms Control, Stanford University, 259–84.

Francis, Corinna-Barbara (1999), 'Bargained Property Rights in China's Transition to a Market Economy: The Case of the High-Technology Sector', in Andrew Walder and Jean Oi (eds), *Property Rights and Economic Reform in China*, Stanford, CA: Stanford University Press.

Howe, Christopher (1968), 'The Supply and Administration of Urban Housing in Mainland China: The Case of Shanghai', *The China Quarterly*, **33** (January–March), 73–97.

Institute of Finance and Trade Economics and the Chinese Academy of Social Sciences (PRC) and Institute of Public Administration New York (USA) (1992), *Zhongguo Chengshi Tudi Shiyong yu Guanli* (Urban land use and management in China), Beijing: Science of Economics Publishing Ltd.

Kirkby, Richard (1990) 'China', in Kosta Mathey (ed.), *Housing Policies in the Socialist Third World*, New York: Mansell Publishing Ltd., 289–312.

Lam, Alexa C. (1996), 'Building a New Foundation: Little by little, Beijing is Shrugging off its Housing Obligations', *The China Business Review* (January–February).

Lee, Yok-Shiu F. (1988), 'The Urban Problem in China', *The China Quarterly*, **115**, 387–407

Lim, Gill-Chin and Man-Hyung Lee (1993), 'Housing Consumption in Urban China', *Journal of Real Estate Finance and Economics*, **6**, 89–102.

Liu, Jianjun (1988), 'The Privatization of Urban Housing', *Beijing Review* (14–20 November), 18–20.

Ma, Laurence J.C. (1981), 'Urban Housing Supply in the People's Republic of China', in Laurence J.C. Ma and Edward H. Hanten, *Urban Development in Modern China*, Boulder, Co.: Westview Press, 222–59.

Pudney, Stephen and Limin Wang (1995), 'Housing Reform in Urban China: Efficiency, Distribution and the Implication for Social Security', *Economics*, **62**, 141–59.

State Statistical Bureau (1997), *China Statistical Yearbook 1997*, Beijing: China Statistical Publishing House.

Tolley, George S. (1991), 'Urban Housing Reform in China, An Economic Analysis', *World Bank Discussion Papers*, No. 123, World Bank, Washington, DC.

Tong, Zhong Yi and R. Allen Hays (1996), 'The Transformation of The Urban Housing System in China', *Urban Affairs Review*, **31** (5), (May), 625–58.

Wang, Ya Ping (1995), 'Public Sector Housing in Urban China 1949–1988: The Case of Xian', *Housing Studies*, **10** (1), 57–82.

Wang, Ya Ping and Alan Murie (1996), 'The Process of Commercialisation of Urban Housing in China', *Urban Studies*, **33** (6), (June), 971–90.

Whyte, Martin King and William L. Parish (1984), *Urban Life in Contemporary China*, Chicago and London: The University of Chicago Press.

World Bank (1992) *China: Implementation Options for Urban Housing Reform*, Washington, DC: World Bank.

Wu, Fulong (1996), 'Changes in the Structure of Public Housing Provision in Urban China', *Urban Studies*, **33** (9), 1601–1627.

Yang, Lu and YuKun Wang (1992), *Zhu fang gaige: Lilun de fan si yu xianshi de xuanze* (Housing reform: the reflection of the theory and the choice of the reality),

Tianjin: Tianjin People's Publishing Ltd.

Yeh, Gar-On and Fulong Wu (1995), 'Internal Structure of Chinese Cities in the Midst of Economic Reform', *Urban Geography*, **16** (6), 521–554.

Yeh, Anthony Gar-on and Fulong Wu (1996), 'The New Land Development Process and Urban Development in Chinese Cities', *International Journal of Urban and Regional Research*, **20** (2), 330–53.

Yu Xuelong (ed.) (1992), *Zhufang gaige yu fanggai jinrong* (Housing reform and finances of housing reforms), Beijing: Knowledge Publishers.

Zhang, Xing Quan (1998), *Privatisation: A Study of Housing Policy in Urban China*, New York: Nova Science Publishers, Inc.

Zhang, Z. [1988] (1993), 'An Overview of Housing Reform', translated and reprinted in *Chinese Law and Government*, **26** (1), 31–53.

Zhou, Min and John R. Logan (1996), 'Market Transition and the Commodification of Housing in Urban China', *International Journal of Urban and Regional Research*, 20 September (3), 400–421.

9. Provision of Social Benefits by Russian Enterprises: Managers' Behavior and Motivations

Elena Vinogradova

1. Introduction

Within the framework of a centrally planned economy Russian enterprises were important providers of various kinds of social benefits to both their employees and members of relevant local communities. In addition to mandatory benefits, i.e. sick pay, maternity allowances, paid vacation, pre-dismissal allowances, etc., they provided a wide range of services based on social infrastructure they had on the books as well as a number of monetary benefits. By the beginning of the reforms the enterprise infrastructure included all types of social assets, providing social services to more than half of Russian employees. More than 30 million people occupied lodging that was on the books and maintained by enterprises, enterprise medical centers and hospitals provided healthcare services to about 32 million, and 5 million children attended enterprise kindergartens (Leksin and Shvetsov, 1999, p. 228). In recent years enterprises in Russia, as in other post-socialist countries,[1] have cut a number of social functions they had performed under the centrally-planned economy. Simultaneously, though slowly and unevenly, new models of social assistance to employees, revision and transformation of traditional patterns, are emerging.

On one level, the substantial decline in enterprises' social provision was obviously due to the general economic situation of Russian enterprises, influenced by the current economic crises as well as by financial constraints created by stabilization policies. But on another level, it was a desired outcome of the policies aimed at the municipalization of social assets of privatized enterprises, which was considered to be one of the most important institutional transformations in the social sector.

It should be noted that the transfer of social assets to municipalities or their retention on enterprise books has never been a result of a voluntary decision by either party. Transfer of such assets is an indispensable condition of enterprises' privatization. With rare exceptions social assets, which were publicly owned in the Soviet period (as were the enterprises themselves), may not be retained as the property of privatized enterprises. According to legislation, during an enterprise's privatization, its social assets must be transferred to the municipality and become its property. In some special cases, depending on the asset and decision of the municipality, assets may be privatized separately. For example, recreation centers may become simply private organizations, purchased by some company or individual.

The policy of municipalization of enterprise social assets was adopted to meet a number of pressing social and economic objectives. It aimed, in the first place, at relieving enterprises of the financial burden associated with social asset maintenance. This would help cut costs which could lead to higher profits, and in some cases provide opportunities for lower product prices and greater competitiveness of enterprises. The municipalization policy was dictated by social considerations, too. As is known, the enterprise affiliation of the bulk of social assets produced a huge differentiation in access to social goods, producing territorial, sectoral and status differentials in social services consumption. The transfer of enterprise social assets to municipalities was expected to alleviate this inequality in the interests of social justice. Asset municipalization also seems reasonable for optimizing management technologies: execution of the relevant social functions fits the activities profile of city administration much more than of enterprise management.

In 1993–95 the transfer of enterprises' social assets progressed quite rapidly, and a large part of them were divested. In 1995 the process slowed down, as the abilities of local governments to accept and continue maintaining these assets had reached the limit. Actually Russian industrial enterprises are still playing quite an important role in maintaining them. According to some estimations, in 1998 enterprises were financing and managing about 20% of previously maintained housing stock and healthcare institutions, about 25% of children's vacation camps, 30–40% of different types of recreation and rehabilitation centers, etc. (Leksin and Shvetsov, 1999, p. 42). As the results of a survey carried out by the Higher School of Economics show, about one-fourth of enterprises that have transferred their social assets to the balance sheets of local governments continued to bear costs for their maintenance. According to the same source, about half of enterprises are still implementing the transfer of social assets, and to all appearances this process will continue for several more years (Survey, 1999).

There is much differentiation among regions and cities, and in some of them the percent of enterprises bearing such costs remains very high. Additionally in many cases, behind the formal transfer of social assets to municipalities the former situation remains: voluntarily or involuntarily the enterprises continue financing the social infrastructure. Special contracts and 'renting' of facilities are the legal forms of this kind of relationship between the municipalities and enterprises.

Social assets divestiture has put forward a lot questions, for example: what is the impact of the transfer of enterprise social assets on the enterprise's economic situation and the related non-monetary benefits of the employees? Since the enterprises have been partially relieved of the burden of social assets financing, are they willing and able:

- to increase the wages and salaries of their employees in order to compensate for a possible loss of previous social benefits?
- to keep some traditional forms of social assistance (not related to social infrastructure) and develop new kinds of benefits, more adequate to the changing environment, like participating in (or creating their own) pension funds, promoting medical insurance for their employees in addition to that required by Russian legislation?
- to create new social infrastructure of their own?
- What is the enterprise's position concerning social assets, providing relevant benefits to employees, their families, and the local population under the current or revised legislative conditions? And finally, are any amendments of the current legislation needed to adjust the policies to the realities?

Unfortunately there is no regular statistical data on the relevant issues, and special surveys devoted to the problem are quite scarce. The most comprehensive information available was collected through a survey conducted by the author under the sponsorship of the EU's TACIS (Technical Assistance to the Commonwealth of Independent States) Project in May–June, 1998 at 92 enterprises based in five pilot cities of the project, namely, Volgograd (26), Astrakhan (20), Tula (19), Veliky Novgorod (13) and Rybinsk (14).[2] Since no radical developments in this field have taken place more recently, the survey data are still able to represent the main problems that have to be managed.

With regard to the survey objectives, included in the sample were enterprises disposing of social assets at the time of the survey as well as enterprises which had such assets within the past five years and then transferred them to municipalities. Those polled were enterprise directors or deputy directors in charge of social matters, in particular, of social assets management.

The collection and processing of data proceeded in three main dimensions. The first one deals with problems of enterprise social assets municipalization and with the socioeconomic implications of this process. The second is connected with maintenance problems related to social assets still on enterprise books. Also, the survey covered issues concerning the current and future status of all major types of enterprise social assets; the questionnaire offered to the respondents dealt with each one of them separately in the respective block: housing, health, childcare institutions, sports facilities, recreation centers, cultural institutions, urban economy. The third dimension of the survey concerned development of other forms of social assistance to employees, both the ones traditionally provided to them by Soviet enterprises and the new ones emerging in the new socioeconomic environments. Analysis of this information gives some idea of the current transformation of enterprise social concepts and performance and their prospects.

2. Municipalization's Social and Economic Results in Managers' Estimates

As noted earlier, the transfer of enterprises' social assets to municipalities was supposed to meet a number of economic and social objectives: to relieve enterprises of the financial burden associated with social asset maintenance, allowing them to become more profitable and competitive; to provide savings that could be channeled into raising wages and salaries in order to offset losses of benefits; to lessen differentiation in the distribution of social services among employees and local communities as well as among enterprises of different sizes and industries; and to free management from functions poorly suited to their technical expertise.

To what extent have these goals been achieved? What has the real impact of municipalization appeared to be at the enterprises, in particular, concerning changes in social benefits provision and remuneration? The survey made it possible to identify some enterprise managers' judgments of how the transfer of enterprise social assets to municipalities has influenced availability of social benefits and remuneration.

According to the data obtained, managers of enterprises that transferred social assets to the city sometimes pointed to a certain reduction in services availability for their employees, though this trend is not pronounced with respect to all types of services. The most negative implications were observed in housing which is, apparently, largely linked with the general severity of the housing problem in cities, including pilot cities of the Project. Nearly 45% of respondents pointed to the much poorer opportunities for their employees to solve their housing problems.

The smallest changes in social service accessibility for employees of enterprises that were former social asset owners, were observed following health asset municipalization (64% of respondents did not observe any changes, 36% pointed to just minor deterioration). In relation to other types of social services, the respondents' opinions are quite diverse, preventing any discernment of trends. But in any case, according to a sizable share of respondents (25–50%) social asset transfer to the local community had a negative effect on employees' possibilities to get the respective services (Table 9.1).

Table 9.1   Assessment of changes in accessibility of services for enterprise employees following social asset municipalization (as a percentage share of all respondents)

Estimate of change in service availability	Housing	Health	Kinder-gartens	Recreation	Sports	Culture
Reduced markedly	44	0	20	25	25	25
Reduced slightly	9	36	18	0	12	25
Remained intact	32	64	50	50	50	38
Hard to say	15	0	0	25	13	12

Were the enterprises willing and able to increase wages and other types of social benefits to compensate for the respective cuts in social services earlier provided to workers by the enterprise infrastructure? The survey showed that divestiture of social assets did not lead to any significant changes in remuneration levels at any of the enterprises included to the sample, and only about 20% managed to increase wages and benefits to a minor degree. While about 10% of respondents did not consider or set such objectives, the majority (more than 60%) of managers reported that they tried but failed to find resources for financing such increases.

Much the same picture was revealed in relation to social benefits, payments and other types of social assistance provided to employees. The saving of resources that were spent in the past on social asset maintenance was not accompanied by any significant increase in other forms of social provision to employees of any enterprise; 23% of enterprises somewhat expanded the scope of services; at 63% the managements failed to find opportunities for this; and at 11% this objective was not considered or set.

This statement is well correlated with the estimations of the general economic effect of social assets transfers. The survey outcome indicates that social asset divestiture did not have any marked effect on the financial state of the majority of enterprises: 23% of enterprises which divested some or other assets said that this was in no way beneficial, half of the respondents (50%) estimated the benefit as 'minor'. The managements of just 15% of surveyed enterprises measured the positive effect of this move as significant (see Table 9.2).[3]

Table 9.2   *Distribution of responses to the question: 'Did the enterprise really profit from social asset transfer?'*

Response versions	Positive responses as shares (in %) of all respondents
Benefited significantly	15
Gained a minor benefit	49
Did not benefit at all	23
Hard to say	11

There appear to be a number of reasons for the lack of tangible economic effects from social asset municipalization at the majority of enterprises. In some cases (about 30% of the sample) it can be explained by the fact that social asset maintenance costs accounted for a relatively minor share of aggregate enterprise costs.[4] At a number of enterprises it is linked also to the current procedure of enterprise asset maintenance cost compensation through tax breaks, soft credits and direct subsidies. Unfortunately, the survey generated only scarce information on this range of issues as the majority of managers preferred to avoid the response. Data were provided by some 30% of respon-

Table 9.3   *Shares of positive responses to the question: 'Was your enterprise granted subsidies, tax breaks?' (as a percentage share of all responses)*

Responses	Subsidies	Tax Breaks
Regional authorities	24	32
City authorities	20	32
Federal authorities	20	28

dents. As is evidenced by the data collected, compensation in the form of sub-sidies and tax breaks is rather common for the surveyed enterprises (see Table 9.3). Obviously, not all benefits and subsidies were directly targeted at social asset maintenance; as is seen from our earlier research, however, decisions on providing subsidies to some or other end are frequently conditioned, explicitly or implicitly, by the enterprise's possession of social assets.

3. Management and Funding of Enterprise Social Assets

In 1992–5, when the transfer of social assets was progressing quite rapidly, the municipal stock of these assets increased by an average of 65%, while in some cities it more than doubled. Initially it was supposed that this increase would be accompanied by a comparable increase of municipal budgets, as a part of financial resources which were previously used by enterprises would be trans-ferred to local tax payments. It was also supposed that another part of these financial resources would be used to increase wages and salaries of the em-ployees, so that they could afford the increasing prices of municipalized ser-vices.

But in many cases (and the survey results presented in this chapter also demonstrate this) it hasn't happened like that, and the capacities of local bud-gets to manage an increased bulk of social infrastructure were exhausted. Mu-nicipalities started to slow down the process, either refusing to accept the so-cial assets in an open way, or forcing the enterprises to continue in one way or another to finance the social infrastructure formally divested from them. So in this or that way the enterprises still keep on their books a substantial number of assets. As noted earlier, they are estimated to retain some 20% of housing stock, 25% of kindergartens and healthcare institutions, 30–40% of recreation and rehabilitation centers. What are the actual characteristics of the process and the managers' attitudes to the situation?

As is known, enterprises, like municipalities, incur the heaviest financial costs of maintaining social assets. The survey data make it possible to specify the distribution of this load among the respective service consumers and asset holding enterprises. The survey showed that tenants of residential buildings and dormitories mostly cover no more than a third of all costs involved. De-spite the institution of some or other forms of health service payment, the contribution of patients to funding health institutions is still meager. On the whole, all of the surveyed enterprises cover over half of the required costs of childcare institution maintenance, and in the majority of cases the enterprise share is as high as 70–90%. Consumers generally cover no more than half of the costs involved in maintaining sports facilities. Almost 90% of vacationers cover no more than half the costs of recreational center maintenance. About 80% of enterprises said that consumers of cultural institutions cover no more than half the costs of their maintenance. In over half of cases this contribution is insignificant, accounting for no more than 10%. The consumer contribution to funding community utilities is just as dismal.

The survey data make it possible also to specify the estimated employees–community ratio for enterprise services consumption. As we can see from the survey data, enterprises' provision of services to community members is rather common; yet the employee share of service consumers varies in relation to different types of services (Table 9.4).

Over 50% of those responding to the respective question said that, in their estimation, enterprise employees account for no more than half of tenants residing in enterprise houses; a similar picture is observed with respect to dormitories. Sports facilities owned by enterprises provide a great deal of services to the city population. Only 25% of respondents said that their employees account for over half of consumers of their sports facility services. Most often, employees of the asset holder account for less than half of consumers of the respective cultural institutions.

Judging from survey results, healthcare and recreational facilities are largely oriented at providing services to the enterprise employees. Based on estimates of 60% of the respective group of respondents, employees account for over half of patients. Patients not associated with the enterprise prevail at just 10% of surveyed enterprises. The asset-holder employee share of those staying at recreational centers is comparatively high. As follows from the data below, it accounts for 70–100% at 41% of enterprises. Yet another quarter of respondents estimated the share as lying within 50–70%.

Based on estimates of surveyed enterprise management, the majority of enterprises are incapable of funding social asset maintenance at a level sufficient for their regular functioning. Only 10% of housing owners said they had the capacity to incur such costs, as many with respect to cultural institutions, 16% of enterprises holding health institutions, 20% with community facilities, 24% with sports facilities, 28% with childcare institutions. The only exception are recreational centers, which are regularly financed by over two-thirds of their 'owners'.

The survey revealed that, given that the city population continues to make up a large share of service consumers (Table 9.4), and despite the institution or expansion of the payment principle with respect to the bulk of social service provision, enterprises' contributions to financing costs of asset maintenance remain prohibitively high (Table 9.5). The estimates of enterprises' capacities to secure financing at a level sufficient for adequate maintenance of assets are rather low.

Table 9.4   Distribution of responses to the question: 'Which share of enterprise social service consumers is made up by its employees?'

Responses	Residential buildings	Dormitories	Health institutions	Childcare institutions	Sports facilities	Recreational facilities	Cultural institutions
	Positive responses as shares (in %) of all respondents						
less than 10%	16	22	0	10	33	9	15
10%–30%	13	5	5	19	10	3	10
30%–50%	22	16	5	22	24	18	40
50%–70%	11	21	15	22	10	24	15
70%–99%	7	12	35	19	10	32	10
100%	0	0	10	0	5	9	5
This type of asset is unavailable	24	19	–	–	–	–	–
Hard to say	7	5	30	–	–	6	5

187

Table 9.5   *Distribution of responses to the question: 'Which part of enterprise social asset maintenance costs is covered by consumers of the respective services?'*

Responses	Housing	Health care	Child care	Sports	Recreation	Culture	Urban housing
				Positive responses as shares (in %) of all respondents			
less than 10%	37	26	23	57	30	63	44
10%–30%	31	31	57	10	45	5	26
30%–50%	14	5	6	14	12	10	7
50%–70%	0	0	0	5	3	0	8
70%–99%	2	0	0	0	0	0	0
100%	0	0	0	0	6	5	0
Hard to say	16	36	13	14	3	15	15

The survey made it possible to identify management opinions on social sector prospects, on the methods of problem solution most acceptable for enterprises. To reveal the most general attitudes, the respondents were asked about their opinion as to who is primarily bearing the actual responsibility for the state of the social sphere in the city, as well as who should undertake it in the future. As shown by the data in Table 9.6, while naturally giving priority to city authorities, the enterprises' managers consider that they also should share responsibility for the state of the social sphere in the city in the future.

Table 9.6   *Opinions of the actual distribution of responsibility for the state of the social sphere in the city currently and in the future*

Subjects of social responsibility	Currently	In the future
Regional authorities	23	37
City authorities	54	67
City authorities and enterprises	23	21
Enterprises	5	2
Other	1	1
Difficult to answer	13	3

The analysis and interpretation of survey results show that managers' estimates of their social asset funding capacity are deeply affected by the current economic and, most importantly, legal conditions. Since current legislation requires enterprises to divest or transfer their social assets, and the only question is one of timing, managers are not willing to invest in those assets which they cannot keep. As was shown above, for all the differences in estimates and opinions on the part of individual enterprises and cities, the main problem created by the legal and institutional framework of asset municipalization is the reluctance of enterprise managements to carry 'worthless' costs. This is the situation least acceptable to them. The lack of positive incentives for maintaining social assets may sometimes breed lower estimates of capacity to fund. *The survey also showed that the majority of managers do, in principle, consider it possible or reasonable to maintain social assets, given the proper conditions. At the same time, the survey-generated results do not validate the widespread view that enterprise managers go on claiming their traditional leading role in social sector.*

Even those enterprises with some capability to provide funding for social facilities are not interested in investing in projects which they are not going to keep, or in properly maintaining facilities that sooner or later have to be transferred to municipal authorities. In this situation they may choose the following strategies:

1. they may try to pressure local authorities in order to make them finally accept from the enterprise lodging, kindergartens or whatever. In the past three years there has been a lot of evidence of difficult conflicts, cases where enterprises applied to courts to make local authorities accept the social assets;
2. they may underinvest in social infrastructure, and these cases are quite common;
3. finally, they may even stop funding social assets, without waiting for the local authorities to accept them. And such cases also exist.

It makes the situation quite difficult and even dangerous in many cases. The facilities which are not funded properly or at all are simply subject to physical degradation. Many of them no longer meet technical and safety requirements. This situation is extremely dangerous in the case of urban utilities (heating, electrical and water supply, public city transportation, etc.), especially taking into consideration the severe Russian climate. There are also serious problems connected with maintenance of housing, of kindergarten buildings, healthcare institutions, stadiums and cultural centers which are becoming places which it is not really safe to attend.

As the number of conflicts between enterprises and municipalities rises, and the municipalization process continues to slow down, it becomes increasingly clear that the problem can not be resolved within the existing legislative and organizational framework. The scale of the problem, its potential economic, political and social consequences, are so substantial that the solution can not be postponed. Some new approaches should be found to deal with the problem.

It is clear that since the municipal administrations do not create financial resources themselves, the increase of their financing capacities is mainly linked with businesses and enterprises. The most obvious way to increase these capacities is to increase the amount of enterprise taxes, either by increasing the rates of existing local taxes, or by imposing new ones. (In fact there used to exist a number of local taxes which were eliminated, and some of the experts propose returning to this practice.) Projects of this sort are now under discussion and should be studied quite seriously. But there are arguments which show that under the current conditions possibilities of this sort would be quite limited. Many companies are not able or pretend to be unable to pay the existing taxes.

Are there any other ways to make the enterprises more involved in maintaining the social sphere, more interested, more responsible? What is the most efficient way to combine the efforts of the local authorities and enterprises?

In the course of the survey the respondents were requested to evaluate the acceptability of a number of alternative solutions relating to the social assets they still keep on their books, taking into account the actual conditions. At the same time, respondents were also asked to describe their behavior in other, hypothetical environments assuming statutory possibilities for enterprises to keep social assets they used to own. The survey showed that enterprise managers who still have social assets insist on the decisive and immediate municipalization of these assets to a rather limited extent. Most pressing seems to be municipalization of housing: the majority of managers (about 70%) are for a complete transfer of housing to municipalities. About half of respondents advocated an all-round transfer to municipalities of public utilities; a little more than 40% seek to unconditionally pass over childcare and health institutions. The shares of those insisting on unconditional municipalization of cultural institutions and sports facilities are twice as small (20% each). The share of those anxious to transfer rest/guest houses and recreation centers is rather small (9%) (see Table 9.7)

So the share of those who are ready to look for compromises, who in one form or another, under these or other conditions are ready to participate in funding social assets, is substantial. It is large enough to study seriously what these forms and conditions may be. As follows from the results of the survey, under current conditions the preferred solution seems to be: 'local administration and enterprise use and finance asset maintenance on a contractual basis'. This solution was supported by 21% concerning housing, 36% for medical care, 27% for urban utilities and recreation centers, 32% for cultural centers, etc. Managers also find it possible that the assets could be jointly run by several enterprises with or without the participation of municipal agencies.

At the same time, if legislation would permit, 27% of enterprises currently keeping housing on their books, and 45% running dormitories, would like to continue owning them. Nearly all (85–90%) enterprises holding recreation and rehabilitation centers would like to keep them on their books. Sixty-one percent of enterprises holding childcare institutions would like to keep them. As regards housing, most of the managers who expressed this desire find it to be an important incentive to workers; 10% are sure that housing is an asset which will strengthen the financial state of the enterprise in future. Recreational facilities are also supposed to be an incentive, and to contribute to the image of the company; many managers argue that these are assets which can

Table 9.7   Distribution of responses to a question: 'Which solution relative to social asset now on enterprise books do you deem the best under the durrent circumstance?'

Responses	Positive responses as shares (in %) of all respondents							
	Residential buildings	Health institutions	Childcare institutions	Sports facilities	Recreational centers	Cultural institutions	Urban economy
Assets are municipalized without preconditions	69	41	42	20	9	21	7
Assets are municipalized upon meeting certain conditions by the enterprise (sharing in maintenance costs to a certain amount and for a certain period, undertaking repairs, etc.)	7	0	10	10	0	0	7
City administration and enterprise are jointly using and financing asset maintenance on contractural basis; enterprise costs are *fully reimbursed* by local budget	15	18	16	10	15	21	7

192

City administration and enterprise are jointly using and financing asset maintenance on contractural basis; enterprise costs are reimbursed in part by local budget	6	18	7	10	12	11	20
Assets are privatized	4	0	3	5	0	0	7
Assets are jointly run by several enterprises *with no participation of municipal agencies*	2	0	7	0	9	4	3
Assets are jointly run *with participation of municipal agencies*	2	12	7	14	9	16	3
Hard to say	9	18	16	23	42	21	13

193

strengthen the financial state of the enterprise in the future, or even generate a profit. Despite the difficulties in financing public utilities many enterprises are prepared to share the costs with municipalities. Given an adequate legal environment, the overwhelming majority of enterprises (89%) that have thermo-electric plants and boiler houses would prefer to keep these assets. According to 67% of enterprise managers holding such assets, this would be justified for technological reasons.

The fact that the majority of polled enterprise managers do not press for unconditional municipalization of virtually all assets (except housing) points to broad opportunities in searching for flexible financing and management solutions. At the same time, support for asset municipalization with continued enterprise responsibility is weak. The solutions most acceptable to managers would be based on contracts governing joint use and shared financing by the enterprise (probably several) and municipality. Thus the survey results provide evidence of a variety of approaches to the problems of social asset maintenance and management which could be perceived positively by enterprise managements. This opens up rather wide opportunities for a dialogue between enterprises and municipalities, a search for an effective way of optimizing the process of subsequent municipalization of enterprise social assets.

4. Social Assistance Schemes Exercised or Planned by Enterprises

Indications of 'paternalistic' or 'social' orientations have been repeatedly identified by sociological surveys conducted among managers of Russian industrial enterprises. The objective of this study was to consider in more detail the specific forms and scale which the formulated (or declared by management) attitudes can take. Subject to consideration, in particular, was the enterprises' readiness to provide employees and their families with both traditional and new types of social services and assistance.

In the case of housing policy, the respondents were requested to describe the management's stance in relation to a variety of measures. As is seen from the survey, the majority of managers believe that the enterprise ought to contribute, in some form or other, to the solution of employees' housing problems: the proportion of those who do not treat this line of activity as one of the enterprise's responsibilities is relatively small. However the share of enterprises capable of undertaking any measures or at least planning them for the foreseeable future are even smaller. The prevailing response to all questions included in the questionnaire turned out to be 'would like to but are financially impotent' (Table 9.8).

The survey data provide evidence that enterprises sometimes practice relatively new forms of social assistance to employees as regards their health service needs. Each fifth enterprise (21%) regularly compensates employees' costs for outpatient treatment, one-third of surveyed enterprises (33%) provide one-off allowances, 22% of respondents mentioned regular reimbursement of employees' costs of hospital treatment, 28% informed of non-recurring compensations. Seven percent of enterprises regularly refund employees' costs for purchased drugs, and 39% do it as a one-shot benefit. Over half of enterprises (52%) entered into agreements with health institutions to provide services to their employees, and 15% of all surveyed enterprises did so with health institutions they had previously kept on their books; 17% of enterprises insure their employees in addition to statutory health insurance.

In response to a question as to what the enterprise is going to do in terms of solving their employees' health problems, 40% of respondents said that this is no responsibility of the enterprise, another 25% found it hard to say. Only one of the surveyed enterprises intends to commission its own health institutions in future; 16% are planning to assist (institute allowances for) their employees especially in need of health services; 13% plan to institute or expand additional health insurance.

Enterprises undertake some measures in support of employees' families with children. Eighty percent of surveyed enterprises maintaining kindergartens provide payment benefits. Allowances for complete or partial compensation of services of childcare institutions not belonging to the enterprise are paid out by 24% of all enterprises surveyed. Responding to a question on future enterprise plans in this area, 43% said the enterprise must no longer involve itself in solving problems associated with childcare, for this is no business of enterprises. Thirteen percent of managers said that their enterprises intend to pay out child benefits to their employees.

Around 70% of enterprises with sports facilities on their books provide the respective sports benefits to their employees. Each tenth enterprise has entered into agreements with sports facilities owned by the city or other enterprises for service provision to their employees. About 5% sponsor professional sports teams, 10% assist amateur teams, 20% children's sports groups. One-fourth of surveyed enterprises sponsor sports championships, 13% other sports events. Only one enterprise reported plans to build new sports facilities, explaining this move as a desire to provide incentives to its employees. The majority of enterprises (82%) possessing recreational centers compensate their employees for the costs of vouchers; one enterprise had commissioned a new rest house.

On the whole, the survey indicates that for all the numerous references to the importance of socially oriented attitudes by enterprise managements, close

Table 9.8 Measures undertaken and planned by enterprises in housing sector (positive responses as shares in % of all respondents)

Measures for solving the employee housing problem	Employees have no such need	This is no job of the enterprise	Would like to but are financially impotent	Can and do	Intend	Other	Hard to say
Rent compensation allowances	1	30	55	5	1	1	2
Loans to employees for purchasing new homes	0	14	72	5	1	1	2
One-off monetary allowance when buying a new home	0	11	76	2	2	0	5
Loan guarantee to commercial banks upon issuing credit on mortgage to employees	3	21	54	3	1	0	13
Home purchase by enterprise and selling it to employees at subsidized prices	0	17	66	2	4	0	7
Home purchase by enterprise and renting it to employees	0	22	60	4	3	0	8
Building apartments by enterprise and selling them to employees at subsidized prices	0	13	67	5	4	1	4
Building apartments by enterprise and renting them to employees at subsidized prices	0	24	59	1	4	0	9

scrutiny frequently shows that, in fact, enterprises tend to abandon a number of traditional social functions. In response to a question on future plans for social assistance to their staff, over 40% of managers said, in particular, that involvement in handling health and childcare problems is no responsibility of their enterprise. Enterprises would like to play a more active role in solving employees' housing problems, but their financial capacities are too scarce for any significant contribution.

5. Conclusion

The survey shows that, contrary to earlier expectations, municipalization of the social assets of the majority of enterprises has not translated, in the current economic environment, into a significantly improved financial state and higher competitiveness. Only 15% of enterprises which divested their social assets estimated the subsequent positive changes as significant. Substantial cost cutting was observed at a mere 8% of enterprises in this group; none of them, however, managed to cut the prices of their products; social asset divestiture did not lead to any significant pay increases at any of them; saving of resources spent in the past on social asset maintenance was not accompanied by any significant increases in social benefits to their employees. Moreover, many respondents pointed to a contraction in availability of some social services, in the first place, in relation to housing.

Despite a frequent lack of any marked economic effect of social asset municipalization, enterprises are nevertheless interested to a greater or lesser extent in completing this process, as long as standing legislation requires divestiture of their social assets. This interest is more closely linked to the disincentives created by mandatory divestiture, in particular, to the unwillingness to invest in the maintenance of assets which will surely not belong to them in future.

Managers of enterprises that still have social assets on their books insist on their unconditional and immediate municipalization to only a limited extent. In situations where social asset transfer to municipalities actually ceased because the latter were absolutely unprepared to take over management and financing, most managers do not demand such unconditional and immediate municipalization (except for housing). Rather, the majority of enterprise managers are prepared for a dialogue and application of contractual forms of joint use and shared financing of social assets. The way is open to a stage-wise, diverse and flexible solution to social asset maintenance problems. The development, piloting and subsequent statutory consolidation of the alternative solutions would meet the interests of enterprises, municipalities and, in the final analysis, of the population.

Notes

1. A cross-country analysis of new phenomena in this area is available in Rein, et. at. (1997).

2. The survey concept, methodology and tools were developed jointly with Steven Whitefield, a TACIS expert, who was responsible for the questionnaire questions on the opinions of the efficiency of social reforms currently under way in Russia. The fieldwork was done by All-Russia Center for Public Opinion Poll headed by E. Duke. The survey was a follow-up of a number of studies carried out within the Project. A fraction of the survey results is an experimental validation of a number of provisions outlined in the report *Municipalization of Social Assets of Privatized Enterprises* authored by V. Leksin and A. Shvetsov, whose findings were used by the author in designing the questionnaire.

3. Several hypotheses were tested within the survey concerning the factors determining economic gains of municipalization, including the general production cost structure, certain privileges given by federal, regional and local authorities to the enterprise keeping the social assets, etc. Unfortunately, presentation of these results is outside the scope of this chapter.

4. A similar situation was exposed by the 1996 industrial enterprise survey. Managers looked at social asset divestiture as a feasible way to performance, but did not give much weight to these measures for, taking into consideration the actual structure of enterprise costs, they expected a much higher effect from the measures reducing other cost components, in particular, easing tax pressure, regulation of natural monopoly product prices and the like. See Vinogradova (1996).

References

Alfandary, G., L. Freinkman Q. Fan (1996), 'Financial Transfers and Russian Industrial Firms', in S. Commander, M. Schaffer and Q. Fan (eds), *Economic Policy and Industrial Restructuring in Russia,* Washington, DC: World Bank.

Commander, S. and M. Schankerman (1995), 'Enterprise Restructuring and the Efficient Provision of Benefits', ERBD/World Bank, mimeo.

Commander, S., U. Lee and A. Tolstopiatenko (1996), 'Social Benefits and the Russian Industrial Firm', in S. Commander, M. Schaffer and Q. Fan (eds), *Economic Policy and Industrial Restructuring in Russia*, Washington, DC: World Bank.

Dolgopiatova, T. (1995), *Russian Enterprises in Transition Economy: Economic Problems and Behaviour*, Moscow: Delo Ltd (in Russian).

Leksin, V. and A. Shvetsov (1999), *New Problems of Russian Cities*, Moscow: URSS, MOSCOW (in Russian).

Rein, M., B. Friedman and A. Worgotter (1997), *Enterprise Benefits after Communism*, Cambridge.

Standing, G. (1992), 'Industrial Wages, Payments Systems and Benefits', ILO, Budapest, mimeo.

Survey of Economic Policy in Russia (1999), Moscow: TEIS (in Russian).

Vinogradova, E. (1996), 'Russian Industrial Enterprises: Employment, Wages, Social Infrastructure', *Society and Economy*, **7** (in Russian).

Vinogradova, E. (1997a), 'Reforming of the Social and Labor Polices of the Enterprises: a Natural Sluggishness', *Man and Labor*, **10** (in Russian).

Vinogradova, E. (1997b), 'Social Mission of the Enterprises: Analyses of Managers' Opinions', *Economic and Social Changes: Public Opinion Monitoring*, **4** (in Russian).

Vinogradova, E. (1998), 'State and Perspectives of Enterprise Social Infrastructure: Managers' Opinion', *Economic and Social Changes: Public Opinion Monitoring*, **6**, (in Russian).

Whitefield, S. and E. Vinogradova (1999), *Social Impact of Economic Restructuring and Privatization. Sociological Surveys*, Moscow: TACIS (in Russian, summary in English).

10. The Political Economy of Pension Reform: Poland and Hungary

Martin Rein[1]

1. Introduction

The focal question of this chapter is: what kinds of welfare society are the Central European countries building as part of their post communist transformation? Can we seek answers to this question by applying the established concepts of those classifications of welfare arrangements which have elaborated in the West? Our main point is to show that these countries do not make up any of the classical 'models' of the welfare state. Why? We think that the explanation partly lies in recent general developments of welfare, and partly in region-specific factors. In general, the theory of the three classical regime models of the welfare state was born in an era when the major framework of national social policies seemed to be determined and fixed for long periods by settled (country-specific) party structures and political arrangements, and by stable economic development. Thus, static models, reflecting established political/economic/social structures, appear in this context to have made intuitive sense. However, the situation has markedly changed in the 1980s, and 1990s. On the one hand, countries radically changed party constellations, reshaping their political institutions as splits within parties between modernists and traditionalists intensified, and sharp economic crises were followed by periods of rapid economic growth. On the other hand, the globalization of the influence of international organizations has become a marked process, leading to what for some observers is the stridently strong influence of external factors on all national social welfare states (European Union, increased role of the World Bank, IMF ILO, etc.). In this new environment, it is not surprising that the actual 'three worlds of welfare' have become blurred practically everywhere, but these new developments have not been reflected adequately in the theory of welfare yet. Change has become the dominant and unmistakably important factor in the 're-making' of the classical models as national social policies have tried to adjust to the new normative, political and economic developments that seem to be entrenched in a new wave of economic liberalism.

As to the region-specific reasons: on top of the new international developments, the Central and East European countries have to struggle with the decomposition of the economic civic and political institutions/structures of their inherited totalitarian state. And at the same time, they must build an utterly new state to guide the process in the formation of their new economic and social orders. In this turbulent environment where it seems that everything needs to be done simultaneously, do they have an option to freely 'choose' among ready-made Western social welfare models of an era which is itself also clearly in transition? Obviously not. But then: do they develop their own new 'model' for balancing within all the challenging factors? Is this 'balancing maneuver' able to build on clear visions of coherent social development, or is it shaped by unpredictable, hectic and anarchic forces?

In order to explore these issues and to reach tentative conclusions, we have to 'concretize' our questions. We do this by limiting the number of cases to consider, and by selecting one singular area that, in our view, aptly indicates the critical points that need to be taken into account. Poland and Hungary are selected as leading actors of the 'transition'. Bunce (1999) argues that while state socialism does appear to represent a reasonably coherent past because 'this political-economic system was internally consistent, elaborate in structure, unusually invasive in practice, and regionally encased', the optimistic assumption that 'eastern-Europe was well positioned to become the eastern half of Europe' quickly proved to be mistaken. 'The dominant pattern of post socialism has been one of variation, not uniformity.' And this is particularly important for our subject. Bunce identifies three post-socialist pathways: the first approach is 'where democracy and capitalism co-exist, in relative and, indeed, mutually-supportive harmony, and where political stability and sustained economic growth are the result' (Poland and Hungary best typify this pathway). The second pathway is 'where authoritarian politics co-exists with semi-socialist economies' (typified by Uzbekistan).The third pattern, 'represents a middle ground, poised between democracy and dictatorship and between socialist and capitalist economies' (typified by Russia). This chapter modestly explores only the first pathway, focusing only on Poland and Hungary and making use of pension reform as a basis for generalization.

Pension reform is selected because this is a key sphere of welfare where: (a) massive economic, labor-market, state, community and individual interests with the involvement of practically all members of society meet, clash and have to reach some compromise; (b) on the funding side, issues are at stake for important actors in the international and domestic capital market; (c) the arrangement of the system has direct effects on investments, thus, on domestic economic growth; (d) the arrangements determine for long periods the social relations between generations of a society; (e) the actual benefits – the pensions – form an important element of people's income and the resources of their households. Thus we hope that analysis of the pension sphere will give us an insight beyond the scope of traditionally understood social policy, and give us some ground to draw conclusions on the more general questions raised above.

To structure our analysis and build up the main arguments, we need briefly to discuss *three key concepts* for describing 'models of the welfare state', and *three aspects* to look at them over time and in space. Table 10.1 is intended to serve as a point of departure for our analysis. This three by three table is a starting point from which to discuss the conceptual framework, and also to introduce the issues we will focus on in our discussion of the three columns: as blurring manifests itself in the regime; linkage in the domains; and mixing of pillars. We point out emerging problems in the transition from intention (policy) to pragmatic realities (practice), and why in the two countries blurring, mixing and linkage does not necessarily point toward clear signs of a harmonic change.

We now wish to elaborate briefly each of the three closely linked ideas which provide the framework for our analysis: domains, regimes and pillars. We start with a static view of the key concepts, tracing the origins and meaning of each idea and discussing some of the conceptual issues that arise in the use of these concepts. Following the discussion of the main idea we consider the dynamics of change in each concept. Change occurs in both a passive and active mode and for this discussion we combine both types of change while recognizing the importance of separating them for some purposes.

2. A Static View of the Three Concepts: The Concept of Domains

Why do we reject the idea that the unit of analysis ought to be the welfare state as a whole and choose instead to focus on specific domains? (This discussion draws heavily on work by Goodin and Rein, 2000.) We explore three different kinds of arguments and the issues that each present: the level of abstraction, the level of coherence, and the level of domain linkage. Social policies of the welfare society are constituted by many domains organized by function. If we wish to ignore domains to reach generalizations about the welfare of the society as a whole, we need to assume essentially common characteristics cutting across these different functional areas of health, education, pensions, etc. We have decided to avoid this pitfall and instead focus on the domain of pensions, which, as we have explained, is one of the largest and most strategic domains of social policy and highlights the kind of process of change that our model of types of welfare state implies.

On the other hand, as we seek to avoid the danger of abstraction we can surrender to another danger in focusing on a single domain when the coherence within a domain is not transferable across domains. Michael Walzer's influential theory of *Spheres of Justice* is relevant here. He argues that each good (in our terminology, functional domain) also has a unique principle for distributing the good (need, merit, free exchange, punishment etc.) that is appropriate to that sphere and to no other. However the autonomy of distributive principles when applied to domains is an assumption that is not always warranted, because it implies a degree of coherence that may in fact be especially misleading. Thus the problem is not only that of a too high level of abstraction, but also that the various domains might point to utterly diverse models of the welfare state. The transfer domain and the service domains present quite different puzzles. For example, if one analyzes the health-care system in Hungary (as a single domain 'modeling' the direction of welfare state development of the country), one can easily arrive at the conclusion that the state still maintains an overpowering control over inputs and outputs, and that civil influence is only minimal – all in all, this is the direct continuation of 'state socialism'. Whereas turning to the domain of income maintenance, the researcher might conclude: Hungary has a classical liberal welfare state. Choosing the 'pension domain', we see the justification of the 'mix/blurring' thesis. Thus, it is of the essence of the story that the various domains follow diverse principles and rules. But if this is the case then it is too much to expect that we can hope to answer our starting question about the 'kinds of welfare society' these economies are moving toward. The lack of coherent development is the major characteristic of their 'social reforms' – thus, it is in itself a strong assumption to see the trend of development pointing toward *any* welfare society (at least, in the sense in which the term 'welfare society' is used in the literature and also in public discourse). It might well be the case that the lack of coherence is simply the outcome of a lasting 'transition process' (which will somehow clear up in the longer run). As a result, the static idea types we create are not really 'intellectually and pragmatically unified packages of programs and policies, values and institutions'. (Goodin et al., 1999, p. 16). But it equally might be the case that this lack of coherence remains the 'normal' state of affairs in the countries in question This can be an unintended but growing danger of the future in Central Europe. This important issue is taken up again in the conclusion of this chapter.

3. The Concept of Regimes

What is the classic model of regimes that has dominated the field of the comparative analysis of welfare states? A brief historical tour is needed here. Re-

Table 10.1   *Preliminary framework for examining emerging cross-national models of the welfare society*

Key-concepts	Dimensions of stability and change		
	Static: ideal types	Passive Change	Active Changing (reform)
Regime	Defined in terms of dominant political arrangements that are stable over time: – liberal – corporatist – social democratic	Blurring over time. A) the state of affairs in welfare policy shows an in-between situation, departing from any ideal types where the various components making up the regime follow different rules, initially belonging to another regime. B) coherence is a key issue that blurred boundaries pose.	A) from one more or less clear model based on need to another based on work (e.g., welfare reform). B) oscillation becomes the main new feature of the regime, which is maintained and reproduced by blurring between the regimes (e.g., from residual to redistribution).
Logic of conditionality	and in terms of characteristics of programs and policies: – residual – industrial achievement – redistributive		

204

		Domain linkage	A) domain linkage as reform
Domain Logic of difference functionalized specializations	Functional areas regulated by fixed purposes, principles and mechanisms, stable over time.	A) one domain takes over the functions of another domain B) regulated by incompatible rules and mechanisms (this makes it different from mix!)	coordination, integration 'clearing up', rules and functions, as interests become crystallized
Pillar Logic of a Pay-provide Divide	Fixed combination of the roles of state/market/community which are translated into: – public pillar – private mandated pillar – voluntary pillar	Pillars lose their clear character: the state behaves like a market-actor, market acts with means initially belonging to the state (e.g., increased role of bureaucratic coordination), civic society use the market to cross subsidize non-profit activities	Changing pillar mix A) shifting burden to one or another pillar (e.g., from state to private or voluntary), and searching for a more equal balance of burdens among pillars and actors in order to avoid the drift toward the dominance of one pillar.

205

gimes are essentially about the variety of ways that the state organizes its distribution of the public transfer system. The focus is unmistakably on the variety of forms for the organization of programs and policies administered in the public sector. But this idealized typology of state action arises from both a recognition and a rejection of the prevalence and dominance of the indirect role of the state in stimulating and financially supporting the private sector. The story unfolds with the seminal inaugural lecture of Richard Titmuss on the 'Social Division of Welfare' in Britain in 1955 and thirty-five years later in the influential work of Esping-Andersen's *Three Worlds of Welfare Capitalism* (1990), based on Titmuss's early work. It is the continuity of thought and the stable structure of argument on which welfare state types are based that we want to stress here.

Titmuss recognized the prevalence of fiscal welfare (tax expenditure); occupational welfare (market-driven social benefits provided by private employers and the state in its role as employer, rather than provider to the general public); and social welfare (direct provision by the state). He argued eloquently that fiscal and occupational welfare were perversely redistributive, multiplying the privileges of the better off in society, and that only public direct spending was capable of redistributing benefits in a fair and just manner to a society's citizens. In his later work he transformed this insight into three models of different ways of organizing social welfare in the public domain. He called his three regime types: residual (means-tested provision for those in need); institutional-redistributive (through universal social protection); and industrial achievement (where benefits and contributions were co-integrated to promote work incentives).

In constructing his index of three types of public regimes, Esping-Andersen also recognized, as did Titmuss, the pull toward private provision of health and pensions, relative to public spending on pensions, although the role of tax expenditures, so important in the 'Social Division of Welfare' is curiously absent in the construction of regime types in *The Three Worlds of Welfare Capitalism*. The term 'regime' in Esping-Andersen's *The Three Worlds of Welfare Capitalism* clearly seems to suggest an extended interpretation of the term 'regime'. See for example the following citation:

> For pensions, our analyses will distinguish what we argue are critical differences between regimes. We will thus examine the degree of program corporatism (number of status-defined separate pension plans); the etatist bias (expenditure of civil-service pensions as a percentage of GDP); the relative importance of private-sector pensions ... and what might be called the social security bias ... (Esping-Anderson, 1996, p. 111)

This description would seem to suggest that Esping-Andersen incorporates into the notion of 'regime' a much broader framework than only the 'public domain,' embracing all participating actors in a certain arrangement of distribution within a domain, 'public' being only one among them.

But this limited interpretation is deeply misleading since the logic of regimes is in fact based on models of different ways of categorizing the tax-transfer structure of public programs in terms of the degree to which public provision relies on means testing, universalist equal flat-rate benefits, and contributory earnings-related social insurance. This interpretation was perhaps valid in the early years of the welfare state when the expansion of the public, as signaled by the increase of the functions and responsibilities taken over by the state, was a novelty. However, the later stages of the welfare state revealed varying arrangements for the very same functions in meeting people's needs, redistributing income, correcting malfunctions in services, etc., and in this context the concept of pillars was a complementary idea.

4. The Concept of Pillars

The idea of pillars is based on a very different logic than the different ways of categorizing public provision. The starting assumption is that society is organized in different social spheres of state, market, and community, including family, and all these spheres must contribute to the design of social protection. When these abstract spheres are translated concretely into systems for the design of social provision they yield three pillars, the content of which can be construed as public, private and voluntary. The specific institutions that constitute the three pillars involve one further level of specificity and here it is clear that there is a variety of forms that each of these pillars can take. The state pillar can be organized on a universal, means tested or contributory design. The private pillar can be based on occupational pensions provided by the firms as employer, as is done in a wide range of countries – for example the USA, the UK, Sweden, the Netherlands – to show that it cuts across liberal, conservative and social democratic regimes. But the private pillar can be seen as individual accounts invested by individuals in the equity and bond market. Voluntary pillars can be built from the civic institutions of society and invested in the market. It is helpful to keep in mind the difference between multi-tiers and multi-pillars. One can have multiple tiers in the public sphere consisting of basic, supplementary and additional pensions. Tiers essentially build on each other, while pillars can also be cumulative, the central idea underlying the pillars being the variety of institutional spheres that constitute the whole. In fact in most countries it is very difficult to get a good statistical picture of the relative size of the pillars in terms of the level of spending or accumulation.

The distinction between regimes and pillars refers at root to two different logics in the design of social benefits. Regimes refer to who gets what and under what conditions. Pillars refers to who pays, and who provides. The regime and pillar terminology also originates from two different intellectual traditions: a social policy tradition focused on the direct role of the state and an industrial relations tradition which has its roots in contractual agreements between employers and employees and in particular those agreements which took the form of firm-provided occupational pensions.

5. The Idea of Change: Blurring, Mixing, and Linking

Thus far we have tried to set out a static view of our three main concepts of domains, regimes and pillars. The static approach based on cross-sectional comparisons at a point in time is most commonly followed by Western scholars. The assumption is that a static cross-sectional snapshot of prevailing policies captures a deep and enduring dimension of a society's basic approach to social welfare, and that the patterns that emerge from such an analysis are stable over time and that countries can unambiguously be assigned to one primary type. We know these strong assumptions are false, but to weaken these premises leads to a morass of complex patterns that make it difficult to make generalizations. Of course, such a strategy does make sense in those situations where policies, 'provide incentives that encourage individuals to act in ways that lock in a particular path of policy development' creating commitments that are difficult to reverse, and reinforcing mechanisms that are self-reinforcing and processes that feed on themselves, building more stability (Pierson, 1997, p. 56). But this argument for path dependency does not apply to the transformation of social policy in Central Europe, where the future form and character of the emerging welfare state in post-communist countries will only partially be shaped by their early history.

Not surprisingly, there has also been a rather large body of literature which has criticized these various efforts at developing a static typology of social policy across countries. This criticism has tended to try to identify an important elision, i.e., a significant dimension that has not been taken into account, such as gender. The critics have in turn responded by developing a new classification that is based on the omitted variable. A good example is the scheme to take account of recent feminist debate, classifying countries on the extent to which they follow a strong, moderate or weak breadwinner model. These difficulties in developing ideal types are, of course, well known and need not be belabored here.

The approach we want to pursue is based on different assumptions; that the quality that is most essential to a classification of social policy is that it also changes over time, that actual social policies are both path dependent and resultant from current competing ideological, social, economic and political forces. Change occurs both across pillars and within regimes. It is therefore useful to use a different vocabulary to describe these different changes. We use the term 'blurring' to describe those situations when distinctive regime models blur the lines of demarcation. This occurs when, for example. a country shifts from universal to means testing to contributory public schemes or the other way round. We use the term 'mix' to describe the shifts across pillars: of state, market and community, and the various categories where the spheres of society are translated into the pillars of pension policy.

At the level of practice social policy involves a blurring of the principles on which to allocate public social benefits and a mixing of the institutional structure which allocates these benefits. Hence the demarcation of clear and unambiguous boundaries delimiting the public and private spheres is not achievable in practice. This blurring is unavoidable since an institutional mix involves the state increasingly in three tasks: regulating markets and community, ensuring that the regulatory rules are complied with, and stimulating individuals, families and institutions to be actively engaged in constituting a mixed system. Even in the Chilean system, which is probably the most privatized system, there is a large governmental role as a regulator, insurer, enforcer, policy-maker and provider of benefits to relieve poverty.

Thus the idea of change we use is not broad and encompassing; it is based on the more limited view that the different regimes for organizing the public sphere become blurred over time, and that the mix of the multi-pillar system shifts over time. While it might be generally accepted in many countries that an individual in retirement requires a balance of all three pillars – a state pension, an occupational pension and some form of voluntary or personal savings – the elements that constitute the relative size of each of the pillars change over time. It is a major premise of this chapter that structural reform can be understood as a political effort to deal with the realities of blurred regimes as described later in this chapter, and that the actual shifts in the relative size of public and private pillars lead to new multi-pillar institutional arrangements. It is important to separate deliberation from actual reform. We sometimes have a public debate about the available opportunities for changing the mix, but nothing changes in practice. We also observe that blurring and mixing actually occur and it appears that nobody has in fact made an explicit choice or even thinks that the changes are desirable.[2]

While pension reform is therefore about change in the blurring of regimes and the mix of pillars, we need to try to identify the mechanisms that create change. It is obvious that change can be both internally and externally driven. A country has a historic legacy; seldom, if ever, does policy start with a clean slate. History matters. But so too do changes in the context in which past action is grounded. We want in particular to consider how the historical legacy is used and abused by the various sponsoring groups and the frames they create to legitimize their claims. How does the tension between legacy and exigency get resolved in practice? In the context of Central European economies in transition, international and national organizations have a high stake in exporting models of pension reform, which typically carry implicit assumptions concerning the time span in which reforms are expected to occur. So the debate about pension reform is concerned not only with the direction a country must go in to change its institutional mix of pillars and regimes, but also how fast change should or will take place. While both the time and direction are important, the time dimension tends to be neglected as attention is riveted on the direction that a change in the mix should take.

Finally, we consider change in the ways that domains are linked to each other. This raises another important question about domains, namely, that they are not autonomous. Here we consider only one aspect of domain linkage, namely, when one domain passes on its functions to another domain and expects the captured domain to absorb the costs. The study of early retirement makes it clear how important domain linkage is in understanding the evolution of pension reform. What we have discovered is an almost universal tendency for pensions to have lost much of their tight relation with old age in some countries, for an increasing number of people draw a pension while at the same time remaining in work. The boundary between social and economic policy has become blurred as the social policy of early exit is passively used to deal with unemployment and an active policy of pension reform is introduced to try to reverse these trends. This dimension of domain linkage is clearly part of the background story of one of the important challenges precipitating the response we have labeled as pension reform. But domain linkages take other forms of interdependency as well. In the case study of Hungarian pension policy, we explore how activities in the health domain can indirectly affect the political career of pension policy.

Fortunately Claus Offe has articulated one argument with both force and clarity. He argued that

> Old design options are monistic, relying on the state, the market or the community as the ultimate guarantors of social order and cohesion. More promising solutions are essentially 'impure': none of the three principles of social order is to be relied upon exclusively, but none is to be denied a role within a composite and complex 'mix' of institutional arrangements. These three components of social order (market, state, and community) ... rely on each other, as each of the

components depend on the functioning of the two others. On the other hand, their relationship is antagonistic, as the predominance of any one of them risks to undermine the viability of the two others ... The problem of designing and defending state-society relations, however, is not that of opting single-mindedly for one of the three, but of engaging in, or at the very least, tolerating a process of the ongoing design, readjustment and fine-tuning of a rich and adequate mix in which all three building blocks of social order have a mutually limiting and variable role. (Claus Offe, 2000)

The vocabulary that we have proposed also accepts that we live in an essentially 'mixed' institutional world and that the challenge of redesigning social policy is to find ways of linking regimes and pillars.

In brief, we claim that social policy requires a mix of institutional arrangements, which in practice raise questions about the demarcation of the fuzzy boundaries of these institutions. This in turn gives rise to the evolving role of the state as the agent stimulating the mix through a variety of indirect mechanisms, the most important of which are: tax incentive; regulation and mandating, which define the rules institutions should follow; and overseeing compliance with these rules. Therefore it is important in developing a typology of types to examine both the direct and indirect role of the state. These concerns bring us back to the central question of this chapter, namely, how the historic legacy gets resolved when confronted with the interests internal to the country and the external interests pulling it toward one or another model for creating a mix of spheres.

6. Pension Reform in Central Europe: the Experience of Hungary and Poland

We recapitulate the argument developed thus far: the question we are trying to answer is what kind of welfare state is likely to evolve in Central Europe in the future. To answer this question we started by asking what can be learnt from the way Western scholars have tried to describe different types of mature welfare states. To understand their answer, a brief historical account was presented. At first influential scholars tried to locate an approach based on regime which is essentially about different approaches to social policy within the public domain. The regime approach describes a historically determined period of post-industrial development, and this period seems to be over. In any event, it is now being challenged by an approach that draws on a mix of the main pillars or spheres of society, including the state, the market and the community. Ideas about regimes seem to have been developed largely by academic scholars, whereas the idea of pillars seems to have emerged from an insider approach, i.e. by individuals with access to key policy-makers and with the opportunity to influence the design of institutions as they emerge over time. But more is at stake than is suggested by this dichotomy. We believe that an analysis of types of welfare societies must combine the following main elements: public regimes and a pillar approach, integrated into a dynamic rather than static picture focused on change over time. The ambition should be modest: focusing on specific domains which constitute the welfare society rather than trying to give an account of all the elements that are constitutive of social policy.

The starting point of our analysis in this section of the chapter is a review of the evolution of pension reforms in Hungary and Poland during the past ten years. Fortunately there is a great deal of published literature to draw on. (We have made particular use of Orenstein, 2000; Turner and Rajnes, 2000; Kornai et al., 2001; James, 1999, as well as her unpublished notes and personal discussions; Chlon, et al., 2000a; Szalai, 2000.) We organize this discussion around three main points. The first is to build on those antecedents – traditions, determinants, functions and malfunctions of the late stage of the communist era – that shaped the immediate legacy of the current policy reform attempts. Secondly, we review the national deliberative policy-making process which has evolved in each country and what the pension reforms look like at this time. Thirdly, we consider the role played in this process by the conflicting positions held by international organizations and adjacent Western countries, like Sweden, and asses their weights in the actual evolution of reform.

7. Policy Legacies

Some analysts interpret past experience as a constraint on the present. In general terms, legacy is both a constraint and an opportunity, and both meanings of the term are relevant. Ideally what we are searching for is a systematic understanding of the 'initial conditions' prevailing in a country that constitute a country's legacy and which offers an interpretative framework for understanding why the countries followed different pathways to reform. One would like to know, for example, why the construction of the three pillars and the balancing of the public–private mix took such different turns in Poland and Hungary? This task is too ambitious for this chapter. What we can do at best is call attention to some selected dimensions of legacy without linking these to the outcome of the reforms.

A brief review of the situation that prevailed during the last stages of state socialism may be a useful place to start a discussion of historic legacies. This is a very demanding task and is a topic which clearly warrants more systematic attention than the cursory review presented here. Yet the subject of how the past shapes the present is too important to be altogether neglected. We argue that under state socialism in Poland and Hungary, social welfare was organized around three interrelated institutional arrangements: the state (central and local government) for the general population; the enterprise, through its provision of a wide range of fringe benefits, for employees of the firm; and the Communist Party, with its own unique institutional form of social protection and social benefits, for members of the political elite (Rein et al., 1998). These three institutional structures were tied together by the party-state where the communist political party controlled the apparatus of the state and the production system of the firm. While many individuals expressed their solidarity as members of the party, the party's leadership was the key driving force in this system of control.

Social policy in general and pension policy in particular played a distinctively special role under state socialism. The continued viability of the state depended on controlling the behaviour of its citizens. One powerful way to keep the population under the direct control of the state was through the use of the social security system to control individuals' everyday lives. In order to do this social security had to carry out a multiplicity of different functions that were largely unrelated to its role as a system of transfer and services. It served within the firm as a system of rewards for compliant behavior and also as a system of punishment by withholding benefits for those who violate the overt and implicit norms. The firm is a small community, so that such actions were clearly visible and widely recognized and understood. But the local government could also perform a similar regulatory function in the way that desirable and much coveted housing units were allocated in the community. The firms also had their own generous housing subsidies for their managers and other selected workers.

In the aftermath of 1956 and during the 1960s, this situation gradually changed as party leaders became more concerned with the expression of discontent and hence the visible use of social security as an instrument of control was mediated; as a result benefits were more uniformly distributed. But even in this new environment, the special schemes and special rules for different occupational groups like farmers, teachers, judges, ballet dancers etc. persisted. This form of special privilege can, of course, also be understood as a substitute for differential wages. But whatever the original motivations for these benefits, the fact that pensions served multiple functions was one of the important reasons why the state was spending so much on its social policy. How this issue of special privileges shaped the efforts to reform pensions is discussed further in the section on Poland, but in general the role they played was to raise the level of social spending as a percentage of GDP to that of many mature capitalist countries in Western Europe.

It is not only in the level, but also in the composition of spending for public pensions that special privileges are visible. Pensions are constitutive of three different programs: retirement, disability and survivors. In 1998, in Hungary 81% of total spending was allocated to pensions and 3% to disability, compared to 54% and 30% respectively in Poland (Schmahl, 2000). 'In Poland, approximately a quarter of the population was covered by some kind of early retirement privilege' (Chlon et al., 2000b, p. 11).

After the fall of communism in 1989, this pattern of expanding the multiple functions of social security continued and accelerated as the pension system, early retirement, disability, partial pensions and minimum pensions were used to respond to declining employment, growing unemployment and decreasing wages. Pension policy became a tacit, non-explicit, but nevertheless key strategic tool in dealing with the economic policy of transition. It was used to keep labor out of the market by de-activating labor, but it was also used to integrate social benefits with temporary, part-time, transitional, informal and illegal work. A new system of benefits created a structure which made it possible for women to combine social benefits with a variety of forms of flexible work: jobs with reduced hours, risky jobs, informal and even illegal work. This fuzzy boundary which blurred the demarcation of labor market and social policy, between social security and labor-market policies, made it possible to pass the costs of employment strategies onto the social security program. The inevitable result was a decline in the value of the benefits and a growing frustration with the management of the public pension system.

In the 1990s critics like Kornai offered a powerful argument as to why the state needed to reduce its level of spending, even in the face of growing need. He argued that people need to be allowed and educated to take over individual responsibility for their lives. However, what change in the mix of the multiple functions of pensions should be shed to achieve this aim, was by no means self-evident. The use of the historic legacy and its transformation was one of the key puzzles in pension reform.

But there are troubles with too narrow a definition of these functions just as there is trouble with the multiplicity of functions. One could readily argue that family and child policy is relevant to pension policy since there is a potential demographic imbalance in the ratio of retirees and current workers, hence a fertility-promoting policy. If one wants to change the mix of functions how can this be done in a way that respects the historical legacy of the country, and when is it right to make a clean break?

Estelle James has argued that a country's implicit debt is an important part of the initial conditions that constrain future action and plays an important role in any general theory of pension reform. The implicit pension debt, defined as the present value of accrued rights of pensioners and workers under the old pension system, is the silent, invisible debt incurred by the country in contrast to the highly visible national debt which is the center of public review. This implicit debt constraints the size of private pension spending. The implicit debt in Hungary and Poland is over 200% of GDP and is the highest among countries for which data were reported (James, 1999, p. 10 and table 1, p. 43).

The argument about debt was advanced by the World Bank as one of the strongest rationales for reform. But critics argue with equal force that the implicit debt simply does not matter. Hungarian experts made similar calculations in the public debate about pension reform in the 1993–96 period. The arguments were not persuasive at that time, as the emphasis on voluntary pensions stressed the capability of civic society in correcting the injustice of the old system.

We have placed the argument about debt in the discussion of legacy to make the point that this kind of fiscal constraint is different from the normative policy legacy of believing that a pension system should provide income guarantees, and limit the range of benefits by establishing minimum and maximum rates of return. This later legacy defines norms of appropriate behavior. There are also norms governing what kinds of policies are legitimate or appropriate in the social and economic spheres of society. Helping family and kin is appropriate in the domestic sphere but such behavior is regarded as illegitimate in the public sphere. But sometimes the boundary separating the economic and social spheres is not so sharply defined, as the norms which treat the disability system and occupational privileged pension as acceptable social norms in a country's legacy.

Most, but not all, countries develop over time regulations and guarantees to protect their citizens against market risks, but sometimes a country anticipates the need for such protection and does not await a local scandal before initiating such rules. Not surprisingly, therefore, Turner and Rajnes observe that Poland and Hungry 'have elaborate guarantees', and minimum and maximum rates of return in their pension funds (Turner and Rajnes, 2000, p. 17). In Hungary there are in fact three different guarantees. There is the guarantee in the PAYG (pay-as-you-go) first pillar; secondly, there is a guarantee for those with a minimum of ten years' contribution in the second pillar; and finally there is the guarantee that is provided if the firm or the sector in which a worker was employed goes bankrupt. One could readily argue that any responsible pension reform would build in all these forms of guarantees and historical legacy is therefore not a relevant consideration.

But more recent policy legacies also play a role in the evolution of pension reform.

In 1993 Hungary had introduced a system of voluntary pension funds in the form of 'mutual benefit societies' funded largely by tax breaks. The idea was to build civil society by allowing groups of citizens to found their own voluntary pension funds. Organization of these third pillar funds had a major structural impact on the course of later pension reform. (Orenstein, 2000, p. 28)

The success of this voluntary program built a constituency which supported a mandatory, funded pension scheme fashioned on the same logic as the voluntary program and subject to the same kind of governmental oversight.

The main point here is that these examples show that past traditions take quite different forms: from norms of building guarantees into policy design, to norms for extending privileges to special occupational groups, to practical considerations like building constituencies for support of future programs, and finally to the fiscal constraints set by the size of the implicit debt. But these different meanings of constraint and opportunity by themselves do not really explain what shaped the policy options for pension reform that were debated in Poland and Hungary and accepted as defining the range of acceptable choice for change. To understand the forces that framed the policy debate about alternative choices we need to examine both the role played by international organizations and the initiatives promoted by adjacent national states with a stake in the policy options developed by their neighbors. At the most general level we are talking here about the processes shaping the diffusion and imposition of innovation.

8. Policy Choice: International and National Organizations in the Diffusion of Ideas.

But while history does matter, so too does the role of international organizations and the influence of neighboring countries. The active diffusion of social policy ideas from external sources is not a new phenomenon. After World War II Britain tried aggressively to export its ideas about a uniform, flat-rate national basic pension based on common citizenship in society to European countries, like the Netherlands and Sweden, where these ideas were accepted. So it is not surprising, in a different historical context characterized by the dominance of liberal ideas, to find international organizations like the World Bank and the International Monetary Fund (IMF) promoting their idealized solutions. The International Labor Organization (ILO) struggled to compete in the idea and influence market.

We have argued earlier in the discussion of regimes and pillars that what is emerging in the specific area of pension reform is a hybrid of both traditions. In order to understand the impact of this development on pension reform in Poland and Hungary we need to elaborate the different variants of this hybrid form. First we elaborate the position promoted by the World Bank in their influential book *Averting the Old Age Crises*, first published in 1994. While this has played a dominant role in framing the pension reform alternatives, there have also been important and influential alternatives as expressed in the position of the ILO and even more importantly in variations of national models. The Swedish variation of a notional defined contribution system is of particular importance for our analysis, because of its special role in influencing the framework of Polish pension reform. But other national variations are also important. In this section we explore these variations before considering their impact on pension reform in Poland and Hungary.

9. The World Bank View and its Challengers

While a three-pillar model is widely accepted, views differ on what are the characteristics of each pillar. The approach of state–market–family discussed earlier may be the most common from a sociological perspective. But in the public debate about pension reform the World Bank position has played a particularly dominant role.

The World Bank takes as its point of departure the functions to be performed and the institutional structure required to carry out these functions. The state is viewed as the only appropriate institution to perform the redistributive function of providing a flat-rate minimum benefit to serve as a safety net on which the other functions would stand. Second is the function of savings to be built in a mandatory pillar to be paid for by individual contributions, where there is a clear relationship between the contributions paid during the working life and the benefits later recouped in retirement. The market, as in the example of contractual occupational pensions, could provide for this function. It could also be provided by the state in the conventional, non-funded, pay-as-you-go defined benefit programs financed from payroll taxes, where the present generation pays for the benefits received by the future generation. At issue here is whether this function should be radically redefined into a fully or partially funded scheme, whose assets would be managed privately and competitively through market institutions. Benefits would depend on the return on investments which would be available in the assets of the funded scheme at the time of retirement. Thus, final benefits would be linked to returns from investments in the funded scheme, i.e., a defined contribution plan, rather than pre-set as some ratio of past earnings as in a defined benefit plan. The third function is voluntary saving designed to supplement the income of people who want more consumption in their old age. Here the individual is responsible for investing his or her own savings or purchasing the services of an investment manager who invests the assets in the market. A multi-pillar system assumes that each of these functions should be carried out by a different institutional agent: the state, the market and the individual (James, 1999, p. 4).

These functions are already carried out in many societies, where in the last stages of their working careers households in the top 60% of the income distribution derive their income from a multi-pillar system which includes state social security, occupational pensions and personal assets. But what is new in the public debate is the apprehension that societies cannot afford the cost of the pension system. What is projected in the World Bank analysis is a near-doubling from 9 to 16% of the proportion of the population over age 60 due to increases in life expectancy and declining fertility of the active population and a dramatic non-sustainable increase in the cost of the contributions required to support the system. These challenges have led to a debate about the crises of aging and the size of the welfare state. It is in this context that the pillar framework proposed by the World Bank opens the possibility at a policy level of drastically altering the regime–pillar mix with a greater role played by both markets and individual personal accounts that could make pensions sustainable and could also contribute to economic growth.

This debate has crystallized around the policy positions adopted by two international organizations: the World Bank and the ILO, and the reform options pursued by different countries (Guillian, 1998). This is a story of the three pillars in a global perspective viewed from the lens of the mandate of these organizations, and signaled by their names: a bank that provides loans in developing countries and a labor organization focused on the social protection of workers. The stakes are high because pillar reforms are, after all, about the heart and soul of a country's pension policy. The position of the ILO is most forcefully expressed by an economist participating in the American debate as to whether public social security should invest part of its resources directly in capital markets. 'There is no financial goal that private accounts can achieve that cannot be achieved at a lower administrative cost by a government system that can invest in private stock and bonds. There are plausible arguments for private accounts, but they are political' (Weinstein, 1998; see also Stevenson, 1998, p. 5). Of course, funds have to be managed and this raises an additional issue of whether the private sector should manage mandated public programs. It is interesting to note that the Swedish personal premiums, where individuals control the choice of investment, or the contractual pension schemes which are managed and financed by firms or unions in the Netherlands and Switzerland, do not appear to be a central issue in the ILO's formulation of the debate. It appears that they are more concerned that workers participating in mandated, privately managed, fully funded, defined contribution schemes must also bear all the financial risk, while in defined benefit plans this is borne entirely by the plan sponsor.

It is now generally accepted that there are a variety of quite different ways to pursue the idea of individual accounts. Therefore 'policy makers must adapt a more nuanced approach to pension reform than that offered by the common interpretation' of the World Bank's position. Leading economists now believe 'that the arguments most frequently used to promote individual retirement accounts are often not substantiated in either theory or practice' (Orszag and Stiglitz, 1999, p. 2).

The positions developed by the World Bank are not only subject to external criticism, but the range of alternative possibilities also changes in light of the actual experience of the World Bank in its efforts to reshape national policy. There are at least three plausible reasons to believe that the World Bank may have changed its mind and revised its views of the shape of the possibility space that is realistically available in the definition of pension options. First, policy is partly shaped by the personnel that work in the Bank and these people change over time. Secondly, there is the role of feedback, not in the sense of formal empirical studies, but the common everyday observation of apparent policy failures. These include the inability to introduce health reform in the face of declining mortality rates; the increase of poverty and the inability to transform the income transfer system; and the limited success in getting many countries to adopt pension reform. Finally, consider the role of scandals in the mishandling of money leading to the claim that budgetary allocations designated for East and Central Europe were circulating back to the West. Some estimates were that 40% of budgeted funds were spent on experts and travel. These are, of course, only plausible speculations and may or may not have contributed to recognition within the Bank of the variety of approaches to reform that were actually emerging in practice.

In a thoughtful paper Estelle James sets out the three main international variations of the multi-pillar model. Important as these international organizations may be in the innovation and diffusion of policy that followed the Latin America model and especially the model pursued by Chile, where the individual workers choose the investment manager for their investment funds options, they are not the only actors in this game. Some countries like Sweden, with its ideas about notional defined contribution and Switzerland, with its commitments to mandated occupational pensions, have also played a critical role in this debate. Switzerland was an early innovator of this form of multi-pillar. The OECD also promoted a model in which employers are mandated by the state to provide an investment plan and to choose the investment manager, sometimes as a part of contractual employer and union negotiations. In the Swedish model there is a first traditional pillar which is expected to decline over time and is designed to protect low wage workers. The second pillar is based on a large, notional-defined contribution plan where lifetime contributions are uprated according to the wage bill growth of the economy and then converted to an annuity on retirement. But the distinctive feature of this scheme is that the notional accumulated capital is then divided by the expected life expectancy at the time of retirement. The result is a reduction in inter-generation transfers since benefits are lower than the traditional defined benefit plan because they are more actuarially balanced. Moreover 'the formula does not include income redistribution elements, as it gives pension rights for actually paid contributions' (Chlon et al., 2000, p. 9). The plan's intention is to make the contributions transparent so that they can serve as an incentive to work. Thirdly, there is a much smaller, premium reserve plan constituting 2.5% of total contributions, which is allocated to a fully funded and privately managed defined contribution plan whose assets are invested according to the choices made by the individual worker. The model is in opposition to a partially funded system with a mandated private pillar (James, 1999, p. 1 and Wadensjo, 1998, p. 5). On these three pillars stands a supplementary contractual occupational pension system which covers about 90% of the population. The pension reform process is not complete until these contractual pensions are integrated into the notional defined contribution system. This process of integration is now under way.

What these variations in the World Bank model suggest is the wide range of other institutional actors with a stake in framing pension options. In addition to the World Bank, the ILO, the Organization for Economic Cooperation and Development (OECD) and the IMF, there are the global profit-making companies with a large financial stake in the capital markets that pension reform generates. We discuss the Hungarian pension reform below, but to anticipate here, Hungary developed a second privately financed pillar. Two of the three leading private funds, controlling 83% of the massive capital generated from the public, is run by the Dutch companies ABN and Nationale Nederlande. Perhaps this can be interpreted as a civilized form of Dutch colonialization. Interestingly enough, these companies do not play such a visible role in the Polish pension system. Moreover it is hard to imagine that Swiss and British firms will not have an interest in the growth market of Central Europe's pension reform.

10. The Impact of these Variations on Pension Reform in Poland and Hungary

The evidence seems clear: national and international alternatives framed the debate in Central Europe's pension reform. While any viable pension reform must ultimately be the outcome of negotiated agreements based on the internal dynamics in each country, countries are also strongly influenced by the diffusion of reform ideas that frame the domestic debate and shape the choices that need to be made. And these options originate with international organizations like the ILO and the World Bank, the European Union, the OECD and Western countries like Sweden. The involvement of international and national organizations in the reform process in Poland and Hungary 'can be divided into two categories: contribution to policy discourse and direct policy intervention' (Orenstein, 2000, p. 12). Examples are not difficult to find. The World Bank offers a pre-set reform strategy along with analytical and technical assistance that helps countries think through their problems. Moreover, they help finance the cost of bringing foreign experts in from other countries that have already reformed, and organize study tours for the press, members of government and legislators, to show them how the multi-pillar system has worked abroad. A report on the successful reform of the Polish pension system stresses the important positive role played by the media in providing extensive positive coverage of the proposed reforms (Hausner, 2001). Journalists participated in study trips to countries that had already reformed their pension systems. Such learning from international experience, partly financed by the World Bank, may have contributed to the positive reception by the press of the reforms. There are many such examples of direct intervention in national social policy formulation. Deacon's study concludes that these international organizations 'have been the most influential ... in post communist social sector reform' (cited in Orenstein, 2001, p. 12).

National scholars who are close to domestic policy-making are troubled about the imposition of outside intervention on an elite, closed policy-making process. Consider the thoughtful position developed by Julia Szalai.

> The argument that Eastern European countries act under the pressure of the huge international organizations and/or Western experts sounds to me a bit as a reminiscence of the anti-colonalization rhetoric: it is the 'colonizers' who – in the name of the civilizing mission – dictate certain things to the 'wild' people of the 'underdeveloped world'. As we know, this argument was always patronizing, and failed to ask fundamental questions about those 'wilds'. Further, it's totally false in the case of Central Europe, which has always been part of the 'civilizing' actor, though on a less developed stage. Therefore, you simply miss the point why Latvians, Poles, Hungarians show so much inclination to introduce reforms in accordance with the World Bank – etc. – recommendations. To find an explanation, instead, the internal social structure, re-shaping of interests, actual 'use' of the new institutions should be analyzed. Such an analysis would reveal at which points these countries genuinely act according to the outer 'recommendations' (see e.g. the new welfare assistance schemes), and at which points they put the World Bank reform-ideas under blockade (see e.g. the health-reforms). (Personal communication with Julia Szalai, June, 2000)

11. National Politics and Policy Outcomes: Poland

The only way to answer the challenge posed by Szalai is by a detailed account of the policy-making process in Hungary and Poland of the type reported in Orenstein's monograph and the more recent volume published by Kornai et al. (2001; see especially the essay by Jerzy Housner who held the position of under-secretary of state to the Prime Minister in Poland). Finally a recent paper with the most current information about Poland is especially useful (Chlon et al., 2000a). We cannot develop such a detailed account here, but we can, at the least, present a brief summary of selected aspects of the process of reform, and some speculation on the plausible connection between the pension reforms in Poland and Hungary and international influence. Let us start with a brief overview of the pension reforms introduced in Poland.

The Three Pillars of Polish Pension Reform
The new pension reform called for the creation of two new pillars, fashioned after the logic of the Swedish pension reform and a zero pillar which is a public, basic income financed from general taxes. The first pillar is based on the idea of notional defined contribution (NDC) and is a pay-as-you-go system. The second pillar is a fully-funded pillar, where individuals choose the fund to make investments on their behalf. A brief elaboration is provided below.

The zero pillar
The zero pillar provides a basic income guarantee, at a level to be determined by parliament, signaling a clear political decision not to develop a program whose cost is to be absorbed from general revenue. To avoid the complexities of setting up a costly administrative structure it was decided not to create a means tested program. What in the regime approach to pension policy was heralded as the foundational structure of a new vision of citizenship entitlement, in the new pension reform has been accorded the status of a 'zero pillar'. The old system is now regarded as a residual program rather than a primary foundation. It is the second, fully-funded pillar and a third voluntary pillar that constitute the basic reform.

The first pillar
The old public PAYG regime introduced in 1950 still remains alive, but it has been transformed to the first pillar and is best understood as a close replica, not of the World Bank's vision of pension reform, but of the social imagination

and design invention of Swedish social policy. Pension benefits under the first pillar in the new system simply depend on the pool of resources accumulated after a lifetime of contributions, available to each worker in the notional fund plus accumulated interest. This is augmented by an inflation index and reduced by a unisex life expectancy index (explained below). So budgetary imbalance arising from a mismatch of contributions received and benefits paid out is therefore no longer an issue. It is important to understand that the Polish pension reform applies only to old age pensions and not to the system of disability and survivors' benefits. On retirement the account is converted into a real annuity, which specifies the actual amount of money the individual will receive over his or her remaining lifetime. This is supplemented by a fully-funded, privately managed second pillar. The total contributions for old age are equal to 19.5% of salary. These contributions are centrally collected by the Social Insurance Institute (ZUS) and then transferred to the two pillars – 12.2% for the first pillar and 7.3% to the second pillar. The long-range plan calls for the contributions to be equally divided between the two pillars, but these are projected plans and not the reality of the present situation.

This explains the logic of the new first pillar system, but not the richness of the institutional details of its design. The devil is, as usual, always in the details, and to be sure the details are technical and complicated, and likely to continue to be changed in light of the identification of emerging new problems encountered during the implementation phases of the reform. But one cannot understand the reform in Poland without attention to at least some important key elements. I want to comment briefly on four details in the design of the first pillar.

First, all young people under the age of 30 are in the new system; those 30–50 years of age can choose between the old and the new; and those over age 50 remain in the old scheme. To make an informed choice it is necessary to compute the present value of the initial capital they are bringing from the old system based on the percentage of their average wage, the number of years they have worked and the number of years needed to be eligible for the plan. This is clearly not a task that an individual worker can compute on his or her own.

Secondly, some groups get credited with income, even if they do not directly contribute. In all such cases the government or someone else has to make the contribution in lieu of the individual. These groups for example include: mothers, students and the military. The treatment of the disabled remains an unresolved issue.

Thirdly, the size and generosity of the annuity is determined by two factors: the first factor is the level of wage growth included in the computation of the index to take account of inflation. Poland decided on 75% of wage bill growth in the economy for this index. The second factor is that each retiring cohort has the indexed notional capital used in computing his or her annuity reduced by a unisexual life expectancy index. In other words, the actual value in the notional account is divided by the average years of life expectancy for the cohort at the point of retirement. Taking life expectancy into account reduces the value of the annuity, but a unisex index benefits women who on average live longer than men. The effect of introducing this index can be quite dramatic. The formula gradually reduces the replacements of the pension to about 50% for both pillars, compared to a 62% replacement rate at its height in 1994. The advantage of this silent system for taking life expectancy into account is that government does not need periodically to raise the retirement age as longevity increases. But including this factor reduces the total costs of pensions by lowering the value of the benefits for each future cohort.

Fourthly, the system is designed to discourage both early retirement and the evasion of paying benefits since the final annuity depends on the size of the notional pool of accumulated benefits. Fewer years of coverage thus means a smaller pool of accumulated assets. Discouraging early retirement was an especially sensitive issue contributing to the escalation of costs in the old system, since early retirement did not require labor force withdrawal. Pensions were thus in effect wage supplements at the last stage of the working career. To offset the benefit reductions which come about from taking account of life expectancy and from using only 75% of the wage bill growth in computing wage credits, there is no mandatory retirement age specified in the law. There is, of course, a minimum age to take up the pension of 65 for men and 60 for women. So if an individual wants to get a higher annuity he or she can do so by working more years, assuming that firms will continue to employ them.

The second pillar

Supplementing the notional account is a fully funded privately managed second pillar. It is privately managed because the investment managers are chosen from a pool of about 12 pension funds, offering different investment portfolios. In the long run, assuming that the contribution levels remain the same, 9% of total contributions will go to the first notional pillar, and 9% to the second mandatory, privately managed and funded second pillar. The long-term projection is that the pillars will be of equal size. However, in the years of transition, the first pillar is substantially larger. As we have seen, about 20% of the wage bill is used to compute the contributions and this implies that 60% of the total amount will go into the notional pillar (12.2/19.5) and 40% into the funded pillar (7.9/19.5)

In the Polish mandatory contribution pension funds, there will be two different types of funds: one that can invest in a wide range of financial instru-

ments and one restricted to fixed income securities. About 80% of all contributors participate in these open pension funds with a projected annual flow
of contributions of about 2% of GDP.

> The mass choice to shift part of the contribution to the second pillar can be
> partially explained by the poor opinion of ZUS in society generally ... the cre-
> ation of pension funds represented a new era, with a wider range of services and
> the possibility of having more control over pension savings. However this also
> means ... the greater financing from the state budget. (Chlon et al., 2000b,
> p. 29)

A separate minimum guarantee will apply for each type of fund (Turner
and Rajnes, 2000, pp. 11–13). In the second pillar, pension fund managers are
obliged to supplement the difference between the actual returns of the funds
and the minimum mandated level of benefits. Financing the minimum benefits
in the first pillar was recently shifted from the pay as you go system to the
state's budget.

Regulation and Oversight

The second pillar needs to be regulated to deal with a variety of administrative
costs such as how to deal with the high start-up cost of putting the system into
place and how to decide on the portfolio structure and in particular whether to
allow unrestricted investments abroad, or whether to limit such investments.
Other issues are how to set up a reserve in the notional system to create a nest
egg for the bad years. To deal with these and other issues a State Supervisory
Board was created. A privatized system is not self-regulating; it redefines the
role of the state and in particular managing its oversight tasks. Because the
pension reform was put into effect very quickly, this means that in practice
important changes will need to be made as new problems are uncovered and
these will fall largely on the regulatory role of the state.

The importance of starting with a cautionary note is suggested by the fact
that although Poland passed legislation in 1997 and 1998 and began implementation in 1999, problems in getting launched were encountered from the
beginning by an accounting mess created by faulty management decisions at
the Insurance Board, ZUS. The Insurance Board phased out the old working
system but did not get the new system up and running in time. Problems have
been encountered in both pillars. In the first pillar all age cohorts covered by
the system are affected from the beginning because individual accounts have
to be established for all participants in the pillar, since these accounts will
determine their benefits at the time of retirement. Here, however, no one will
see anything in practice until the ZUS (Insurance Board) gets its accounting

system finished (at end 2000 at the earliest). However, the PAYG pension rights nevertheless are already accruing according to the new rules. The accounting problem affects the financial account of the funded second pillar even more, because money needs to be transferred to the individual's choice of fund manager immediately. People were given about a year to choose a fund and that period is just about up. Many have already chosen a management fund, which means that money should already be noted on an account and transferred to the account in practice. Obviously the Insurance Board is managing as best as they can until an accounting system is installed (personal correspondence, Ed Palmer, summer 2000). Compounding these problems in transition is the estimate 'that there are around 60% of documents with errors in all individual documents delivered for 1999' (Chlon et al., 2000b, p. 30).

Of course, the accounting problem can also be interpreted as an important, but still minor, annoyance. But in a turbulent policy environment it can also suggest a continually evolving process of redesign, which can modify critical elements in the design structure. Rather than providing the institutional details of the new reform plan I want to consider first the familiar dispute between the Ministry of Finance and in Poland the Ministry of Labor. This is a recurrent theme in the evolving story of stalemate and resolution in pension reform and the Polish experience helps to deepen our understanding of the conflict. Three sources of conflict emerged in this account.

First, the basic underlying struggle was the difficult choice between incurring budgetary deficits or imposing major cuts in pension expenditure. One conventional way of coping with this situation, in Poland and elsewhere, was to make ad hoc legislative adjustments. But the Constitutional Court ruled that 'the practice of periodically and temporarily suspending a portion of the state's commitments to pensioners for fiscal reasons was unconstitutional' (Hausner, 2001, p. 215). This proved to be an advantage because it set the stage for the need to find a way of resolving the conflict by introducing a major structural reform with a permanent legislative change introduced by appropriate rather than ad hoc legislative reform.

Secondly, at another level the differing views of the two ministries represented differing views about the economic viability of the current PAYG pension system entrapped in the political pressures and bargaining of what Hausner calls 'socialist branch corporatism'. In this system certain occupational groups achieve special privileges. Historically the mining and heavy industry groups acquired this special status. The mining industry was the main debtor in the social insurance fund. But there are modern versions of this form of corporativism. In the 1990s the legal lobby created a new privilege by passing new legislation governing the courts that excluded courts and the prosecutors' office from the universal pension system. Creating what Hausner fears could be a 'a dangerous precedent ... a new privilege that limited the possibility of cutting back on existing privileges' (Hausner, 2001, p. 222).

Thirdly, also underlying the different positions was a deeper conceptual issue of what constituted the risks of social protection. Social security in most systems was about the replacement of wages by leveling a tax or contributions from wages set by a ceiling and a floor to cover the costs. Returns to capital or property are not part of this system. In Poland this issue surfaced in a court decision which had to decide whether the legal doctrine of social insurance recognized funding systems. This is, of course, a familiar narrative.

But when the three examples are considered together they also highlight the less-recognized, continuing struggle between the economists and the lawyers. The different intellectual perspectives of these professions provided the background to the substantive issues that divided the two ministries

Given these deep splits in the underlying rationale on which a reform initiative could proceed, for many political observers the possibility of reaching agreement on a pension reform 'seemed impossible' (Hausner, 2001). But the start of a breakthrough to the stalemate was the invention of a new institutional design which 'bypassed normal ministerial and parliamentary channels and set the agenda for debate and negotiation' (Haggard et al., 2001, p. 106). The creation of this initiating authority was reinforced by the technical expertise of a Polish national seconded from the World Bank to manage the everyday details of producing a reform proposal. Two additional factors seemed to have played decisive roles in reaching a consensual agreement among the competing actors. The first was the availability of financial resources from the privatization of industry which could be used to finance the transition from a PAYG to a funded system. Second was 'the positive role played by journalists' in informing and changing public opinion. We briefly comment on each development.

The role of the media, not as a protagonist but as a mediator of the competing frames in the reform controversy, seems to have been a decisive factor in reshaping public opinion. The reform debate received a great deal of media coverage – after all this was an issue that deeply affected virtually the whole population. But how was the media kept informed about the technical complexities of any sustained debate about pensions? The journalists were invited to take part in study trips organized by the Office of the Plenipotentiary to Latin American and other countries that had already initiated pension reforms by introducing mandated and voluntary private pillars. These study trips were generously financed by the World Bank. Information was certainly important in informing the public about the implications of the reform for present pensioners and those 30–50 years of age who were given the choice of opting either for the new system or remaining in the old system. 'Without the support of the middle-aged population, which had the most to lose if reform did not take place: it is difficult to carry out any type of reform whatsoever' (Hausner, 2001, p. 226).

An extremely contentious and divisive issue centered on how the money from privatization should be distributed. The Ministry of the State Treasury estimated that at the end of 1996 the book value of the country's privatized resources was 141.8 billion PLN, with the market value being both larger and more uncertain. But the issue was how to use these resources. The Solidarity union was committed to a plan of universal impropriation as opposed to expropriation. A non-binding referendum was held with a majority of a low turnout supporting the union position. In its simplest form the issue concerned whether the available money would be distributed to eligible citizens or groups; to pension funds; or to the state to help pay for the financial gap between the PAYG contribution system and the funded pension pillar (for details see Hausner, 2001, pp. 222–5). The decision to transfer revenue from privatization not to the pension funds or directly to the citizens, but to the state budget, was an important victory for the reformers who favored a funded multi-pillar system.

Interpreting Polish Pension Reform

How can we understand the Polish pension reform? Orenstein argues that while 'only domestic actors have veto power over reform, international organizations have a powerful agenda-setting capacity through the formulation and diffusion of reform ideas' (2000). But these international actors do more than shape the discourse; he believes they are actively engaged in 'direct policy intervention', meaning they shape the outcome as well. But the question remains as to how decisive these forms of direct engagement are in determining the outcome. He argues that a plausible hypothesis is that more fundamental pension reform is *only* likely to occur as a result of the World Bank's intervention. He cites as evidence that Poland implemented a notional, defined contribution first pillar because a World Bank official, Rutkowski, was designated to be the head of the Plenipotentiary responsible for pension reform and this official believed in the validity of this approach.

Nelson appears to reach a different conclusion. 'Yet there is little in either reform [Poland and Hungary] to indicate that the World Bank dictated or even strongly influenced the specific choices and design details that emerged from the process of analysis and negotiations' (Nelson, 2001, p. 245).

But other interpretations are also plausible. The Polish reform is after all not the outcome of the disagreement within the World Bank. Rather it is the outcome of the innovative ideas promoted directly by Sweden, which has aggressively exported its ideas about social policy. These ideas are in important ways in opposition to the reform strategy promoted by the Bank. In particular, Sweden had developed the notional defined contribution concept and provided trust fund money to Latvia in 1995 to finance a Swedish team showing Latvia how to model and establish such a scheme. Latvia subsequently implemented the scheme. The same team of Swedish consultants brought the idea to Poland and influenced the redesign of the Polish first pillar. Accepting the Swedish model in Poland was certainly facilitated when Rutkowski, a World Bank employee, was seconded to manage the routine day to day running of the pension reform efforts, including the drafting of reform proposals. He believed in the Swedish model from the personal experience of seeing it implemented in Latvia, but the ideas on which the model was based were in opposition to the ideals of pension reform developed by Estelle James in her influential book *Averting the Old Age Crisis* (1994). But as the outline of the Polish pension reforms shows, the reform ideas are after all Swedish and it is equally likely that Swedish consultants played as decisive a role in Poland as they did in Latvia (informal discussion with Ed Palmer in Sweden, correspondence with Agnieszka Chlon in Poland and Estelle James at the World Bank).

There is no doubt that Poland introduced many innovations in the detailed design of the Swedish scheme. As reviewed above, it appears that Poland is planning to go much further than Sweden in projecting that the notional and funded pillars would eventually be of equal size. And this is clearly an important difference in conception, but again intention cannot be equated with actual implementation. A more detailed analysis shows significant further departures from the Swedish model, including the following: the treatment of transitional arrangements for accrued rights; the indexation of notional accounts (average wage growth vs. wage bill growth); the benefit formula (there is a pre-indexation in the Swedish formula which is non existent in Poland); and finally the treatment of non-contributory periods, which are financed from the state budget, such as army service, maternity leave, etc. However the main difference in the treatment of non-contributory periods for social security is in the approach to disability. In the Polish system, contributions to the old age system are not paid for by disabled people; they are in Sweden (personal correspondence with A. Chlon, 11 September 2000). Despite these important differences in key features of the design of the two systems there is the strong impression that borrowing rather than innovating is the dominant story.

Any interpretation of the case needs to weigh the relative importance of legacy and current political context and the role of Western experts in the diffusion of innovation. While both readings of the case are clearly present, the emphasis given to one or another of these themes creates a different interpretative story. One view stresses that the political feasibility of the reform (in the broad sense of the term) mattered much more than what the 'experts' said, and indeed played the decisively important role. In this interpretation, the role of outside experts is played down and can even be the subject of an interesting and perhaps important sociological study in its own terms. Szalai has proposed the interesting idea of experts ghettoized into the 'international circle', but having little contact with local politicians. It would be interesting to analyze the careers, attitudes, aspirations and ultimately double-edged solitude of those young experts in the region who once had put their hopes of occupational mobility into the hands of the international organizations, received excellent training, and then try to 'translate' this knowledge to home circumstances. To what extent are international experts who are nationals in the study they are working in caught in a double bind, between their life within the international community and their domestic loyalties (Szalai, personal correspondence, summer 2000)? My own reading of the story is that the structures of the notional defined contribution part of the system do differ in Poland and Sweden. At the same time, and without doubt, Poland and Sweden started basically 'from the same ground', i.e., with a similar conception of a multi-pillar system that is quite different from the model promoted by the World Bank and the model followed by mandated occupational pensions in Switzerland and Australia.

12. National Politics and Policy Outcomes: Hungary

After the transition from communism, Hungary, unlike Poland, managed to keep its pension costs relatively stable at around 10% of GDP despite a 25% increase in the number of pensioners attributable to increases in disability and early retirement programs. Hungary managed to keep costs down by a series of ad hoc adjustments in pension levels, as benefits declined in real terms between 1990 and 1995 by 25%. At its peak in 1992–95 the contribution level paid by firms as a proportion of the gross wage bill reached 44% (23.5% for the formally separated health fund, and 20.5% for the pension fund). Another 10% was also shared between the two funds, with 6% allocated to pension insurance administration and 4% to the health insurance administration. Thus, the overall contribution level was as high as 54% (Simonovits, 1999, p. 215). These contributions were collected together, and later divided administratively. This is a tax-collection system but distributed according to the earnings-related principle, with both a minimum payment and a ceiling for both benefits and contributions. Note, however, that the ceiling of contributions applies only to the employee's contribution, for the employer contributions have no ceiling.

These rates, combined with the declining value of benefits, not surprisingly led to a problem of growing evasion in the payment of contributions. Non-compliance was rather widespread, extending beyond the private sector to the large government-owned firms such as the Hungarian Railroads (Simonovits, 1999, p.215). Before the reform both Hungary and Poland pursued a policy of 'indirect subsidizing of state-owned firms by foregoing collection of social security contributions from troubled firms' (Kochanowic, 2000, p. 16). These events cumulatively led to a PAYG balance deficit of about 2% of GDP between 1990 and 1995 (Orenstein, 2000, table 1, p. 6).

These developments led to increased pressure for reform, though such trends, by themselves, did not induce any significant reforms. The reform movement was initiated as early as 1980. A major first step was to separate social security from the state budget, thus creating an independent 'pension fund'. This was followed in 1992 by the decomposition of the single fund into separate health and pension funds. Later separate entitlement regulations for pensions and other benefits were redrafted together with the introduction of higher age limits for entitlement, but the retirement age was only finally raised in 1996.

The next major step after elections were held in 1993 was the creation of separate self-governing bodies for each fund with their own administration and elected self-government. But the struggle for power over the control and direction of the social security system continued when, after the most recent elections, the government decided to eliminate these self-governing boards and to re-establish more centralized control. The reform process legislated in 1993 also led to the creation of a voluntary pension system, funded by individual contributions. Voluntary pensions were given a strong impetus by the introduction of tax breaks, designed to encourage citizen groups to create their own pension funds. For 'the average pension contribution there is a 50% tax deduction' (Simonovits, 1999, p. 220). This was clearly more than a symbolic movement. By late 1997, voluntary pension funds had managed to attract some 700,000 members, which rose by the end of 1999 to 1.1 million, 14% of the population aged 18 and older.

Later this move proved to be instrumental because it contributed to the evolution of a multi-pillar system. Firms already established to manage voluntary pension funds were among the major stakeholders, but, as Nelson explains, the process of access and influence of these funds in the struggle over reform is less than transparent (Nelson, 2001, p. 250). What we do know is that by late 1997 over 250 pension mutual funds were established, with 15% of the labor force as members (Nelson, 2001, p. 251). This measure is somewhat misleading since the essence of the voluntary funds is that not only employees can become members. Thus, it is not very accurate to express the spreading of coverage as a percentage of the labor force.

It is more accurate to say that some 11% of the population aged 15–60 became members of these funds by late 1997. Sponsors of the voluntary pillar apparently recognized that it was in their best interest to support a mandatory pillar that would be under the same regulatory authority and would make it easier for the voluntary pillar to supplement the mandatory pillar. But this longer-term development was not foreseen and in the short run the introduction of voluntary pensions did little to address any of the problems that the public pension system faced. Neither did the new mandatory private system recognize the strategic importance of these voluntary funds for the future evolution of a multi-pillar system. To a large extent, these stories are best understood as independent developments. Of course, by making less tax revenue available because of the taxes forgone to finance the voluntary scheme, in the short run the introduction of the voluntary pillar also only increased the overall fiscal burden.

In general, the logic of the multi-pillar pension reform strategy that Hungary pursued and passed into law in mid-1997, to come into effect in January 1998, was to decrease the relative size and cost of the public regimes over time. By this time, the public scheme had lost its universal character and had in fact never been a flat-rate system. If, however, universalism means that everybody de facto has access to it, the pension system is still universal. In our sample, analyzed by Robert Gale at Tarki, some 97% of the population above retirement age receives pensions.

This regime-type program had been transformed into a safety net for low-wage earners financed largely by employer-based contributions. It was perhaps never envisioned that the public regime would over time ultimately be replaced. The idea was not 'replacement' but the creation of a channel for higher and better-controlled additional pensions. If we examine the regulations, it seems clear that no one could seriously envision 'replacement'; only a more modest aim is realistic, since only 10% of the wage bill was to be paid in the name of the employee by the employer, and in fact only 6% was, although the original design called for 8%. To make everything more complicated, the figure for the wage bill was actually raised to 11%, with part set aside for the second pillar. These changes in the figures establish an important point, namely, that the 'transition will turn out to be a process of adjustment to continuously changing circumstances and requirements, very much in the way that pension systems have evolved in the past' (Simonovits, 1999, p. 228).

The second important point to make in this maze of figures, is that a huge amount of wage-level-related contributions made by the employer, plus the 4% of the employee's contribution, most of which goes to the health fund, still remains within the public social security program. What could at best be expected is that a second pillar that depended exclusively on contributions plus investment income would create a system where the benefit–contribution linkage would become more transparent. This benefit was in turn to be supplemented by the resources available in a third voluntary pillar.

It is hard to understand why decisions went the way they did and different writers give different accounts of the events and their meaning. The danger lies typically in over-interpreting an event and using it as evidence in a causal argument about mechanisms and outcomes. Interpretation is especially hazardous, since the process is still evolving and it is easy to confuse governmental promises with actual facts. With these caveats in mind we offer a brief account of what happened and what is happening.

Most observers conclude that the debate about pension reform in Hungary as well as Poland centered on the strongly entrenched positions held by two government bureaucracies, the Ministry of Finance and the Ministry of Welfare, and the unions. What is unclear is whether the Ministry of Welfare held an independent position on pensions, since it 'officially' declared itself independent from social security matters in 1989, and apparently maintained this position over time. Siminovits is the only Hungarian source I have found that asserts the multi-pillar system has its roots in World Bank ideas. In reference to the three pillars he says 'The most visible part of the reform was worked out by the Ministry of Finance in 1996 following the ideas of the World Bank (1994 and 1996), it has created a three pillar system' (Siminovits, 1999, p. 218). Julia Szalai and others seem to argue that the three pillar model was strictly the outcome of national political forces struggling for control over the decision-making powers of the social security system, constrained by the economic realities. International organizations are simply not part of her story. The way she puts it is:

> pension funds were the logical and organic result of the coming together of processes which have different origins, but which over the course of time have become entwined and have amplified one another ... and led to the extreme delegitimization of the social security system ... we must contemplate with some surprise the fact that the new institutional system ... stepped fully armed, nevertheless almost without antecedent, onto the stage of Hungarian market economy (Szalai, 2000, p. 8).

Thus there is some disagreement about the identification of the main actors in the struggle over pension reform, and especially about the strategic role played by the World Bank. It is generally acknowledged that in Hungary the unions also exerted their influence, the important partner being MSZOSZ, the major trade union confederation. As discussed above, one forum that opened to express their opposition was part of the move to decentralize the command economy by removing health and pension spending from the central budget and placing it in two social insurance funds. These funds were placed under the control of union representatives elected from the population at large (Haggard et al., p. 94).

Both ministries and the funds agreed to retain the voluntary pillar already in place. So the issue focused on the disagreement within the public administration about the first and second pillars. Not surprisingly the old established party leaders were now seeking a new way to convert political power into economic power. Those agents who have a fair measure of influence or control over the established social security funds were competing for influence and control of the social security fund. A brief account of the narrative from this perspective should start with the decline in public trust in the management of the first pillar, i.e., the old social security system. Consider first the evidence for the distrust and political struggle to find a solution in the creation of a multi-pillar system of a mandated funded private pillar and a voluntary pillar.

Nelson tells the story about the board's use of the autonomous social insurance pension funds. 'Despite legal safeguards the board's control over large flows of money permitted financial maneuvering widely believed to have benefited the union as an institution, key leaders and political parties' (Nelson, 2001, p. 248). Other observers seem to believe that the most serious scandals came from the health fund rather than the pension fund.

The channeling of money from the pension funds into individually managed accounts set the stage for strong public receptivity to a system of privatized pillars. Control over these huge amounts of money was the central political issue underlying pension reform, with all sides seeing an opportunity to use the multi-pillar pension reform to promote their agenda. So the deep disillusionment with the public social security system became a struggle between the relative size and rules in the first and second pillar. The trade unions wanted control over a funded system as the public system continued to erode in value. In this new context of pension reform, the 1993 creation of a voluntary pillar gave the unions some scope to gain control over social security through a parallel voluntary funded system based on the principle of self-government. Other protagonists in the battle for control wanted to renationalize the social security fund to take control away from the unions by using the second pillar as a tool for reform.

Most accounts report that the Ministry of Finance wanted to create a mandatory private pillar which would eventually phase out the existing public PAYG system. But as discussed earlier, it does not seem that such a vision was realistic in the short term. The ministry might have hoped that over a longer time horizon such a development would occur, but since the time period is not clearly specified it is difficult to judge how much weight should be given to this objective. As for the role of the Ministry of Welfare, it is perhaps more accurate to say that it wanted to reform the existing public regime since it was the strong self-governing body of the pension fund. In addition some experts and the most influential trade union leaders took this position.

Most accounts argue that while there was opposition outside of the government, the deadlock over pension reform was a result of the strong opposing views of the Ministries of Finance and of Welfare. It is not difficult to understand why observers writing about pension reform juxtapose the positions of the two ministries and view them as fighting out a conflict about the future evolution of social policy that was held by international and national organizations with a stake in the outcome of the reform. It is easy to interpret the normative and political issues in terms of the respective roles of these organizations and to interpret events as a compromise that was eventually reached when a new Minister of Finance was appointed and the parties accepted the pressure of upcoming political election, which set a time constraint on the deliberative process. In this view the Ministry of Finance established the main framework document which defined the logic and details of the reform. As Orenstein explains, 'The Ministry of Finance, backed by the World Bank resources, emerged from the commitment building process with the main lines of its reform proposal intact, and a government commitment to establish a mandatory, funded pillar in Hungary' (Orenstein, 1999, p. 32). Haggard et al. offer a somewhat different spin on the narrative. 'In April 1996, the new Minister of Finance, meeting with representatives from welfare and with key Socialist Party leaders, agreed that if the others would publicly announce their acceptance of the principle of a private pillar, the Ministry of Finance would abandon the specifics of its own proposal and negotiate all details' (Haggard et al., p. 101).

In essence Hungary developed a multi-pillar system that is at once public, mandated, private, and voluntary. But the negotiations continued about the relative size of the pillars and the rules governing the management of the funds. Eventually the period of qualification for full benefits in the first pillar was lowered from 35 to 20 years, and for the moment the relative size of the second, mandatory funded pillar is still negligible, but growing.

The latest figures available in official publications show that by the end of 1999, the newly established pension funds have collected about 0.8% of GDP and 8% of the social security pension budget (the source of the GDP figure is the Central Statistical Office). Other details about the relative size of the second pillar can be discerned from a breakdown of the payroll tax. The most recent data are as follows (all as percentage of gross wage): the employer pays 33% of which 22% goes to the pension fund, 11% to the health fund. The employee pays 11% out of which 8% belongs to the pension fund, 3% to the health fund. If an employee switches to a private pension fund, the 8% contribution is divided between the national fund (2%) and the private fund (6%).

As discussed above, the principle of self-government of the Independent Social Insurance Boards was abolished when the new government came into power. Thus the pension reform is still very much in the course of development. It is continuously evolving in the context of competing interests and distrustful public opinion. The very creation of the second pillar heralded an important step in the continuous struggle to achieve some measure of autonomy from the shadow of the basic social security program which, under the terms of the reform, now constituted the first pillar. But the reform did not eliminate the widespread distrust and alienation from the state's first pillar. Some strong evidence for this distrust was the enormous public popularity of the newly emerging second pillar. For the general alienated public, when given an opportunity to make a free choice, an astonishing 90% of those theoretically eligible joined the second pillar while maintaining their primary commitment in the first pillar. Szalai describes these developments as 'a major social upheaval' (Szalai, 2000, p. 1). Another way to express these same numbers is to use the working rather than the eligible population as the base. Thus some 50–55% of the working population have switched (2.1 million out of 3.8 million).

The new second pillar provides individuals with only a fraction of their future pension income. Their major source of income in the short run continues to be the old PAYG public system. It is a precondition that you have to be employed in one form or another to be able to join the second pillar. Indeed, there are hardly any unemployed in the private funds. But in principle any of them could have gone to the private funds. The 'employer's' share of contribution is paid by the central budget in the case of the unemployed. The adult population comprises about 7.9 million (18 years old and above; 1996 figure). The 1.1 million voluntary fund members make up about 14% of that number.

This signals not so much confidence in the new fund, which after all had no track record. If this analysis of the Hungarian reform is broadly correct then it would seem that the multi-pillar system implemented was a bargaining outcome that forged compromises among the competing ideas and interests.

Egalitarian ideas softened the logic of the second pillar as a funded, privately invested fund by introducing a design that included floors or minimum guarantees, which consists of a pension of at least 25% of the mandatory defined benefits plan after 15 years of contribution. There is no ceiling in the second pillar. But, of course, depending on the administrative rules which shape actual practice, quite different outcomes continue to emerge.

What does a comparison of the pension reforms in Hungary with that introduced in Poland suggest about the imposition of outside models? Poland started with the same structure as the Swedish notional defined contribution scheme, but when political considerations entered into the process of reform, the final shape of the Polish system was clearly different. The main differences are reviewed in the discussion of the Polish reform, with the most striking difference being the relative size of the first and second pillars. But the basic question remains how significantly different are these design features in the newly emerging Polish pension system? My conclusion is that while they are clearly important, they represent variations on what is essentially a Swedish approach to pension reform.

What conclusion can we reach about the reform in Hungary? What emerged was a multi-pillar model more or less in a World Bank cast, even though we can recognize that other international organizations like the EU also promoted the three-pillar system. And as in Poland the Hungarian system that emerged had design features that were distinctively different from the presumed prototype that may have guided its development. Can one conclude then that it is mainly the World Bank that influenced the Hungarian story, much as Sweden mainly influenced the Polish story? Perhaps reaching such a conclusion seems rather arbitrary, given the many variations of the theme that emerged and in particular the continued dominance in the short run of the public pay-as-you-go system. But on the other hand, it does seem to be the case that Hungary and Poland have emerged with different models of a multi-pillar system, even though the long run outcome of this process is still indeterminate.

13. The Future of the Welfare State in East Europe

What conclusions can we draw from this review of pension reform in Poland and Hungary? Several different interpretations can be derived from the narrative of pension reform reviewed above. One reading of these events is that this is a story about the diffusion of ideas. In this narrative entrepreneurs creatively copy and modify the patterns that are found in the institutional domain of one country and try to transfer these idea to the same domain in their native country. It is through actions of these agents that ideas about institution building are diffused across countries. Offe applies this general diffusion model to Central and East Europe. He describes these agents as:

> opportunists ... to emphasize the ability of these actors to make use of 'windows of opportunity' and to capture options for willing agreements on new rules as they emerge ... This somewhat messy logic of exploiting opportunities for institution-building as they emerge without relying upon the guidance of a master plan; the logic of creating standards and benchmarks according to unforeseen and generally unpredictable chances of compromise; ... these are all elements of what can be observed in ... the [successful] cases of post-communist reconstruction ... Such creative opportunism is probably the closest ap-

proximation to the notion of institutional design that we find in the real world of politics. (Offe, 2001, p. 9)

But the same evidence can be interpreted through a different lens. Offe gives emphasis to the creative role of the local configuration of actors, but it is easy also to view the process not in terms of accommodation, but of imposition, especially when the key agent is a powerful international organization with a mission that derives from the specialized mandate of its financial sponsors. This was the interpretation offered by the many critics of both the process and outcomes of the pension reforms. But when judged not as a contest among competing frame sponsors, but against the standard of outcomes, many surprises emerge. Viewed from this perspective one reaches a somewhat different conclusion. In a study of private pensions in Hungary, Szalai argues that 'The first results are exciting. The whole process goes against all expectations: this system is not exclusively for the rich (as some leftist critics expected), neither does it express the strengthening of some business-interests to gain huge profits ... '(personal correspondence, June 2000).[3]

But even if it is difficult at this stage of the process to specify the practical outcomes of these reforms, they do represent something of a sea change in thinking about the social policy of pensions. If the other domains of traditional state functions in health, education, family and housing were to follow a similar pattern, then the welfare states of Central Europe's traditional welfare regimes would become virtually obsolete.

But this vision of the future for Central Europe has been sharply criticized as resting on too narrow an interpretation of the welfare state seen through the lens of a hybrid mix of regimes and pillar paradigms as developed in Western countries and imported to Central Europe. Lessenich, through the perspective of a critic rather than an opportunist, in Offe's terminology, reads the evidence of reform and reaches a very different conclusion. He focuses on the tripartite formula of mainstream economics, namely liberalization, stabilization and privatization, and concludes that this simple recipe of market-induced and market-led modernization starts with 'state desertion', and following this model Central Europe will draw its inspiration less from Western Europe and more from Latin America (Lessenich, 2000). This position opens an intellectual debate about the emerging welfare state types for Central Europe.

The evidence to support the view that Central Europe will follow a Latin American model cannot easily be summarized because it is drawn from a broader look at the political economy of development rather than a narrow view of pension policy. However, we limit our comments to those points that are relevant to the kind of pension reforms discussed above. The essence of the argument is that 'political capitalism' makes 'it possible for the economic elite to externalize production costs to third parties [primarily state budgets] and to engage in the safe business of rent-seeking ... in sum, a polarized society in which the affluence of the political-economic power elite contrasts with the distress of the ever more impoverished society' (Lessenich, 2000, p. 6).

But for our purposes the interesting point in Lessenich's position is that structural change in the economy is no less a function of the welfare state reforms initiated after the breakdown of communism. Whereas the inequalities found in the former paternalistic welfare state were generated by granting public employment guarantees and through the dispensation of social benefits at the company level; it is now being reproduced through the re-oriented social policy in post-communist regimes. The hallmark of the new social policy is 'the gradual squeezing out of public social policy'. The pension reforms in Hungary and Poland are prime examples. The first steps in this process have already been taken in the decade-long struggle to partially privatize the pension system. This point is forcefully made in a quote from the writings of Guy Standing of the ILO. 'Pensions systems are likely to become a major source of socio-economic differentiation in the next few years ... the major dividing line being that between the affluent private and miserable public pensioners' (Lessenich, 2000, p. 9). In Standing's view the institutional syndrome of 'state desertion' is interpreted as the retreat of the state from social policy that 'is at the core of the miseries of post-communist transformation' (Lessenich, 2000, p. 12). To achieve this aim neo-liberal social reform has singled out privatization as its main reform (Kochanowicz, 1999, p. 8). In other words the privatization of pension reform can best be interpreted as initiating this process. Latin America is the metaphor for a social syndrome of a weak civil society, re-privatization in the economy and a society with 'huge disparities in wealth and income, steadily falling real wages and correspondingly high ... poverty rates' (Lessenich, 2000, p. 11). To reinforce the point that this is a real danger for Eastern Europe, the author cites the extreme welfare gap in the border area between East and West Europe and particularly between Poland and Germany. He concludes that the hope for a realistic 'catching up process will remain a dream' (Lessenich, 2000, p. 12).

By comparing and contrasting 'international' ideas, we can point out that even the alleged 'established' ideas on models (which seemed to work elsewhere) and images on how Central Europe should perform its transformation toward them seem to envision utterly differing societies. If one adds to the uncertainties of these visions the limitations that 'legacies' and local politics provide in the societies in question, then there is only one single thing which is clear: the easy fitting into any of the static models is not a probable scenario.

Can we say something about any more probable scenarios? Not too much. The Latin-Americanization ideas have the strength of calling public attention to some of the warning facts in politics and economic development, and also to signs of social disintegration in Central Europe. However, 'Latin-Americanization' is at best a probable 'danger' but not a fact. All in all, none of the prevailing 'models' seems to work for the present. Thus, we should claim 'openmindedness', flexibility, external and internal responsibility, and – above all – thorough researching. Path-corrections based on research, carefully and flexibly modified regulations should assist 'reform' – instead of the major current of the day, i.e., identifying dreams with facts, particular interests with the universal good, and so on.

Notes

1. Acknowledgements: I have benefited greatly from the advice of three economists: John Turner at the Department of Labor in the United States, Ed Palmer at the National Social Insurance Board in Sweden and the Department of Economics, Uppsala, Sweden; and Estelle James the World Bank. Their contribution to my thoughts on the subject is evident throughout this chapter. But I have also had the unusual privilege of detailed discussion and correspondence with Julia Szalai, Institute of Sociology, Hungarian Academy of Sciences. She is a close observer of Hungarian persion reform and brings the analytic perspective of a value critical approach informed by an insider's view, grounded in years of research on the subject. While I have tried directly to attribute her insights in her own words, I fear that I have not been fully able to acknowledge all the subtle ways that she has contributed to my thinking and inspired my imagination. She brings her commitment and value-led involvement to the subject and not only her sharp intellect. She has enormously enriched my understanding and, beyond that, made the journey exciting.

2. The theme of choice with change and change without choice is discussed in more length in Rein (1970).

3. The evidence is elaborated in an as-yet unpublished paper by Szalai (2000).

References

Adema, Willem and Marcel Einerhand (1998), 'The Growing Role of Private Social Benefits', in *Labour Market and Social Policy Occasional Papers,* No. 32. Paris: OECD.

Best, John, R. and B.D. Kale (1996), 'Older Workers in the 21st Century: Active and Educated, a Case Study', *Monthly Labor Review* (June).

Bunce, Valarie (1999), 'The Political Economy of Postsocialism', Paper presented at the Central European University, 26–29 March.

Chlon, Agnieszka, Louise Fox and Ed Palmer (2000a), 'Notional Defined Contribution Systems: How are they Implemented', Mimeo, September.

Chlon, Agnieszka et al. (200b), 'Pension Reform in Slovakia – Background and

Options: Can Lessons be Drawn from Other Transition Economies', Final Draft, 19 June 2000.

Esping-Andersen, Gosta (1990), *The Three Worlds of Welfare Capitalism,* Oxford: Polity Press.

Goodin Robert and Martin Rein (2000), 'Regimes and Pillars: Alternative Welfare State Logics', Summer.

Goodin Robert and A. Smitsman (2000), 'Placing Welfare State: The Netherlands as a Crucial Test Case', *Journal of Comparative Policy Analysis: Research and Practi*ce, **2**, 2000.

Goodin Robert, Bruce Headey, Ruud Muffels and Henk-Jan Dirven (1999), *The Real Worlds of Welfare Capitalism*, Cambridge: Cambridge University Press.

Guillian, Collin (1998), Paper presented at the Fifth International Seminar on Issues in Social Security, Sigtuma, Sweden, 13–16 June 1998.

Haggard, Stephan, Robert R. Kaufman and Nattgew S. Shugart (2000), 'Politics, Institutions and Macroeconomic Achievement: Hungarian Fiscal Policy Making in Comparative Perspective', in Janos Kornai, Stephen Haggard and Robert R. Kaufman (eds), *Reforming the State*, London: Cambridge University Press.

Hausner, Jerzy (2001), 'Security through Diversity: Conditions for Successful Reform of the Pension system in Poland', in Janos Kornai, Stephen Haggard and Robert R. Kaufman (eds), *Reforming the State*, London: Cambridge University Press.

Hemerijck, Anton and J. Visser (1998), *A Dutch Miracle: Employment Growth, Welfare Reform & Corporatism in the Netherlands,* Amsterdam University Press.

James, Estelle (1999),'Reforming Social Security Around the World: Common Solutions, Contrasting Solutions', Paper presented at the Swiss Statistical Bureau, Conference on Social Security, November.

Kochanowicz, Jacek (2000), 'Leviathan Exhausted: Ideas on the State in Post Communist Transformation', *East Central Europe/L'Europe du Centre-Est*, **27** (1) (June).

Kornai, Janos, Stephan Haggard and Robert R. Kaufman (eds) (2001), *Reforming the State*, London: Cambridge University Press.

Lessenich Stephan (2000) 'The Southern Image Reversed: The Dynamics of "Transformation Dynamics" in Central and East Europe', *East Central Europe/ L'Europa do Centre-Est*, **27** (1) (June).

Nelson, M. Joan (2001), 'The Politics of Pension and Health-Care Reforms in Hungary and Poland', in Janos Kornai, Stephan Haggard and Robert R. Kaufman (eds), *Reforming the State*, London: Cambridge University Press.

Offe, Claus (2000), 'Civil Society and Social Order: Demarcating and Combining Market, State and Community', *Archives of European Sociology*, **XL** (1).

Offe, Claus (2001),'Institutional Design', Paul Barry Clarke and Joe Foweraker (eds), *The Encyclopedia of Democratic Thought,* London: Routledge and Kegan Paul.

Orenstein, Mitchell A. (2000), 'How Politics and Institutions Affect Pension Reform in The Postcommunist Countries', Policy Research Working Paper 2310, The World Bank, Development Research Group, March.

Orszag, Peter R. and Joseph E. Stiglitz (1999), 'Rethinking Pension Reform: Ten Myths About Social Security Systems', Paper presented at the World Bank Conference on 'New Ideas about Social Security', 14–15 September.

Pierson, Paul (1997), 'Increasing Returns, Path Dependence and the Study of Politics', Center for European Studies, Harvard University, mimeo.

Rainwater, Lee, Martin Rein and Joseph Schwartz (1986), *Income Packaging in the Welfare State: A Comparative Study of Family Income*, New York: Oxford University Press.

Rein, Martin (1970), *Social Policy: Issues of Choice and Change*, New York: Random House.

Rein, Martin and Lee Rainwater (1986), 'The Institutions of Social Protection', in *Public-Private Interplay in Social Protection*, New York: M.E. Sharpe.

Rein Martin and John Turner (1997), 'Work, Family, State and Market: Income at the Last Stages of the Working Career', *Lien Sociale et Politiques,* Fall.

Rein, Martin and Eskil Wadensjo (1997), *Enterprise and the Welfare State*, London: Edward Elgar Press.

Rein, Martin, Barry L. Friedman and Andreas Wörgötter (eds) (1997), *Enterprise and Social Benefits after Communism,* Cambridge: Cambridge University Press.

Schmahl,Winfried (2000a), 'Pay-As-You-Go Versus Capital Funding', in Gerald Hughes and Jim Stewart (eds), *Pensions in the European Union Adapting to Economic and Social Change,* London: Kluwer Academic Press.

Schmahl, Winfried (2000b), 'Change and Choice in Social Protection: The Experience of Central and East Europe' Vol. 1, European Community, Phare, Consensus Program, Table 2, mimeo.

Simonovits, Andras (1999), 'The New Hungarian Pension System and its Problems', in Katherine Muller et al. (eds), *Transformation of Social Security Pensions in Cental-Eastern Europe*, Versuca-Verlag.

Stevenson, Richard (1998), 'Squaring Off, at Last, On Social Security', in *The New York Times,* 29 November.

Sundèn, Annika (1998), 'The Swedish NDC Pension Reform', mimeo.

Szalai, Julia (2002), 'The Hungarian Private Pension System: A Sociological View', November, mimeo.

Teles, Steve (1998), 'The Dialectics of Trust, Ideas, Finance and Pension Privitization in the US and UK', Paper delivered to the Association for Public Policy Analysis and Management, October.

Titmuss, Richard M. (1958), 'The Social Division of Welfare: Some Reflections on the Search for Equity', in *Essays on 'The Welfare State'*, London: Allen & Unwin (originally given as lecture in 1955).

Titmuss, Richard M. (1974), *Social Policy*, London: Allen & Unwin.

Turner, John A. and David M. Rajnes (2000), 'Limiting Workers' Financial Risk Through Risk Sharing: Rate of Return Guarantees for Mandatory Defined Contribution Plans', May.

Wadensjo, Eskil (1999), 'Swedish Pension Reform and its Expected Consequences', mimeo.

Wadensjo, Eskil (1998), 'Sweden: Revisions of the Public Pension Programmes', mimeo, October p. 5.

Wagner, Peter (1994), 'Dispute, Uncertainty and Institution in Recent French Debates', *The Journal of Political Philosophy*, **2** (3).

Walzer, Michael (1983), *Spheres of Justice: A Defense of Pluralism and Equality*, New York: Basic Books.

Weinstein, Michael M. (1998), 'A Study Cuts through the Usual Blather on Social Security', *The New York Times,* 2 December.

World Bank (1994), *Averting the Old Age Crises,* Oxford: Oxford University Press.

11. Labor and the Politics of Human Capital Accumulation[1]

José Pineda and Francisco Rodríguez

---

1. Introduction

Recent trends toward deregulation, privatization, greater reliance on markets and globalization have not occurred in a social vacuum. They have been accompanied by a systematic loss of bargaining power and reduction in the membership of labor unions. Whatever – if any – the relationship of causality is between these variables is not our concern in this chapter. We will deal with another aspect of this event that is often put aside – the effect that labor's loss of bargaining power has had on its ability to affect social policy. Indeed, we will argue that this loss has been associated with substantial declines in the resources that are devoted to the formation of human capital and therefore on the long-run income-generating capacity of workers.

Our analysis is based on the idea that economic power is correlated with political power. In the words of Robert Dahl (1971): 'extreme inequalities in the distribution of such key values as income, wealth, status, knowledge and military prowess are equivalent to extreme inequalities in political resources ... A country with extreme inequalities stands a very high chance of having extreme inequality in the exercise of power' (p. 82). According to Dahl's argument, a group's share in national income is a good predictor of its capacity to affect policies. Consistent with this hypothesis, we will argue that countries that have experienced marked increases in capital shares have also experienced steep falls in the amount of resources that they devote to social programs which benefit workers. The induced effect of these falls on the well being of workers in the long run can be substantial.

In the next section we will present the main stylized fact that merits explanation: that higher capital shares are strongly negatively correlated with increases in social spending. Section 3 will go on to discuss the possible explanations for this correlation and will argue that we need to understand the correlation between political and economic power postulated by Dahl in order to make sense of it. We argue that increases in capital shares lead to falls in the bargaining power of labor that are associated with deteriorations in its capacity to affect social policy. The result can often be a collapse in expenditures on

244

education, health, social security and redistributive programs. These collapses can have significant effects not only on the distribution of income, but more generally on the perspectives for long run economic growth. Those effects, together with some further implications, are discussed in Section 4.

2. Social Spending and the Distribution of Income

During the last two decades, a number of countries have suffered significant decreases in the amount of resources that they devote to redistribution and investment in human capital accumulation. As Figures 11.1A and 11.1B show, in Venezuela and Chile there has been a virtual collapse of educational spending per student in primary school (as a percentage of per capita GDP), which has declined by about 50% for Venezuela and by about a third in Chile. Gen-

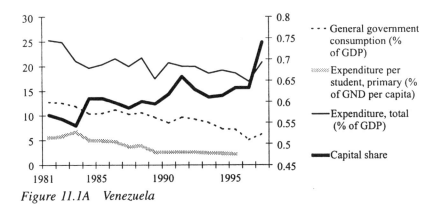

Figure 11.1A   Venezuela

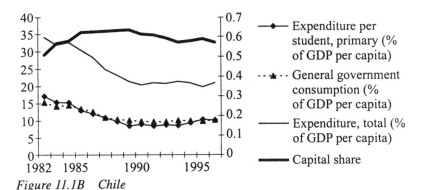

Figure 11.1B   Chile

eral government consumption, an often used proxy for redistributive activities in developing countries, also fell by between one-third and one-half in both countries, as did total government expenditures. These collapses in redistribution have occurred not only in developing countries like Chile and Venezuela, but have also taken place in a number of developed countries. Although the resilience of the welfare state to attempts to dismantle it has significantly varied between countries (see Pierson, 1994), a number of OECD countries have also seen substantial cutbacks in the amount of resources they devote to redistributive activities. In Figures 11.1C and 11.1D we show the two striking examples of Ireland and Belgium, where there have been substantial falls in government consumption and expenditure per primary school student. The real collapse in these countries' educational policies, however, has occurred in the form of a substantial reduction in the amount of resources devoted to higher education, a type of spending which we would expect to be highly redistribu-

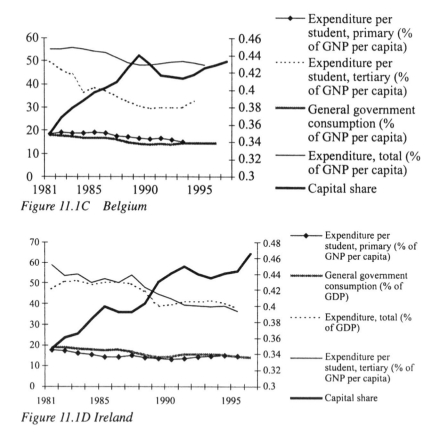

Figure 11.1C   Belgium

Figure 11.1D Ireland

tive in rich countries like Ireland and Belgium.

In the four cases shown in Figure 11.1, these changes in the political equilibrium have been accompanied by changes in the factorial distribution of income. In Venezuela, capital's share of GDP has risen by about 20 percentage points in the period under study. In Chile, Ireland and Belgium, the increases have been more moderate – from 7 to 10 percentage points in GDP – but still substantial. Furthermore, as our four cases illustrate, a substantial part of the deterioration in labor shares occurs toward the beginning of the sample, *preceding* the shifts in spending on redistribution and human capital accumulation. This fact by itself suggests that it is unlikely that the policy changes have caused the changes in income distribution. Indeed, it appears rather that somehow income distribution is having an influence on the process through which these policy changes are determined.

Indeed, a similar phenomenon can be identified at the level of all OECD countries. Table 11.1 shows the changes in capital shares and spending for 17 OECD countries between the 1980s and 1990s. On average, capital shares have risen for these countries by just under 2 percentage points in GDP – not a large change, but not a negligible one either. During the same period, public spending on education and expenditure per higher level student have fallen by about a tenth and government consumption has fallen by about 5%. And although social security taxes as a proportion of GDP have risen by about 3%, this rise is more than anything an artifice of the aging populations of OECD countries – the percentage of GDP devoted to each person over 65 years of age has actually dropped by about 5%. Furthermore, all the aforementioned vari-

Table 11.1   OECD changes in factor shares and policies

	1980–89	1990–97	% change
Capital share	0.387	0.405	4.630
Public spending on education	5.980	5.367	-10.256
Expenditure per student, higher education	44.246	40.177	-9.196
Social security taxes	10.19	10.53	3.310
Social security taxes per person over 65	78.511	74.755	-4.784
Government consumption	17.615	16.766	-4.820

ables had experienced significant rates of growth during the 1960s and 1970s, so that the changes of the 1980s and 1990s constituted a significant reversal of earlier trends.

The correlation between capital shares and spending on redistribution and human capital accumulation goes beyond these striking cases. We used a data set of 91 developed and developing countries to explore whether these findings can be generalized beyond the OECD. Figures 11.2–11.4 show the partial correlations for three variables – public spending on education, public spending on health, and government consumption – with capital shares, after a set of other relevant explanatory variables are controlled for (see Appendix I for details about the data set). There is a robust, negative correlation between all three of these spending variables and capital shares.

The econometrics behind these results is discussed in detail in Pineda and Rodríguez (2000). The results are extremely robust to controlling for outliers, alternative functional forms and alternative right-hand-side variables. The negative relation with capital shares is present for public spending on education (as a percentage of GDP), public spending on primary education (both as a percentage of GDP and per student as a percentage of per capita GDP), public health spending, social security taxes, government consumption and total government expenditures. An increase of one standard deviation in capital shares

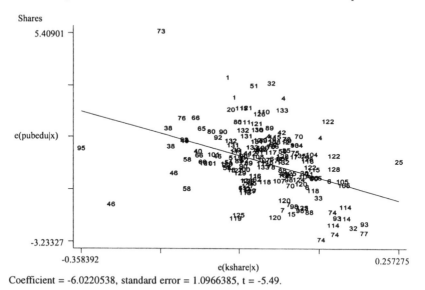

Coefficient = -6.0220538, standard error = 1.0966385, t = -5.49.

Figure 11.2   Partial correlation between public spending on education and capital shares

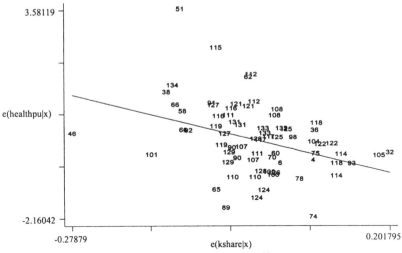

Coefficient = -4.4629612, standard error = 1.4324741, t = -3.12.

Figure 11.3 Partial correlation between public health spending and capital shares

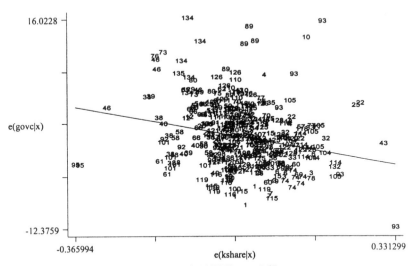

Coefficient = -11.191266, standard error = 2.4468779, t = -4.57.

Figure 11.4 Partial correlation between government consumption and capital shares

(14 percentage points) is associated with a fall of 0.97 percentage points of GDP in public education, 0.85 percentage points of GDP in social security taxes, 0.70 percentage points of GDP in public health spending, 2.18 percentage points in GDP of government consumption, and 1.69 percentage points in GDP of total public expenditures.

One tempting explanation for this correlation is that low levels of spending on human capital accumulation and redistribution cause low labor shares. If the elasticity of substitution between capital and labor is greater than one, then a factor's share will be an increasing function of its quantity, so that policies that raise the amount of effective labor will lower capital's share.[2] Despite its intuitive appeal, this reverse causation explanation cannot account for the observed relation between capital shares and our spending indicators. In Rodríguez and Pineda (2000) we present the results of Granger causality tests that show that changes in capital shares *precede* changes in the spending variables. Furthermore, we show that when a country experiences a positive terms of trade shock that affects its capital share through the effect of product prices on factor prices it also experiences falls in redistribution and human capital accumulation. As these falls can certainly not be causing the changes in the country's terms of trade, this evidence offers strong support for the hypothesis that changes in the functional distribution of income cause changes in the composition and level of government spending.

Another alternative hypothesis for our finding is that countries with high capital shares are precisely those countries where the marginal product of capital is high and investments in capital are profitable. These societies would tend to devote fewer resources to human capital accumulation – because such investments have low payoffs – and therefore see a relatively small contribution of human capital to GDP. Although such a hypothesis could well be consistent with much of our evidence, there are a couple of striking facts in the data that shed doubt on this interpretation. For example, even though there is a strong negative correlation between capital shares and public health expenditures, there is virtually no correlation between capital shares and *private* health expenditures. One would, however, suspect that if the efficiency of investing in health were the driving factor behind the correlation, it would drive private investment at least as much – if not more – than public investment. Similarly, we find that the negative correlation between capital shares and education spending is robust at the cross-country level for spending in primary education. Only as countries become richer do secondary and higher education tend to present negative correlations with capital shares. The fact that the correlation becomes important precisely when the type of educational spending under consideration starts to have a greater redistributive impact suggests that its source lies not in decisions of efficiency but in the politics of redistribution.

3. The Politics of Redistribution

By one account, the evidence shown above seems paradoxical. This is because traditional political economy theories of redistribution would not predict such a correlation. Indeed, most political economy models of redistribution share the characteristic that redistributive spending increases when income distribution becomes more unequal. This is because in these models the determinant of redistribution is the tax rate preferred by the median voter. As Meltzer and Richard (1981) first showed, majority voting over a a redistributive tax rate will produce as the political equilibrium a tax rate which is identical to that most preferred by the median voter. When the median voter is poorer – relative to average income – she will have greater incentives to vote for redistributive taxation. An increase in income inequality causes the income of the median voter to fall relative to average income, therefore raising the incentives she has to support redistribution.

In modern day income distributions, capital income tends to be much more unequally distributed than the income derived from labor. In the United States, for example, 84% of net worth and 93% of net financial wealth is held by the top quintile of the wealth distribution (Wolff, 1998). Therefore it is logical to expect that the median voter will have a much smaller proportion of capital income than the national average. As capital income is held mainly by the top quintile of the distribution, the median voter will have high incentives to vote for high levels of taxation of capital income in order to benefit owners of human capital. It should therefore be the case that as capital's share in GDP increases, the incentives of the median voter to redistribute income will be enhanced. If the median voter theory is an adequate characterization of redistributive politics, countries with higher capital shares should experience more redistribution and investment in human capital accumulation, not less. The median voter theory is thus clearly inconsistent with the correlations shown in Figures 11.2 to 11.4.[3]

It is apparent that we need to look for other theories of politics in order to understand cross-national variations in the level and composition of government spending. In particular, the median voter theorem's assumption of an egalitarian distribution of political power among voters seems unrealistic in the study of large cross-sections of countries, most of which have either undergone dictatorial experiences or are very fragile and imperfect democracies. Indeed, the use of the median voter theorem has even been questioned for advanced industrial democracies, where a number of writers have emphasized the fact that one cannot understand the key characteristics of certain policy decisions without appealing to the role of asymmetrically distributed power and political influence on the political process. Grossman and Helpman (1992) and Magee (1997) have driven this point home in the study of US commercial policy, making clear that the patterns of protection observed cannot be explained without bringing interest groups into the analysis. Their case seems all the more compelling when we move to the study of countries with a less engrained democratic tradition.

A more complex view of politics that brings in political influence and money into the story can help make sense of the observed negative relation between capital shares and our government spending variables. In particular, if economic power and political power are correlated, then we should expect to see a negative relation between the share of resources in the hands of the owners of physical capital and the level of taxation directed at accumulating human capital. This is because we can expect the owners of physical capital to be less interested than workers in greater rates of public investment in human capital. Capital shares, in that sense, may be simply proxies for the magnitude of the political power that is in the hands of capital owners.

The microfoundations for the correlation of political and economic power are worked out in Rodríguez (1999) and Pineda and Rodríguez (2000). In particular, it is easy to write a model of interest groups in which capital shares are negatively linked to the political clout of the owners of human capital. For example, if there are increasing returns to scale in political influence – derived for example from some fixed costs of political organization or from the greater difficulties of solving free-rider problems when the number of participants is large – then politically mobilized groups will be primarily composed of higher income individuals. This would be totally consistent with existing empirical evidence that indicates that higher income individuals are much more likely to participate in political associations and lobbies. Rosenstone and Hansen (1993), for example, use data from 19 National Election Studies to study political mobilization in the United States. Besides confirming the well-known finding that wealthy Americans are more likely than poor Americans to take part in political activities, they also find that 'the prosperous are two and a half times more likely than the poor to attempt to influence how others vote and over ten times more likely to contribute money to campaigns' (pp. 43–4). But political lobbies formed primarily by higher income individuals would tend to pressure for lower redistribution to the poor. This would be true even if these lobbies formed by rich individuals do not coordinate among themselves: for example, if rich individuals pay bribes in order to evade taxes the induced lower effective tax base diminishes the possibilities for financing redistribution and investment in human capital. As capital's share of GDP increases and the resources through which rich individuals affect the political system grow, they are more capable of moving policies closer to their preferred points. Higher capital shares are likely to be associated with a higher deviation of resources into rent-seeking activities and with enhanced political power of the owners of physical capital.

The result that capital shares lead to lower redistribution and human capital accumulation in a political economy model with interest groups, however, does not depend exclusively on the assumption that only the rich are organized politically. Indeed it also emerges naturally from a context in which both the owners of physical capital and the owners of human capital are politically organized, as is shown by Pineda and Rodríguez (2000). In that paper, we present a model of political influence and interest groups in which there exist organized labor and capital lobbies. There is no a priori assumption on who is politically more organized – indeed, given their greater numbers, it is perfectly plausible for the owners of labor to be able to mobilize more not fewer economic resources into the political arena. The main intuition of the model, however, is preserved: as capital shares increase, both the capacity and the incentives for political organization of capital are raised relative to those of labor. In equilibrium, the political clout of capital is higher when capital's share in GDP rises.

It is important to point out that the intuition for this model relies on the assumption that the substitutability between capital and labor be sufficiently high to avoid the perverse case in which workers want less investment in human capital accumulation than capitalists. If the substitutability between capital and labor is low, then changes in factor quantities are likely to have substantial effects on factor prices. In particular, higher levels of human capital can induce substantial drops in the relative wage rate, leading therefore to a fall in the real income of workers. For an elasticity of substitution substantially below one, it is quite plausible for workers to be opposed to higher levels of human capital accumulation that would diminish their total income. Furthermore, if such high levels of complementarity exist, capitalists would be the more interested in high levels of human capital accumulation, as high levels of human capital can considerably raise the marginal product of capital.

The important issue here is not whether the owners of physical capital benefit from human capital accumulation – which they undoubtedly do – but rather what group prefers higher levels of investment in human capital. If workers' preferred stock of human capital is higher than capital's, then the basic intuition of our model holds: workers want higher stocks of human capital than capitalists, and anything that induces a shift of political power from labor to capital – such as a shift in the functional distribution of income – will lead to a fall in the investment in human capital that arises in political equilibrium. The basis for our results would, however, be upset if workers were to desire lower levels of investment in human capital than capitalists.

The case in which capitalists desire more human capital accumulation than workers, although illuminating theoretically, is in our view unlikely to hold in reality. In Rodríguez and Pineda (2000) we show that in order for that reversal of interests to occur it is necessary for the elasticity of substitution between capital and labor to be substantially smaller than one – indeed it must be lower than one-third for a good number of economies. This contrasts starkly with the empirical evidence on these elasticities of substitution, which indicates that they are much higher. For example, Betancourt and Clague (1981) estimate elasticities of substitution at the industry level for 17 industries using UNIDO data and come up with an average value of 0.91. Indeed, the main debate in the literature on elasticities of substitution has revolved around the issue of whether these elasticities are equal to one or not. Note also that the economy-wide elasticity of substitution – which is the one relevant for our model – will be higher than industry-level estimates, as it incorporates inter-industry substitution. Therefore the very low elasticities of substitution that are necessary for there to be a reversal of interests between capital and labor appear at best unlikely for the great majority of countries.

An alternative possibility that is raised by our results is that they perhaps respond simply to cross-national variations in the efficiency of human capital accumulation. It could, for example, be the case that high levels of human capital are simply a reflection of a high marginal return to human capital. If countries differ in the productivity of physical and human capital (perhaps because of differences in the endowments that can be combined with these) then high capital shares are likely simply to be a reflection of low returns to human capital. Indeed, whatever the reason is behind differences in human capital accumulation across countries, if the elasticity of substitution between capital and labor is strictly greater than one, one would expect to see these differences automatically generate differences in capital shares.

There are several reasons why we are skeptical that this interpretation lies behind our observed correlation. First of all, as we pointed out in the introduction, it is striking that the correlations observed are present when the redistributive component of the expenditure is high (as in the case of primary schooling) or when the investment in question is publicly financed (as in the case of health) but not when it is not redistributive nor when it is privately financed. It seems unlikely that shocks to productivity would hit nations in such an asymmetric way – only enhancing the productivity of public investment in redistributive human capital accumulation – systematically. Furthermore, the fact that our correlation is present between capital shares and government consumption indicates that even if the effect of the policy on effective investment in human capital is low or non-existent, as long as it has a redistributive component capital owners will be more likely to curtail it the more powerful they are.

Furthermore, we point again to our evidence on the direction of causation. If cross-country differences in human capital accumulation were the cause of differences in capital shares, then one would expect evidence of that pattern of causation to present itself in causality tests. However, the causality tests that we discuss above all point in the same direction: changes in capital shares appear to precede changes in human capital accumulation, and changes in capital shares induced by exogenous changes in the terms of trade are associated with changes in human capital accumulation. Although we do not discount the possibility that investment in human capital accumulation does affect factor shares, the cross-national evidence appears to be picking up mostly the channel of causation going from capital shares to the composition and level of government spending.

4. Implications for Economic Growth

There is a broad – although not total – consensus in the economic growth literature that human capital accumulation is an important source of differences in economic growth. A typical estimate from a cross-country growth equation implies that raising the average years of secondary schooling of the male population by one standard deviation raises the economy's growth rate by 1.1 percentage points (Barro and Sala-i-Martin, 1997, p. 431). Yet some countries have very low levels of investment in human capital. While Haiti, Guatemala and Indonesia all devote less than 3% of their GDP to education and health expenditures, most OECD countries as well as some developing countries like Costa Rica and Panama devote more than a tenth of GDP to it. It is apparent that if poor countries were able to raise their rates of investment in human capital they could significantly alter their long-run prospects for aggregate well-being.

One implication of our research is that one way to attack these causes of underdevelopment is by policies that affect the primary distribution of income between capital and labor. Policies that protect or enhance the bargaining power of labor at the level of the productive process are also likely to have positive effects on the efficiency of the economic system at large. This is because, contrary to the commonly held view that unions put a damper on economic efficiency, stronger labor organization is likely to affect the distribution of economic as well as of political power. Stronger unions will also be able to pressure at the national level for policies toward human capital accumulation that are consistent with equity and economic efficiency. Indeed, our econometric estimates show that countries with high capital shares have lower economic growth rates – even after the effect of initial GDP, government consumption, terms of trade shocks and a set of continental dummies are controlled for. It is only when one introduces proxies for the stock of human capital in the regression that the effect of capital shares on growth becomes statistically insignificant. These results strongly suggest that human capital accumulation is a channel through which high capital shares negatively affect growth.

Labor organization can affect the functional distribution of income. Figure 11.5 shows a simple scatter plot of the partial correlation between union density rates and capital shares, after controlling for the log of per capita GDP. It is strongly negative, indicating that unionization can significantly raise labor's share in GDP. By significantly affecting the primary distribution of income, labor organization can also have positive long-lasting efficiency effects.

There is an interesting connection between our discussion here and the theories of economic growth that proliferated in the postwar years. These theories established a connection between the factorial distribution of income and economic growth that was actually the opposite of what we are proposing. The works of Michal Kalecki (1971), Nicholas Kaldor (1960) and Stephen Marglin (1984), among others, emphasized the negative effect that greater equality in the functional distribution of income could have on the perspectives for a growth strategy based on the accumulation of physical capital. These authors derived their results from the analysis of two-class models similar to the ones we have discussed. Their analysis, however, occurred within a basic description of the

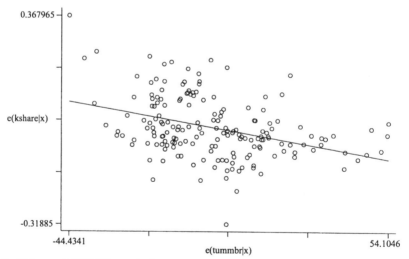

Coefficient = -0.00189873, standard error = 0.00036922, t = -5.14.

Figure 11.5 Capital shares and union participation rates

economy in which economic growth depended exclusively on the accumulation of physical capital – in the spirit of the neoclassical growth model then in vogue. As income distribution worsened, these authors emphasized, there would be more resources in the hands of owners of capital. Therefore more resources would be channeled into investment, leading to higher economic growth.

Although we share with this earlier literature a belief in the primacy of the distribution of income between factors of production for understanding economic growth, there are a few points that distinguish our analysis from theirs. First, their analysis was still deeply marked by the neoclassical model of economic growth, in which physical capital accumulation is the moving force behind economic progress. In our analysis we borrow from the contribution of the new growth theories to the understanding of economic development, in particular the variants of new growth theory that emphasize the role of human capital in economic growth.[4] The key difference between these new models of growth and traditional neoclassical growth models is that in the latter a fundamental type of saving is carried out by the owners of human capital. Earlier analyses assumed that the only ones who could save in significant amounts were the owners of physical capital. But the new growth theory recognizes that the role played by the owners of human capital is as important – if not more – in determining economic growth as that of the owners of physical capital. Workers save when they accumulate human capital, and due to the massive externalities associated with the accumulation of this factor of production, rates of return on human capital are likely to be larger than on physical capital. The new growth theory turns old growth theories on their heads, making workers in effect have a higher marginal propensity to save than capitalists.

Furthermore, our model emphasizes the role of politics in determining savings. Although important individual decisions do of course have an effect on the rates of accumulation of human capital, it is undeniable that the bulk of decisions concerning human capital accumulation – in particular in developing countries – are taken via the political process. Our explanation centers on a rich view of the political process that allows for differential power and access to affect the political equilibrium. In contrast, earlier explanations centered on individual or class incentives for savings as the primary determinant of factor accumulation.

Our analysis underscores the point that there need not be a contradiction between redistributive policies and economic efficiency. Indeed, the bulk of the evidence seems to point to significant efficiency payoffs from greater redistribution. In this sense our story is consistent with the empirical evidence found by Alesina and Rodrik (1994) and Persson and Tabellini (1994) of a negative relation between inequality in the distribution of income and economic growth.[5]

The design of optimal economic policies too often occurs with little regard for the effect these policies may have on income distribution. A common example is trade liberalization, where substantial evidence of detrimental effects of trade liberalization on inequality is often put aside as the inevitable side-effect of greater efficiency.[6] A view of economic growth that emphasizes the feedback effects that distribution has on politics will perhaps help us understand why there are good efficiency reasons to oppose such policy changes: because they may induce changes in the political equilibrium which in the long run will prove even more harmful to prospects for increased well-being.

Appendix I

For Figures 11.2 through 11.5 we used a panel of data for developing and developed economies (91 economies in total) from 1960 to 1997. In order to abstract from business cycle effects, we use five-year averages of all our variables. A detailed description of the data used and its sources is given below.

Gross domestic product (GDP). Source: World Bank (1999).

Capital share (KSHARE). Equals the ratio of operating surplus plus depreciation to GDP at factor cost. KSHARE13 and KSHARE23 assign, respectively, one-third and two-thirds of the income from unincorporated enterprises to labor's share. Source: United Nations Statistical Office.

Total spending on pubic education. The percentage of GNP accounted for by public spending on public education plus subsidies to private education at the primary, secondary and tertiary levels. Source: World Bank (1999). Primary Source: UNESCO.

Expenditure per student on primary, secondary and higher education. The percentage of GNP per capita accounted for by public spending on public education plus subsidies to private education at each level. Source: World Bank (1999). Primary Source: UNESCO.

Public health spending. Consists of recurrent and capital spending from government (central and local) budgets, external borrowings and grants (including donations from international agencies and non-governmental organizations) and social (or compulsory) health insurance funds. Expressed as a percentage of GDP. Source: World Bank (1999).

General government consumption. Includes all current expenditures for purchases of goods and services by all levels of government, excluding most government enterprises. It also includes capital expenditure on national defense and security. Expressed as a percentage of GDP. Source: World Bank (1999).

Government investment (capital expenditure). Spending to acquire fixed capital assets, land, intangible assets, government stocks, and non-military, non-financial assets. Also included are capital grants. Data are shown for central government only. Expressed as a percentage of GNP. Source: World Bank (1999).

Total government expenditure. Includes non-repayable current and capital (development) expenditure. It includes expenditures financed by grants in kind and other cash adjustments, but does not include government lending or repayments to the government or government acquisition of equity for public policy purposes. Data are shown for central government only. Expressed as a percentage of GDP. Source: World Bank (1999).

Union participation rates. Total trade union membership as percentage of the total labor force. Includes workers of both sexes in the public and the private sectors. In some countries, the union membership may include unemployed and retired workers who pay their dues. Based on the number of active contributors declared by the trade unions themselves and on labor force estimates. Source: Martín Rama and Raquel Artecona, 'A Database of Labor Market Indicators across Countries', unpublished, The World Bank, Washington, DC, 1999.

Notes

1. We thank participants at seminars in Brown University and the International Labour Organization for their comments and suggestions. All errors remain our responsibility.

2. Note, however, that this is not true when the elasticity of substitution is smaller than one.

3. By this we refer to median voter theory as an attempt to explain cross-national variations in policies. This is not to say that a more restricted statement of the median voter theory, where its range of application is restricted to the societies that have well-functioning democratic systems, may not be consistent with a subset of the data.

4. See in particular Lucas (1988), Uzawa (1965), Mankiw (1995) and Mankiw et al. (1992). In particular, the latter two papers incorporate human capital in a neoclassical Solow-style growth model and thus lack the constancy of asymptotic growth rates commonly associated with endogenous growth theory. However, in their emphasis on the role of human capital in economic growth, all of these papers mark a significant advance with respect to the conventional one-sector modelo of economic growth.

5. Regrettably, these authors relied on a variant of the Meltzer–Richard hypothesis as the microfoundations for their theory. In the interpretation, inequality generated political pressures for redistribution which harmed capital accumulation. Therefore, although inequality was harmful for economic growth, the harm was actually caused by the attempts to redistribute income. However, although the link between inequality and growth seems well established in cross-country data, the intermediate channel relied on by Alesina and Rodrik (1994), and Persson and Tabellini (1994) has found no empirical support (see Perotti, 1999), suggesting that explanations such as the one proposed in this chapter may have greater power in accounting for the growth–inequality nexus.

6. On evidence that trade liberalization has associated with increased inequality in developing and developed economies, see Wood (1994) and Hanson and Harrison (1998). In this case in particular, it must also be emphasized that the evidence in favor of a positive effect of trade policy on growth is at best empirically very weak, and at worst non-existent (see Rodríguez and Rodrik, 2000).

References

Alesina, A. and D. Rodrick (1994), 'Distributive Politics and Economic Growth', *Quarterly Journal of Economics*, (May), 465–90.

Barro, Robert and Xavier Sala-i-Martin (1995), *Economic Growth*, New York: McGraw Hill.

Betancourt, Roger and Christopher Clague (1981), *Capital Utilization: A Theoretical and Empirical Analysis,* Cambridge: Cambridge University Press.

Grossman, Gene and Elhanan Helpman (1994), 'Protection for Sale', *American Economic Review*, **84** (4), 833–50.

Hanson, Gordon and Ann Harrison (1998), 'Who Gains from Trade Reform? Some Remaining Puzzles', *NBER Working Paper No. W6915*, Cambridge, MA: NBER.

Kaldor, Nicholas (1960), *Essays on Value and Distribution*, Glencoe, IL: Free Press.

Kalecki, Michal (1971), *Selected Essays on the Dynamics of the Capitalist Economy*, Cambridge: Cambridge University Press.

Lucas, Robert E., Jr. (1988), 'On the Mechanics of Economic Development,' *Journal of Monetary Economics*, **22** (1), 318–34.

Magee, Stephen (1997) 'Endogenous Protection: The Empirical Evidence', in Dennis C. Mueller, *Perspectives on Public Choice: A Handbook*, Cambridge: Cambridge University Press.

Mankiw, N.G. (1995) 'The Growth of Nations', *Brookings Papers on Economic Activity*, **0** (1), 275–310.

Mankiw, N.G., D. Romer and D. Weil (1992), 'A Contribution to the Empirics of Economic Growth', *The Quarterly Journal of Economics*, (May).

Marglin, Stephen A. (1984), *Growth, Distribution, and Prices*, Cambridge, MA: Harvard University Press.

Meltzer, Allan and Scott Richard (1981), 'A Rational Theory of the Size of Government', *Journal of Political Economy*, **89**, 914–27.

Perotti, R. (1996), 'Democracy, Income Distribution and Growth: What the Data Says', *Journal of Economic Growth*, **1** (June), 149–87.

Persson, T. and G. Tabellini (1994), 'Is Inequality Harmful for Growth?', *American Economic Review*, **84**, 600–621.

Pierson, Paul (1994), *Dismantling the Welfare State? Reagan, Thatcher, and the Politics of Retrenchment*, Cambridge: Cambridge University Press.

Pineda, José and Francisco Rodríguez (2000), 'The Political Economy of Human Capital Accumulation', College Park: Univeristy of Maryland, mimeo.

Rodríguez, Francisco (1999), 'Inequality, Redistribution and Rent-Seeking', College Park: University of Maryland, mimeo.

Rodríguez, Francisco and Dani Rodrik (2000), 'Trade Policy and Economic Growth: A Skeptic's Guide to the Cross-National Evidence', *NBER Macroeconomics Annual 2000*, NBER.

Rosenstone, Steven J. and John Mark Hansen (1993), *Mobilization, Participation and Democracy in America*, New York: Macmillan.

Uzawa, Hirofumi (1965), 'Optimal Technical Change in an Aggregative Model of Economic Growth', *International Economic Review*, **6** (January), 18–31.

Wolff, Edward N. (1998), 'Recent Trends in the Size Distribution of Household Income', *Journal of Economic Perspectives*, **12** (3), 131–50.

Wood, Adrian (1994), *North-South Trade, Employment, and Inequality: Changing Fortunes in a Skill-Driven World*, Oxford: Clarendon Press.

Index